DIGITAL ARCHAEOLOGY

Digital Archaeology is a unique edited work addressing the changing and growing role of digital technologies in all aspects of archaeology and heritage management. Exploring the wide potential of IT across the discipline, this book goes beyond the prevailing notion that computers are merely a methodological tool, and considers their influence on the very nature of archaeological study.

Blending rigorous archaeological theory with the extensive practical knowledge of professionals in the field, *Digital Archaeology* is a highly accessible text that shows and discusses the ways in which computing can be holistically incorporated into archaeology. The book discusses elements of archaeological theory and reveals how computers can be used to reintegrate theoretical questions into the application of field work and analysis.

Beginning with a history of the growth of computing within the field, the book goes on to look at examples of how and why different technologies have been implemented into archaeological theory and method. It includes GIS, virtual reality modelling, internet publishing and archiving, and on-site digital recording using such examples as the integrated digital recording of the Ferrybridge Chariot and other case studies from around the world. This volume also discusses ways in which technology can now be used in normal excavations and how this affects the study of archaeology as a whole, from planning to publication.

Thomas L. Evans is Head of Geomatics for Oxford Archaeology and a Research Associate at the University of Oxford's Institute of Archaeology.

Patrick Daly is currently a British Academy Reckitt Travelling Fellow in Archaeology based at the McDonald Institute of Archaeological Research, University of Cambridge.

DIGITAL ARCHAEOLOGY

Bridging method and theory

Edited by
Thomas L. Evans and Patrick Daly

Routledge
Taylor & Francis Group

LONDON AND NEW YORK

First published 2006
by Routledge
2 Park Square, Milton Park, Abingdon, Oxon OX14 4RN

Simultaneously published in the USA and Canada
by Routledge
270 Madison Ave, New York, NY 10016

Routledge is an imprint of the Taylor & Francis Group

© 2006 Thomas L. Evans and Patrick Daly

Typeset in Sabon by
RefineCatch Limited, Bungay, Suffolk
Printed and bound in Great Britain by
The Cromwell Press, Trowbridge, Wiltshire

British Library Cataloguing in Publication Data
A catalogue record for this book is available from the British Library

Library of Congress Cataloging in Publication Data
Evans, Thomas L. (Thomas Laurence)
Digital archaeology: bridging method and theory / Thomas L. Evans
& Patrick Daly.
p. cm.
Includes bibliographical references and index.
1. Archaeology—Methodology.   2. Digital
electronics.   3. Electronic digital computers.   4. Archaeology—
Philosophy.   5. Antiques—Collection and preservation.   6. Cultural
property—Protection.   I. Daly, Patrick T., 1975–   II. Title.
CC75.7.E93   2005
930.1′028—dc22   2004028972

ISBN 0–415–31048–2 (hbk)
ISBN 0–415–31050–4 (pbk)

TLE

TO DR CARMEN ELISA OQUENDO CIFUENTES
My wife, my love, my best friend. Without her support and affection, this would never have been completed.

PD

TO EZRA, MIKE, AND PHIL
For the push down the road to where I am now – the blame or credit lies at least partially with you all.

CONTENTS

FIGURES AND TABLES

Figures

Tables

NOTES ON CONTRIBUTORS

Paul Backhouse is currently Manager of Graphics and Digital Media at Oxford Archaeology. He deals extensively with the preparation of both academic and popular publications and reports, and is responsible for all WWW, interactive media and presentations done by OA. He helped to develop the data and metadata standards and dissemination formats used by Oxford Archaeology. Furthermore, he is a specialist in archaeological web development, and interactive educational media.

Matt Bradley is the Geomatics Officer and GIS Co-ordinator for Oxford Archaeology. He has 15 years experience working as a professional archaeologist and archaeological surveyor on sites in Britain, Germany, Holland and the Middle East. He has worked for Oxford Archaeology since 1997. His current work includes building, earthwork, topographical and landscape survey as well as the design and implementation of GIS, survey and CAD strategies and spatial decision support.

Kenneth Brophy is currently a lecturer in archaeology at the Department of Archaeology, Glasgow University, and has previously worked as an aerial photographic liaison officer with Royal Commission on the Ancient and Historical Monuments of Scotland. His current research projects include excavations at multiple stone rows in Caithness and Neolithic cropmark enclosures in lowland Scotland, and landscape study around Cairnpapple Hill, a henge in West Lothian. Furthermore, he is working on a book on cursus monuments in Scotland.

Henry P. Chapman is a Research Fellow and part-time lecturer at the Wetland Archaeology and Environments Research Centre at the University of Hull. Employed previously as a landscape investigator with the Royal Commission on the Historical Monuments of England, and as a researcher with the English Heritage Humber Wetlands Project, he specializes in later prehistoric landscape archaeology and the applications of GIS and technical survey for the interpretation and management of archaeological landscapes. He currently works on projects focusing on environmental change and the impacts on human perception of the landscape.

Patrick Daly is currently a British Academy Reckitt Travelling Fellow in Archaeology based at the McDonald Institute of Archaeological Research, University of Cambridge. He has worked as a Visiting Academic at the Institute of Archaeology, University of Oxford, and an Assistant Professor in the Faculty of Arts at An-Najah National University, Nablus, Palestine. He has conducted field work in Britain, the Middle East and Malaysian Borneo, focusing on periods of social transformation brought about through foreign intervention and occupation. He has been involved in the use of GIS in archaeology for about ten years, and has published a number of articles and chapters related to digital methodology.

Graeme P. Earl is a Research Fellow in the Department of Archaeology, University of Southampton, specializing in computer techniques for the analysis and presentation of archaeological data. He is particularly concerned with the development and implementation of multimedia resources for archaeology, including the uses of virtual reality and other techniques for the interpretation of archaeological sites and for providing access to online archives. Previously his work focused on multimedia methods for presenting data and the use of computer aided design and modelling packages for the representation of archaeological remains at the site of Quseir al-Qadim, Egypt. He has recently begun working on a three-year AHRB research fellowship using network analyses in the study of Roman towns in southern Spain.

Thomas L. Evans is currently the Head of Geomatics for Oxford Archaeology and a Research Associate at the Institute of Archaeology, at the University of Oxford. He has worked extensively in both academic and commercial research in Britain, across Europe and in North America. His research interests focus upon the nature of identity and its interrelationship with landscapes as reflected through spatial analysis. He is currently working upon the development of the practical uses of technology in archaeology, the investigation of social reproduction through 'Landscape of the Dead' and the examination of Iron Age 'Communication and Combat' as represented by two-wheeled vehicles and their relationship to the landscape. He is a specialist in the integration of geomatic approaches such as geodesy, GIS, quantitative methods and technological recording methods into archaeological practice and the development of theory.

Michael Frachetti is a Research Associate of the University of Pennsylvania Museum of Archaeology and Anthropology. His primary research focus is on the prehistoric development and organization of Bronze Age pastoral societies of the steppes and deserts of Central Asia and Eurasia, and their interactions with contemporary civilizations of the region. His recent field research has been based in Kazakhstan, though he has also conducted fieldwork among pastoralists of Finland, Tunisia and Morocco. He has applied GIS and Remote Sensing techniques to the study of social and environmental landscapes for the past ten years.

Benjamin Gearey is a Research Fellow and part-time lecturer at the Wetland Archaeology and Environments Research Centre at the University of Hull. Following his PhD at the University of Plymouth, he worked at the University of Exeter before taking up a position with the Humber Wetlands Project. His research interests include Holocene human-landscape interactions and the archaeological record, and the archaeoenvironmental record of mire systems.

Marcos Llobera is currently a Leverhulme Research Fellow at the University of Southampton, UK. His major interests are landscape research in archaeology, mathematical and computational modelling (especially GIS methods) and archaeological theory. Much of his research concentrates on the design and development of new methodology aimed at addressing in a more formal manner the complexities inherent in the reconstruction of past landscapes, in particular their social and experiential aspects. Currently he is also the co-director of two landscape projects: LA BALAGNE (north-western Corsica) and ALCOI (eastern Spain) Landscape Projects. He has now taken up a position in the Department of Anthropology at University of Washington (Seattle), USA.

Gary Lock is a University Lecturer in Archaeology at the University of Oxford based in both the Institute of Archaeology and the Department for Continuing Education. He has a long-standing interest in the use of computers in archaeology, especially the application of GIS to landscape studies based on his fieldwork projects in England, Spain and Italy. He is an editor of the *Archaeological Computing Newsletter*, and has published many papers and books on computer applications in archaeology, including *Virtual Pasts: Using Computers in Archaeology*, *Archaeology and Geographic Information Systems: a European Perspective* (with Zoran Stančič), *Beyond the Map: Archaeology and Spatial Technologies*, and *On the Theory and Practice of Archaeological Computing* (with Kayt Brown).

Carol Palmer is a Post-doctoral Research Associate at the University of Sheffield. She is presently working on a NERC-funded project investigating the modern ecology of weeds found on archaeological sites in Europe and the Near East. Her research interests are in the ethnography of farmers and pastoralists in the Middle East, archaeobotany, plant ecology, and statistical approaches to data analysis. She recently held the

Council for British Research in the Levant Post-doctoral Fellowship at the University of Leicester and is a member of the Wadi Faynan Landscape Archaeology Survey.

Julian D. Richards is Reader in Archaeology at the University of York. His research interests focus on early medieval archaeology of England and on computer applications in archaeology. He has directed excavations of the Viking cemetery and Heath Wood, Ingleby, and is currently examining Anglo-Scandinavian settlement patterns in the Yorkshire Wolds. Since 1996 he has been Director of the Archaeology Data Service and the e-journal *Internet Archaeology*. He has published numerous books and articles on computer applications.

Ezra B. W. Zubrow is currently Professor of Anthropology at the University at Buffalo, Senior Research Scientist of the National Center of Geographic Information Analysis, Honorary Fellow of the Department of Archaeology at University of Cambridge, and a member of the Graduate Faculty of the Department of Anthropology of the University of Toronto. He is one of the founders of the use of GIS in archaeology. His primary research interests are in theory, methodology and field areas concerned with spatial phenomena. His methodological interests are geographic information systems and sciences, quantitative and statistical analysis applied to spatial and demographic topics, and archaeometry. His area interests focus on environmental extremes and wetlands and he has done fieldwork in the colder extremes of Northern Europe, Scandinavian and Finnish Arctic, the drier extremes of the Southwestern, Mexican and Middle Eastern deserts, as well as the more humid extremes of the tropical wetlands of the United States, Philippines, and India. He also is one of the inventors of a solar powered parallel processing computer and he plays the banjo and cello.

ACKNOWLEDGEMENTS

As with most collaborative projects, there are many individuals and groups whose assistance has proven crucial to the production of this volume. The original concept for a session at the Theoretical Archaeology Group's TAG 2000 session was the brainchild of André Tschan, and though his own illness prevented him from attending the session or contributing to this volume, his initial contribution to this project was invaluable. Similarly, Vuk Trifkovic helped organize and contribute to that session, and his involvement in the early stages of turning that idea into a published volume was essential. Other contributors to the *Archaeological Theory for a Digital Past* TAG 2000 session also proved essential in both bringing about that endeavour, and invigorating the debates and ideas that eventually led to the production of this work. We would particularly like to thank Chris Gosden, Ian Hodder and David Wheatley for their contributions to that session, which were inspirational.

Also of great importance to the completion of this book was the support and assistance given to us by Oxford Archaeology which gave us both time and use of their facilities and personnel in the development of this book. Similarly, the University of Oxford provided encouragement, facilities and a forum for discussion and inspiration. Last but not least, we would like to thank Celia Tedd and Matthew Gibbons who nursed this book over many of the hurdles and whose help and patience allowed us to develop the book into its final form.

Part I

WHERE WE'VE BEEN AND WHERE WE ARE GOING

INTRODUCTION
Archaeological theory and digital pasts

Patrick Daly and Thomas L. Evans

We live in a digital age; a world where computers are omni-present, but in which we are only just beginning to understand how to productively apply them to our lives. In a very short period computers have come from being great number crunching machines to being 'neat' and 'nifty' gadgets, from being almost inaccessible to being everyday devices that we have come to rely upon – perhaps too much. Yet, despite the presence of computers in our offices, homes, cars, planes and, in fact almost every device in the modern world, we do not always know how to utilize them to their best advantage. This is certainly the case in the study of archaeology. To this end one can say that digital archaeology is not so much a specialism, nor a theoretical school, but an approach – a way of better utilizing computers based on an understanding of the strengths and limits of computers and information technology as a whole. This volume presents an overview of some of the more useful and innovative applications of computers to our understanding of the archaeological past. It shows good examples of how technology is being integrated into our approaches to theory, practice and indeed demonstrates how they are assisting in the marriage between the two.

Digital Archaeology explores the basic relationships that archaeologists have with Information and Communication Technology (ICT) and digital technology to assess the impact that such innovations have had on the very basic ways that archaeology is performed and considered. To this end this volume is intended not just for IT or ICT specialists in archaeology, nor for adherents to any one specific theoretical school, but for all those who are interested in and concerned with better understanding how digital approaches have impacted archaeology. It examines the ways that technologies can and do bridge the gap between what have become discrete branches of the same discipline. All of the contributors to this volume are interested in better ways of utilizing computers and computer based technologies in the pursuit of an archaeological past. Towards this end, all of the papers in this volume discuss the formation, current state, and the potential use of ICT in different aspects of archaeology, and/or demonstrate different specific applications which holistically integrate the substance and theory of archaeology with digital approaches. In all the contributions, the explicit aim has been to focus upon how ICT and other digital techniques are integrated into archaeological theory and practice in ways that expand the limits of what is possible within archaeology.

The idea of this book began in the spring of 2000, when André Tschan gathered Vuk Trifkovic and ourselves to discuss the idea of holding a session at the Theoretical Archaeology Group held in Oxford that year (TAG-2000). Its title was *Archaeological Theory for a Digital Past*, and it consisted of an all-day session that delivered a full range of interesting and stimulating papers, all ultimately concerned with how ICT has been productively added to the 'archaeologist's toolbox' in all facets of the discipline, from field work to data analysis and publication. Sadly, and indeed ironically, before the conference even took place, André developed an inner-ear disorder that prevented him from being in the presence of electronic equipment for extended periods and so was unable to continue with the project. The world of archaeological computing has been a far less interesting one ever since. In spite of this, *Digital Archaeology* continued on.

Since we began, however, both technology and this project have changed. Some of the papers presented at TAG were too dated by the time the volume could be prepared, some authors who participated in the conference were forced to bow out due to other obligations, and others were added because their work had appeared or indeed had gained relevance due to the changes in the digital world. As a result, this volume has changed just as both technology and its application to archaeology have changed.

Yet, in other ways, this volume remains essentially the same work that was conceived of in early 2000. It is an examination of how approaches to archaeology, both methodological and theoretical, need to intelligently utilize the world of Information and Communication Technology and how this can redefine the potential of archaeology in the twenty-first century. As such, this volume is divided into different sections based upon a natural division suggested by Ezra Zubrow, author of Chapter 1. To ensure that the holistic nature of the applications presented in this book are clearly demonstrated, authors were encouraged to provide a much broader context, including an almost equal part of substance, digital methodology, and theoretical consideration.

Thus the book begins, not surprisingly, at the beginning, with Zubrow's *Digital Archaeology: A historical context*. As its title promises, this work provides the context and sets the stage for the rest of the work. A unique combination of general historic overviews and personal observations, Zubrow's work discusses where we have come from, and guides us down the road of how digital archaeology might best be applied. Like any good contextual overview, Zubrow's work also suggests the structure for the rest of the volume, defined by five areas of impact that computers have had and can have in archaeology:

1   ICT and digital techniques are changing the actual practice of recording and representing archaeological data;
2   the influence of the advancement in computers on the use of quantitative methods in archaeology;
3   how ICT has created modelling processes to better understand the interaction between people and their environment;
4   how digital techniques have allowed the development of virtual, hyper and alternate realities;
5   and finally how such approaches have vastly increased the dissemination of information to both professionals and the public.

On their own, each area represents a separate aspect in which digital archaeology is developing, but together represent a manner in which our present approaches to archaeology are being changed, challenged and developed to create new paradigms. As such, Zubrow leads us to the important and perhaps paradoxical conclusion that the development of ICT and digital techniques has now entered a stage in which a combination of factors have begun to make even fairly sophisticated analysis and techniques accessible to a non-dedicated ICT specialist. This increasing egalitarian integration of ICT and digital techniques through all aspects of archaeology has enormous implications, both with regards to digitally empowering archaeologists, and bringing non-ICT specialists deeper into the mix and debate. It holds the potential end result of increasing interaction between different theoretical paradigms and digital approaches. Taken to their conclusions, digital techniques will ultimately redefine the roles of all involved in the archaeological process, from the digger in the field, to the interested public. Recognizing this is the first step to taking an active part in shaping these roles, rather than letting them be haphazardly assigned.

To define these roles we begin by noting what in many ways is the most basic impact of the introduction of ICT to archaeology: the gathering and management of data. Thus the second section of this book examines some of the ways in which computing and technology is changing the recording and interaction with data on site, and the ramifications of these changes in terms of data management. The examples given in this section both come from the front lines of the world of contract archaeology and cultural resource management – the world where most archaeology is actually done. Unfortunately, this side of archaeology is often underemphasized or even excluded from much academic consideration and publication, yet it is here that most data is recorded, and where most archaeological work is performed. Indeed, many of the most innovative and influential uses of computer based technologies in archaeology have and are developing out of this world, both in terms of practical data gathering, and indeed in the very ways in which computers can be used to shape the considerations of the excavation process. The growing incorporation of ICT in all aspects of commercial archaeology can and has actually served as a valuable link between the commercial, academic and heritage management sectors. Here also are the projects and circumstances where the use and management of such technologies are put to their greatest limits, and where problems, when they occur are most readily and drastically noticed.

The effectiveness of digital technology in field archaeology and the impacts that this has is well illustrated by Bradley's account of the practical use of real-time recording on two very different sites: the historic buildings of Dorchester Abbey, and the excavation of the 'Ferrybridge Chariot burial'. In both of these projects, reflectorless total stations were linked directly to computers, allowing the results or detailed data capture to be shown as recording was taking place. In both cases, this allowed fuller, more informed decisions to be made regarding the excavation and/or the recording of the buildings, and for reflective interpretive analyses to be accessed during the recording processes.

In a broader consideration, Backhouse discusses some of the problems created by the use of computer based applications in archaeology from the perspective of contracting archaeology (or Cultural Resource Management). He notes how the ease and availability of digital techniques have resulted in the creation of a mountain of data that must be both managed and archived without the clear knowledge or understanding of how and when the presence of such information is to be useful. He then goes on to discuss the ways in which the Framework project (jointly run by Oxford Archaeology and Wessex Archaeology) has not only addressed this problem, but has used information technology to integrate archaeological theory and archaeological method and re-introduce the importance of the excavator's perceptions into the final interpretational processes. This use of ICT has had a significant impact, both in the empowerment of the excavators, and in the ability for the final report writers to better gain the 'digger's eye view' of each pit and trench as it has been excavated. It has, in a sense allowed us to better utilize not just the technology, but that most important of all archaeological resources, the archaeologists.

Yet some elements of archaeology cannot be productively done in the field, and indeed can only be attempted through the examination of collected datasets. The third section of this volume discusses this by focusing on quantitative archaeology: the statistics and number crunching of large datasets. As is pointed out by Zubrow, even basic statistical analysis required massive investment in both time and resources just 30 years ago. Desktop computers with standard and effective software packages have dramatically changed this, to the point where most projects have a database of some sort, and the capacity to conduct a full suite of statistical procedures. This ability to manage, manipulate, and work with large and complex datasets most certainly alters the very nature and scope of the questions that can be asked of the data, and the answers received.

In his chapter, Evans explores the use of simple statistics and large datasets to understand theoretically based questions. He illustrates this with a case that examines how patterns related to concepts of gender and identity can begin to be seen when exceptionally large datasets are examined using even mundane quantitative approaches. An illustrative case, his chapter shows how information technology allows one to begin addressing theory through the use of properly defined questions and how the increasing ability to work with large and complex datasets and statistical procedures influence this. He does this using easily accessible quantitative methods, hinting at the patterns and perceptional expansions that can be obtained through the use of more sophisticated methods.

The fourth section is dedicated to one of the most informative developments in the archaeological use of computers, the use of Geographic Information Systems (GIS) in the modelling of real world processes in the attempt to simulate and perhaps gain new insights into the interaction between humans and their environments. This is an area in which a significant amount of focus has gone into over the past decade, and many of the more talked about developments in ICT in archaeology have focused. As the general use of GIS and related techniques have now become well established in the literature, we have included several chapters which focus on less conventional aspects of archaeological inquiry, as well as an innovative and informed appraisal of technique and exploration of techniques commonly applied in landscape archaeology. Using GIS, these papers examine a variety of significant developments in our ability to more fully understand the archaeological world in particular issues of scale that are inherently relevant in both landscape studies and ICT.

One of the key ways in which GIS has influenced the study of landscape is the ability it has provided for us to examine different scales of human interaction within an overall methodological framework. It has allowed us to explore multiple scales simultaneously, allowing each to feed into the other. The first demonstration of this is by Palmer and Daly, who use a combination of ethnoarchaeological survey and Geographic Information System (GIS) analysis to study nomadic pastoralists living in the Wadi Faynan area in southern Jordan. In their work they examine and bridge the distinct but related scales of large 'regional' issues and the more intimate social practices related to individual sites and families.

In his contribution, Frachetti furthers the interrelated study of scale in his use of GIS and remote sensing to examine the mobile societies of the Eastern Eurasian steppes. His approach, which more fully utilizes some of the more sophisticated elements of GIS programs, examines the landscape and how different elements of scale impact the nature of the human interaction within it. He notes not only the issues of the pragmatic use of space, but also introduces elements of cultural modelling into the system, testing elements of our assumptions about pastoralists, and their relationship with the world about them.

Yet the study of scale is only one aspect of GIS, and in his chapter, Llobera provides a much needed leap forward in the use of digital approaches to explore the visual patterns of past landscapes. Breaking from the growingly mundane uses of GIS, Llobera develops the use of the cumulative viewshed as a tool for exploring development of visual structures within landscape. Through the introduction of such operational approaches, Llobera shows new techniques that, when properly applied, could have drastic impacts on the study of human interaction with the landscape.

The fifth section discusses the development of virtual realities, and how they impact our perceptions and understanding of the past. This side of archaeology is developing into one of the main and most important inter-faces between archaeologists and the rest of the world – connecting archae-ology into the mainstream world of multimedia and the internet, presenting information in ways that can easily grasp the imagination, attention and interest of the non-professional public. But such techniques also provide further research potential – allowing archaeologists to explore different aspects of the past in new and creative ways. Moving beyond the simple illustrative and visually exciting factors that characterized their introduc-tion, this section shows elements of how the creation of virtual realities can expand our ability to study and understand the archaeological past.

In their chapter, Gearey and Chapman blur the boundaries between GIS modelling and virtual reality through the intelligent use of both to explore issues of palaeovegetation and the landscape. Using known environmental factors Gearey and Chapman use GIS to build up the vegetative elements of archaeological sites and explore the perceptual impact of different approaches to the sites, showing how, if used creatively, such modelling and uses of differing virtual reality approaches can change our perception of the impact of given sites based upon the important data frequently neglected in many such studies. This is followed by Earl's in-depth examinations of the technical realm of virtual reality (VR) modelling, showing how improve-ments in our technical capacity to simulate the real world can be used to impact our ability to understand it. He illustrates how changes coming out of cinemagraphic approaches to VR can impact our study of the past. Yet he not only sings its praises, but also examines the limitations that such approaches have, discussing both the drawbacks and the advantages that arise from each.

The sixth section of the book discusses what is perhaps the most signifi-cant impact of the digital revolution upon archaeology and indeed the rest of the world: the dissemination of information. This part is the foundation for an inspired and innovative way to make archaeology a truly inclusive discipline, increasing the possibilities for people to present and access the past regardless of their relationships to it. Furthermore, it is one of the main vehicles for encouraging multi-vocality and pluralism, while changing the very definition of how data can be structured and presented – redefining who can be involved in an informed interpretative process.

Richards' discussion of the developments of digital publishing gives an in-depth look at the issues involved with publishing across the various digital media, and discusses the ways that electronic publishing has and will continue to impact archaeology. Lock's chapter on the use of digital resources in the educational environment examines how technological resources are being used in the learning environment. Avoiding the technophillic approach, Lock discusses the realities of how computer assisted learning can work to build a better educational environment, and how broader developments in this field are beginning to resonate in archaeology. The development of such approaches can potentially re-structure how archaeology can be taught.

Finally, Baines and Brophy discuss one of the key elements faced when using ICT for the structuring of ideas into a predetermined format. They examine the strengths and problems involved in the creation of digital thesauri for archaeology. Using concrete examples, they show how lack of control can lead to meaningless word searches, but how important subtleties in meanings can be lost with the introduction of too strong a digital hierarchy of words. This is a valuable contribution to the theoretical discussion of the very nature of the categories into which we put archaeological data and how this translates in an ICT environment.

Digital archaeology should exist to assist us in the performance of archaeology as a whole. It should not be a secret knowledge, nor a distinct school of thought, but rather simply seen as archaeology done well, using all of the tools available to aid in better recovering, understanding and presenting the past. In the end, there is no such thing as digital archaeology. What exists, or at least what should exist, are intelligent and practical ways of applying the use of computers to archaeology that better enable us to pursue both our theoretical questions and our methodological applications.

1

DIGITAL ARCHAEOLOGY

A historical context

Ezra B. W. Zubrow

Introduction

Archaeology has always been concerned both with telling the story of the past and telling stories about the past. Archaeologists and archaeology are a strange mixture of scientist and science and storyteller and narrative reconstruction. As practitioners we try to draw a coherent picture that encompasses both human meanings and general processes. This is a difficult enough task in today's world where one may interview agents, hear stories first hand, and directly measure the impacts of actions. It is far more difficult for archaeologists who try to derive these same stories and processes from the fragmentary detritus of material remains that have survived the vicissitudes of time.

There is a gap and one frequently finds problems associated with the gulf between the stories and numbers. There is a certain empowering quality about people in narratives for they are agents who do things out of love, fear and desire. Yes, they empower peoples and cultures, but perhaps they do so falsely. The numerical and digital worlds are seldom agents of change; rather they are the group phenomena upon whom general processes act. The gulf has an archipelago and it still is possible to cross over to the other side, albeit increasingly infrequently. Members of populations are empowered individually, and what is more certain, one knows that no matter how empowered one is, when one is dead, one joins the numbers of the dead.

So in any case, it is not surprising that stories told in everyday life about the past often coexist uncomfortably with the digital world of measurement, computers, and the statistics of prehistoric material cultures. There are other disjunctions between narratives and digital archaeology. They range from the commonplace to the abstruse – mistaking a correlation for a causal connection or confusing a lack of independence with types of co-dependence. One mistakes anecdotes for statistical evidence, individual cases for averages and the informal logic of context for formal logic. Conversely, one assumes the average is the only story – forgetting the diversity of the extremes for repetition requires uniformity.

10

Purpose

It is against the above background that the aim of this paper is to provide a historical context of the relationship between digital developments and archaeology, emphasizing theory rather than particular case examples. The latter are ably presented elsewhere in this book. Of particular interest is the role that digital archaeology has played in giving a methodological foundation to theoretical perspectives and also whether or not digital archaeology has had an impact on the development of theory.

Two views

There are two distinct and ultimately contradictory views. The first view is digital developments are essentially methodological. They provide a set of tools, similar to any other set of tools in the archaeological tool kit for solving problems that are generated by a variety of theoretical or narrative concerns. From this viewpoint, digital archaeology is no different than the myriad of dating or environmental reconstruction techniques that range from radiocarbon dating to palynology. Many would see these techniques as being 'a-theoretical' or even 'anti-theoretical'. Although there may be underlying 'theoretical' assumptions, the techniques are universal and may be used by any theoretical position. Digital developments impact archaeology similar to dating developments and they equally may be applied by cultural historians, 'processual', 'post-processual' and 'post-post-processual' archaeologists. At worst, they may need to be tweaked for differing theoretical viewpoints by making sure they do not reflect particular 'theoretical biases'. Equal application of the digital techniques will produce the same results – no matter who is at the research helm.

The second view is digital developments create or at least influence the creation of theory. It suggests digital innovations determine the scope of theory in many ways. The digital domain emphasizes the very large and the very small and makes possible a re-emphasis on the individual as the primary actor. Indeed, if one believes that it reconstructs human mental processes it may be a proxy for theory itself.

The digital revolution and the digital village

There are intellectual and technical revolutions. Sometimes they occur contemporaneously. Thomas Kuhn (Kuhn 1970) suggested that every few centuries major discoveries create new paradigms of thought, research and application. The previous paradigm frequently fails from both its increasingly obvious inconsistencies and the increasing complexity necessary to understand the new phenomena. The paradigms follow a type of 'intellectual dialectic' with synthesis conflicting with antithesis and both being replaced by a new synthesis. This new synthesis, in turn, develops an antithesis and the cycle repeats itself.

The digital revolution in which archaeology participates has several aspects impacting the present paradigm. First, digital technologies offer a way to represent the real world – whether physical, sound or image – in a compact and efficient package. Second, they allow one to count, do statistics, manipulate and evaluate measurements in a variety of summary and analytical forms. Third, they allow one to efficiently model and simulate real world processes in order to understand complex interacting processes of humans in their environments. Fourth, they make possible the creation of virtual worlds that are independent of actuality. Fifth, digital technologies allow one to transmit all of these manipulations, representations, and words around the earth at almost the speed of light to an increasingly worldwide audience.

The result of course is that archaeologists are becoming part of the increasingly widespread digital village. This village is characterized by a lack of contiguity, distance and identity. Distance between archaeologists – between archaeologists and their sites – and between archaeologists and their artefacts are becoming systematically less important.

Archaeologists communicate with their laboratories, colleagues, and even

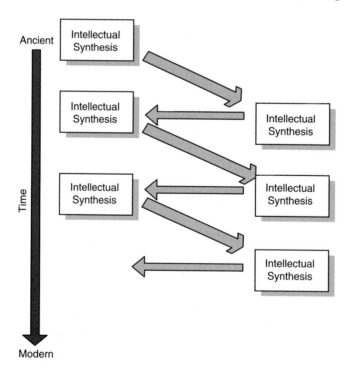

Figure 1.1 Intellectual dialectic.

homes from the field through the expanding networks of cellular and satellite phone systems throughout the world. They bring computers to excavations and surveys for 'in field' computing. Communication is through wire or more frequently wireless connections to the internet. One brings more and more powerful computing to the field where communication problems are significant. Scott Branting, Jeff Tilson and I have developed a modular, field 'parallel processing' machine (with four processors) that runs on solar power. Thus, even when the digital wireless communication systems are insufficient sophisticated field analysis may be undertaken.

A new village is defined by archaeologists, including other specialists such as geologists, palynologists, geographers, economists, etc. as well as the broad general public. The lack of identity in this digital village has important consequences. The boundaries among professional archaeologists, amateur archaeologists, other professionals and the general public become increasingly fuzzy and even disappear. One cannot assume the background or qualifications of an archaeologist or member of the non-archaeological professional public who sends one an email or is responsible for an archaeological ezine, web-site, or e-journal. Given that the digital village is so open one cannot tell who reads and views archaeological web pages or e-journals. The content, such as locations of archaeological sites or artefacts, must be better protected in the digital world. The ease for antiquities to be sold legally or illegally is enhanced through reputable markets such as eBay and less reputable markets where antiquities are sold between individuals who never need to reveal their real name or even location. Finally, the illicit trafficking in antiquities also is hindered by new digital methods to trace and track stolen artefacts.

It is important to note that the digital village is changing at an increasingly rapid rate. There is a process of cyber mutation which means that information technology changes very quickly. It cannot be linked to any single technology or media. In the same way that ink is extinct, both sizes of floppy disk are dead, and CDs and DVDs are on their way out, new digital and e-technology are created, which in turn recreates the village in numerous ways. This paper was composed on four computers using a jump disk that fits one gigabyte onto the same keychain that has my automobile keys. Linux replaces Windows, open systems replace closed computing, and graphics replace text. Soon the PC will be as dead as the 'passenger pigeon'. But for the purposes of this paper it is not where the technology is moving that is important, but rather where the archaeologists are moving. Some are cyber-techies, others digital scholars, others are the 'Luddites' complaining about abandoning their pens and papers. It would appear each archaeologist chooses where on the scale of cyber-innovation and retrogression they are comfortable. There is a role for each of them.

Multiple reflections: epochs and mythos

Epochs

A construal based upon epochs suggests that the digital revolution is one more in a long history of technological developments. Prehistory is defined as the record of humanity's tools and technologies. The toolmaker and tool user are well-developed metaphors central to archaeological discussions. They move through well-defined stages. All of us describe epochs by their most important technological developments. Whether it is the Paleolithic, the Mesolithic or the Neolithic, Mumford's Eotechic, Paleotechnic, and Neotechnic periods or finally, Ong's Oral, Chirographic, Typographic, and Electronic ages (Ong 1982), eras are represented by their icons. Thus, the plough, the factory and the computer represent an agrarian, industrial and information age. Each tool has been used to conquer nature. This is not a new argument, and it has been discussed from Bacon (Bacon 1787; Bacon and Montagu 1825) through Kapp (Kapp 1978). Technology is a tool to control nature, and archaeologists – similar to other workers – use their new tools to find and control the past.

Mythos

There is a perspective that suggests new technologies create new worlds. They guarantee for the believers 'new utopias'. The factory system, telephone, automobile, television and nuclear energy have each promised a new and glorious age. There is a 'mythos' about technology (Carey 1992: 130). One hopes that the 'new' will provide where the old has failed. Our faith is unsheakable even when presented with the non-conforming reality that it delivers occasionally and unpredictably. Sometimes it delivers a version of 'utopia'; more frequently not.

There is a redemptive and messianic quality about the myth for the new technocrats. Refugees fled and solved their Old World problems by moving to the New World – a type of redemption for European migrants. As Turner (Turner 1985) suggested one left the Eastern seaboard, crossed the frontier, and homesteaded 'west of the Mississippi'. It was a type of deliverance for early American colonists fleeing the developing establishment in the East. Similarly moving from one type of information technology to another conforms to this pattern of salvation for twentieth-century technocratic migrants. Each innovation is grasped even though the transformation from one technology to another has major costs. The archaeological technocrats of digital archaeology conform to this redemptive pattern.

New technology not only abolishes the old – the old technology, the old environment, and the old practitioners – it becomes the new environment. Not only is technology relevant for methodology, it is determinative of some aspects of theory. For some archaeologists it becomes a variety of 'technological determinism'.[1] Technology has becomes a new religion, thus taking up a new technology is a form of religious experience. The archaeological participants in the digital village are then 'not boys [and girls] with their toys' but participants in an entire new belief system. Conversely, this 'religious-like' experience takes on technological meaning and may be extended into 'hard determinism'. Namely, not only are all processes mechanical, but 'mechanization (itself) is a mechanism'. It is self-referential. Digital archaeology by its nature must grow out of the increasing use of digital technology. By creating and recreating technology, one determines the future and refines the solutions to the problems with which one must be concerned. Digital archaeologists create problems that require digital solutions.

A couple of final points are worth mentioning. First, it is dangerously naive to assume that redemption is mono-causal. It equally is unsophisticated to suggest that one might be saved by technology as by a single school of theoretical thought. Second, it is important to ask from where within society technological progress originates. This paper proposes that those who have the power to introduce a new technology will usually also have the power to either create or stimulate a consumer class to use the technology. Once that happens, there are new practices, relationships and identities that supplant the old.

Historical enabling and correlations

If one takes an admittedly simplistic view of the history of archaeology and the history of digital innovation within archaeology, some trends are clear. One is that computing has enabled some aspects of archaeology, but not others. Another is the correlations between developments in archaeological theory and events in archaeological computing. Many readers will not know the character of analysis prior to the introduction of the electronic calculator and the digital computer.[2]

As a boy of 13 in the 1950s, I remember being taken to a joint archaeology–economics laboratory at the University of Colorado where both archaeological site reports and economic tax studies were being prepared (Wormington and Lister 1956; Nevada: Legislative Tax Study Group and Zubrow 1960) The laboratory consisted of a large room and around its entire periphery were mechanical calculators. Each was the size of a standard typewriter with a keyboard of numbers and a long metal tube offset to the right containing the number registers. There must have been 30 of these Dreiden calculators. They could add, subtract, multiply and divide with a loud clacking sound as the mechanical registers moved numbers. In order to do simple statistical tests such as cross-tabulations, chi square, multiple regressions, or Kendall's tau, the problem would be divided among 25 or so students. Each would be assigned a calculator and part of the calculation. After a week the results would be recombined. It surely limited not only what one could actually do but also to what one could aspire.

In a similar vein, I remember having dinner with Albert Spaulding, John Fritz, Natalie and Richard Woodbury, and Paul Martin in Vernon, Arizona in 1968 (Dunnell *et al.* 1978; Martin 1962a; Martin and Chicago Natural History Museum 1962a; Martin *et al.* 1973). Spaulding commented that the real tragedy of W. W. Taylor (Taylor 1967) was not that his *Study of Archaeology* produced sufficient theoretical and historical criticism to sow discord throughout the profession but that Taylor's ambitions were so far ahead of the technology. Taylor envisioned a substantive method to make archaeological analysis more 'scientific' and more 'analytical' but there was no technology to accomplish those cross-correlations and cross-tabulations that his imagination demanded. His professional life was an unfulfilled foresight.

In contrast, the studies of Longacre (Longacre 1970), Hill (Hill and Gunn 1977), and Deetz (Deetz 1971; Deetz 1977; Deetz *et al.* 1992) were enabled by the development of the large mainframe computers that made possible for the first time more sophisticated large-scale statistical analyses for the end user. Not only were they developed but they were academically accessible in university computing centres with early packages of statistical software. It was not until the beginning of the 1960s that such calculation intensive tests as factor analysis were available to archaeologists. These trends continue through many technological digital developments including the replacement of the card reader by the tape drive, the terminal, the digitizer, the floppy disk, the zip disk, etc. Even more recently, trends in modelling and simulating prehistoric environmental processes have been made easier through the existence of distributed computing, and even understanding aspects of the ancient mind is now possible through the progress in expert systems and artificial intelligence.

Table 1.1 is an idiosyncratic gaze back at some general correlations I see between the history of computing and archaeological theory.

The general correlation is clear. As computing has pervaded archaeology, there has been a shifting emphasis that may be generalized. There was a 'decreasing scale both in machines and questions'. From the large-scale mainframe computers, regional data sets, and behavioural models, there has been a change to small personal computers and a corresponding interest in site and sub-site specific data. Models change to agent orientation and are beginning to analyse the individual and the manner in which individuals operated prehistorically. This increasing 'individualism' in machines, models and data is made possible as a result of the increasing processing power and language sophistication. In short, the digital archaeologist has moved from applications of the mainframes concerned with prehistoric

Table 1.1 History of computing and archaeological theory

Date	Archaeological school	Types of theories and problems	Computing machines – hardware and software	Subjects of use
Pre-1930	Natural observation	Descriptive	Calculating machines	Statistical analysis
1930–65	Cultural history	Temporal and geographic gapsmanship as well as reconstructive	Mainframes, Fortran, Cobol	Statistical analysis, data storage and manipulation
1965–80	Processual	Systemic, hypothetical, nomethetic, behavioural, group oriented	Mini's Vaxs, PC, Pascal, C, Basic	Causation, modelling, simulation, GIS
1980–95	Post-processual	Individual, interpretative	PCs, C++, Prolog	Expert systems, non-causative, AI, field use, GIS
1990–	Cognitive	Individual, experimental and hypothetical, reconstructive	Work stations, PCs, parallel processing, super computing, visual basic, numerous specialized languages	AI, GIS, individual modelling, visualization, webography

subsistence and environment to the laptop PC and view sheds in less than five decades; all of this within a single professional lifetime.

Post-processual and cognitive archaeology

It is my contention that the theoretical underpinnings of post-processual archaeology impacted the use of digital innovations unfavourably. Post-processual archaeology suggests that the individual and the individual mind are unique and that the primary methodology for understanding an individual is interpretation. Fundamentally, it follows the agendas about practice that have been developed by the 'critical scholars'. Post-processual theory and digital technology are incompatible (Whitley 1998). Post-processual is interpretive, digital is analytic. Post-processual is deconstructive, digital is reconstructive. Post-processual is narrative, digital is measured (Hodder 1992; Hodder 1995; Hodder 2001).

Neither post-processual nor cognitive archaeology as presently understood are completely capable of recreating the ancient mind (Renfrew and Zubrow 1994). Narrative inevitably requires leaps of faith regarding both the veracity of the ethnographic present and its relevance to the past. There also is a huge diversity in thought, aesthetics, and even perception. I think therefore 'I am', 'I dream', 'I believe', 'I perceive', – 'I know' is just the beginning. The realities of Frakes' ethnoscience (Frake and Dil 1980; Ellen and Fukui 1996) are just beginning to permeate the non-anthropological sciences. From this perspective, although digital processors can simulate intelligence or vision, they cannot, as presently constructed, duplicate the operational activities of thinking or interpreting, let alone believing. Computers function numerically and sequentially while there is considerable evidence that the human mind does not do so. Multiple tasks and simultaneous thoughts frequently occur in everyday life. Additionally, digital machines operate according to algorithms – rules that computers follow step by step. However, human mental activity such as interpretation is not limited to rule based behaviour. Differing strands of understanding are connected in new and unusual ways. Thus, it is not surprising that those favourite subjects of the post-processualist such as 'art', 'insight', and 'belief' do not follow algorithms.

Post-processualists must reject 'common sense knowledge' and causation that follows rules and that therefore may be described algorithmically. Post-processualists follow the dictums of E. T. Bell:

> ... put common sense back where it belongs, on the topmost shelf next to the dusty container labelled 'discarded nonsense'.
>
> (McCarthy 2000)

> The law of causality, I believe, like much that passes muster among philosophers, is a relic of a bygone age, surviving, like the monarchy, only because it is erroneously supposed to do no harm.
>
> (Russell 1917/1963)

It appears that digital machines may emulate the human mind but cannot raise themselves to the level of consciousness.

On the other hand, the importance of recognizing the contribution of the individual human mind and culture in constraining and diversifying computing and digital representation is an important input of the post-processualists. As a result I believe that I shall see more and more archaeological studies that include a significant role for 'public participation'.

Cognitive archaeology takes the opposite position. There are generalities about the human mind that are not unique and individuals share similar thought processes including common sense knowledge and an understanding of causation. There is a psychic unity to human kind. For cognitive archaeologists, digital archaeology has an ambitious goal. It must take what one knows about the world in general and about the past world in particular, and try to model the goals of individuals in the past. It does this through a combination of measurement programs that model the senses, algorithms that model thought processes and goal orientation, relational databases that recreate memory, and expert systems that retrodict individual thinking. Common sense knowledge and reasoning about causation are at the core of AI, because both humans and intelligent machines start from a situation in which the information available to it has a common sense character. Parallel computing creates the possibility of non-sequential, non-linearity, and simultaneity.

These programs are 'self-teaching' in that they can perform inferred actions including self-correction for achieving their goals. In order to reach past behaviour, past thinking must be combined with past environments. Other digital programs and data structures for representing the past environment exist. Thus today, one may have prehistoric virtual people thinking and making decisions with consequent behaviour that may be tested against the past (Costopoulos 2001; Costopoulos 2002). Even the amount of memory that these virtual people may access varies. Limited memory produces more successful hunter-gatherer specialists; more extensive memory better generalists (Costopoulos 2004).

I believe in the latter cognitive position. However, it is not the intention to argue here for why one view is better than another. Rather, I wish to point out that irrespective of theoretical perspective there is a clear confluence of archaeological theory and digital technology. What is important is that technology enables theory and conversely one's theoretical position surely influences how one judges or if one is willing to use such digital innovations as artificial intelligence. Indeed, what problems one addresses, what technology one uses, and what methods one will find acceptable will be dependent upon where one sits on the post-processual/cognitive fence.

Space, geometry, time, visualization and communication

GIS and digital technology in the third millennium

The third millennium is here. For archaeologists, who spend their lives understanding the increasing rate of innovation in the past, it is a daunting notion to seriously prognosticate the next century. Although trends may be foretold, the careful scholar knows there is a long distance between extrapolation and reality. With that said, it seems likely that the digital revolution will continue to impact archaeology through both a myriad of technological changes, as well as changes in the very conceptions of space, geometry, time, visualization and sound.

I give short shrift to technological changes here. The trends are clear and one needs to follow the engineering, computing, and digital literature more than the archaeological literature to be fully aware of them. Surely, the increased power of computing, increased parallelization of computing, greater distribution of computing, and increased use of large-scale databases are inevitable, as are their concomitant data mining and pattern recognition. Similarly, smaller computers will be matched to an increasing use of wireless networks whose range and complexity will increase. There will be a wider range of technology that will increase digital functions with increasing capabilities for digital vision (cameras in all their forms), digital sound, digital memory and even digital identity. Robotic machinery based on digital technology will improve (including the robotic archaeological field digger) and software will become more and more accessible. The command line driven programs are being replaced by menu driven programs that will become the voice driven software of the near future.

Some archaeologists already are technologically quite sophisticated including mobile GPS and image capturing systems directly tied to 'in field' computing and remotely tied by the internet to large-scale processing (Sherwood 1998; Riley 2001). The collection of archaeological and environmentally relevant spatial data is increasing many-fold. Innovations in this area are taking place on many fronts – including in-field digital data collection, in-field digital data analysis, long distance data analysis (field to home base or home base to specialized parallel and supercomputer systems), digital photography and documentation as well as digital soil and environmental data collection.

Instead, I want to focus upon the changes in the theoretical and methodological world that will continue for at least a decade or two. The conception of space, itself, is changing. The distinction between spatial reality – that phenomena in which humans, and other organisms, exist, move, and subsist – and the cultural construction of space will become more important as geographers continue to examine spatial perception and spatial language. Archaeologists will increasingly apply it to understand how prehistoric societies perceived, organized, and used space.

Traditionally space (and secondarily time) constrains individual activities, the environment, and the ability for individuals or populations to impact their environment. Both individuals and populations have limited spatial and temporal reaches. This physical limit has been called a prism. It is a physicalist, concrete, observable realism and is not concerned with individual experiences or intentions. This type of representation assumes a set of necessities. They are outlined in Figure 1.1 and one models them with the standard sets of digital spatial and data layers compiled in graphics, maps and relational databases (Lenntorp 1976; Lenntorp 1978).

One expects that as cultural constructions of prehistoric landscapes, domestic spaces and religious areas become more prevalent, these 'physicalist' premises will be relaxed. Recent ethnographic work illustrates many

There is an indivisibility of human beings and many other entities.
There is a limited life span of existence of all human and other physical entities.
There is a limited ability to participate in more than one task at a time.
All tasks are time demanding and are finite regarding both space and time.
Space is Euclidean.
Time is linear.
Movement uses time.
Space has a limited capacity to accommodate events because no two physical objects can occupy the same place at the same time.
Every physical object has a history or biography.

Figure 1.2 List of spatial physical realities.

societies where each of these postulates is broken. Humans are divisible; some entities, including spiritual ones, are eternal; one may participate in many aspects of society simultaneously. Multi-tasking need not be sequential. Time is not linear but circular. Some movements are infinitely fast, etc. Space is non-Euclidean (geometries may be haptic, affine, etc.) (Piaget 1997) and spatial transformations become far more interesting when one makes use of 'island directions' or 'one dimensional geometries' which may inform archaeologists more about some social behaviour than does Euclidean geometry. Culturally space does not need to be continuous with both large gaps in conception as well as perception. Thus, patchiness of the environment may be replicated in the patchiness of the cultural space.[3]

Today, many of the cultural constructions of prehistoric space have been limited to viewsheds. Archaeologists have emphasized the visible rather than the invisible. What is visible and invisible are not just matters of sight but of what are culturally perceived. It may be visible but not culturally seen. So, one need not have binary 'viewsheds' of visible and invisible, but one may have graded viewsheds with differing degrees of visibility. Conversely, it may be culturally seen but may be invisible. If this is not evident, consider a blind person who has a culturally perceived space that is not necessarily visible to them. So, one may recalculate the relationships after dropping out the visible or the invisible and new cultural geometries and representations become apparent. 'Viewsheds' already are extended to 'soundsheds' and 'smellsheds'. The use of 'touchsheds' and 'tastesheds' are sure to follow.

Digital maps, whether digitized or remotely sensed, will increasingly be an analytical and representative tool for archaeologists. For all of their positive assets, scalability, portability, accuracy and ease of analysis, there are problems that will become more important in the next decades. There will be an increasing recognition of the problem of 'God's view'. The aerial image, the space photo, and the digitized map have remarkable credibility for being 'real'. If the digital image the archaeologist is using is taken from a satellite, it must be real. Unfortunately, frequently this perceived reality is greater than is justified. These images or maps are 'made' from the combination of different images taken or digitized at different times and created from combining different wave lengths. In other words the 'land cover' one sees may be a combination of images from March and October, digitized in three different periods and then averaged to make the image.

There are inherent limitations to digital maps. They are simplifications of reality – powerful simplifications – but simplifications, nevertheless, created according to rules of scale and projection. A perfect one-to-one map is a second reality and probably cannot exist. Digital maps are not the disembodied view from nowhere; rather they are located in culture, space and time. The common 'mental map' has neatly publicized this distinction (Smith and Jokić 2003). Nearly everyone has seen the 'urban centric' posters of New York or some other city with the region's attractions in the foreground, and the rest of the world vanishing into the distant background. My favourite is the Australian map of the world in which Ayers' Rock is located in the centre of the page, and the familiar landmarks of Europe and North America are 'upside down' and 'distorted' in wonderful ways. These limitations have been well addressed by type of projection, projection point, and scale since the days of Mercator. I expect the continuation of new projections to solve new problems (Wilford 2000; Crane 2003).

It is said that in the computer world obsolescence occurs every three years. In the more specialized digital world of GIS, it is occurring more frequently. For the last decade there has been considerable work in archaeology and GIS. Most of it has been the making of maps, predicting the location of sites, or its use in cultural heritage management (Allen *et al.* 1990; Gillings *et al.* 1990; Gaffney and Stančič 1991; Lock *et al.* 1992; Lock and Stančič 1995; Petrie 1995; Wescott and Brandon 2000; Wheatley and Gillings 2002). In truth, a few of these have been theoretically simplistic, continuing to do the same archaeological and spatial problems but raising the technological bar. However, far more have raised new theoretical and substantive issues including prehistoric 'spatial cognition', 'spatial representation', 'pedestrian transportation', 'spatially informed heritage and social policy', and 'spatial ritualization' to name a few. The changes are more than new problem specifications or technical changes. They are both simultaneous. Merged together they create new subject matter. For example, sophisticated 'network' solutions for modelling prehistoric irrigation systems are being replaced by full digital hydrological models and then tested against prehistoric and modern data showing how the conceptions of the spatial use of water have changed over time. In the next decade these innovations will continue the process of creating a deeper understanding of the spatial organization of prehistoric society.

The importance of digital innovations for time is equally relevant but less well understood. New, better, and cheaper digital counters make dating more accurate and more accessible. Furthermore, time absolutely is inseparable from the intricacies of human behaviour. Cultural constructions of the past incorporate time. Whether or not it is linear will impact its digital representation. Anyone using variable subscripting to indicate time recognizes it makes a significant difference for digital modelling if one assumes that smaller precedes larger or vice versa. Similarly, it makes a difference if digital time moves in a forward or backward direction; if it is divided into equal discontinuous segments or is continuous; if its periods are defined by first and last dates only or by first, middle and last dates or by some other system.

In the context of GIS, yesterday's digital geography is not today's. One knows the 1990 road map or digital remotely sensed satellite photograph of a year ago may not be useful for finding a house in a new subdivision. The question is how old is 'yesterday' and how are the periods defined. Maps are of a moment or a period. Sites, buildings and artefacts are ephemeral, entering and leaving maps at particular times. For example, the prehistoric landscape changes not only according to prehistoric periods but to modern ones. Consider a field attempt to relocate archaeological sites listed in the state historical preservation office files. The number and type of sites varies by the prehistoric period, but it also varies by the 'modern' period. For example, it was found that more than 40 per cent of the sites in a particular period were either not where they were expected to be or could not be found at all. Initially, this was thought to be caused by errors in location and that was sometimes confirmed with a digital gps. But, sometimes it was caused by the fact that the site although properly located was no longer there. It had been destroyed since discovery.

For some temporal systems, other types of digital modelling are necessary. Perhaps the clearest discussion for the layperson of temporal systems is *Einstein's Dreams* (Lightman 1993). In this short book, ten of Einstein's dreams are recounted. In each he is walking by the same lake. Everything is the same except the structure of time . . . and this makes all the difference. In each, causation and perception change. Sometimes you cannot tell 'whether the fat lady is singing' or 'just warming up'. In any case, whether it is greater accuracy, new digital conceptions of periodization, or the use of different temporal systems, time will be one of the most important areas of innovation for the archaeological digital village in the coming decades.

Time, space, and reality become reconfigured in digital visualization of archaeological sites and artefacts. Digital reconstructions of archaeological sites and their environments are becoming more important. One needs only note the Chinese (Yasuda and Miyatsuka 2003) and Turkish fortifications (Summers and Branting 2003) as examples. Digital reconstructions now exist for sites in six continents. Individual objects such as vases, mummies and human fossils have also been reconstructed using this technology.

Various digital systems have been developed to make it easier (Vote *et al.* 2000; Eos 2003) and a variety of models have been developed and tested (Roberts and Ryan 2001). One issue that I want to emphasize has philosophical, methodological, ontological and archaeological implications. It is the problem of indicating the different types of reality in visualization. This issue will become more and more important as digital archaeology becomes more widespread. The merging of differing realities already is a problem in the popularization of archaeology in either the tourist (travel – Jorvik Viking Centre) or the entertainment (movie and television media – Disney) industries. Where does the Discovery channel end and archaeological reality take over? In any visualization of an archaeological site, what part is based upon observation, what part is based upon 'connecting the material dots – interpolating', what part is based upon 'extending the material dots – extrapolating', what part is based upon ethnographic analogy, what part is based upon a theoretical stand, and what part is based upon informed speculation? I believe that each of these should be differentiated and shown visually in the image. Otherwise, when one sees the 'walls of Petra' one is simply buying 'a kettle of fish'.

A differentiated fusion of these realities could be symbolized in a visualization by a clever use of digital graphic design where different amounts and types of transparency, colouring, and texturing correspond to different types of the reality (e.g. interpolation 10 per cent transparent, extrapolation 20 per cent transparent, ethnographic analogy dimple textured, etc.). Thus, a wall might shade into increasing and decreasing transparency depending upon what parts of it are based upon interpolation and what parts are based upon extrapolation. However, this process may rapidly become more difficult as the number of types of modelled realities overwhelms the number of visual denotation systems. In the case of visualization, there should also be digital reflexivity. For example, it would make sense for a wall to have a gradient showing to what degree the visualizer believes it is purely speculative or not.

Finally, as in the case of digital computing, the archaeological digital village is being connected by an increasingly complex digital communication network. The technology is an array of digital equipment and information creating the physical network infrastructure (wiring, digital switches, modems, optical fibre, wireless and other satellite technologies). There is digital software used to send and receive digital data across the network (email packages such as Pine, Elm, Webmails, Mulberry, etc.) (Young 1998; Graham 1999; Furht 2000; Schwartz *et al.* 2000; Gattiker 2001), a videoconferencing system (Intel ProShare) (Schaphorst and NetLibrary Inc. 1999; Rhodes 2001) or a Web browser (Netscape or Microsoft Internet Explorer). These may be combined in powerful ways such as the ACCESS GRID.

The results of the increased digital communication already are seen in archaeology. Field research, data analysis and articles are frequently undertaken by individuals who are not located in the same institution, city, province or country. Examples are numerous. The Stage III project which Tjeerd van Andel and Nick Shackleton developed was an international attempt of numerous fields from five countries to assess the current state of the relatively mild part of the last glaciation. Among its other digital achievements was the running of the world climatic models for the period providing daily, monthly, and seasonal weather maps for Europe during part of the Paleolithic (Van Andel and Shackleton 2002). In another example I cooperated with Patrick Daly on a joint field project along the Russian Finnish border that included archaeological staff from Finland, England, Ireland, Germany, Cuba, Canada, and the United States (Zubrow *et al.* 1999). The analysis was done by people who were neither contiguous nor coterminous. Today, research results are distributed by list-server and by the web. There are archaeological electronic journals, ezines, blogs, and even an anthropological web search engine. The result is that new information is known faster and is spread far more widely than ever before. Archaeology has always been a relatively small but widespread profession. These trends in digital archaeology will both broaden the profession and decrease the spread among the practitioners.

Conclusions

Digital archaeology has its problems and its limitations. But, the dilemmas are challenges calling out for solutions and the boundaries are expanding so rapidly that the limitations are becoming mute. Three of the more pressing problems are the data size, complexity, and toys issues.

- The data issue is that digital analysis and representation have insatiable data appetites. There is never enough data. As archaeologists increase the sophistication of their problems and the methodological techniques for collecting more data become increasingly available, the amounts of expected data are raised. Where once provenience to the metre square was acceptable, now provenience to the centimetre is commonplace; where once remote sensing by proton magnetometer was considered new information, now entire arrays of magnetometers, resistance meters, and seismographs are considered essential.
- The complexity issue may be divided into two parts. First, digital archaeology is possible because so many of the digital technologies rely

on many independent components working together flawlessly. In general, as the digital complexity increases (from numbers to text to graphics, to sound, to multi-dimensional motion, to reconstructive video technology, and real time multiple video conferencing) there are increased problems in implementation and successful operation. More parts mean more chances for component failure or failure in their inter-actions with other components. A consequence is that modern archae-ology is less independent. The day of autonomous researchers, the archaeological Livingstones or the 'Indiana Jones' of the world is gone. For as the work becomes more digital and less independent there is both a perceived and substantive increased need for professional intervention from other fields to make archaeology work. The day of the digital archaeologist as a specialist to keep the digital components of archae-ology running smoothly is already here in some research laboratories and is spreading to governmental, university, commercial and museum based laboratories. The second aspect of the complexity issue is that given the large amounts of data, the sophisticated methodologies, and complex analytical techniques that make up digital archaeology, the archaeologist will often have trouble tracing cause and effect. What is the routing of the changes and their effects through all the intermediary steps? Additionally, similar to the problems of a physicist[4] (Heisenberg 1958; Price et al. 1977) one may have trouble differentiating what is caused by the digital techniques and what is caused by the archaeo-logical and anthropological processes. Of course, the irony is that using more digital techniques just compounds the problem.

• The third problem is the 'digital toys' issue. There is a tendency to use digital technological solutions simply because one has the 'toys' avail-able. For many archaeologists, archaeological engineering is one of the more pleasurable of archaeological occupations (Florman 1976; Hacker 1989; Hacker 1990). It comes second only to the actual field work and the discovery of the new artefacts. Usually, it is far more enjoyable than the 'drudgery' of writing grant proposals, preparing collections, and the usual humdrum of academic, bureaucratic, and museum politics. The archaeologist's pleasure that is found in ancient materials is reflected in the emotional comfort they find in technology. For many archaeologists, a childhood spent hunting for objects makes using technology for understanding those same objects a comfortable environment. Second, it is commonly assumed that being field-focused, adventure-focused, travel-focused, and technology-focused that archae-ologists tend not to be particularly people-focused.

It took more than 200 years for the printed book to change the nature of scholarship and research; it is clear that it has taken less than 50 years for the digital revolution to change the face of modern scholarship. As

I have shown, the impact of the digital world on archaeology has been considerable. The sharp growth in the percentage of distant co-working relationships has already been noted. This article was written by a North American archaeologist for archaeologists presently residing in the Middle East and Europe.

In summary then:

- Digital archaeology is not strictly methodological; it enables and impacts particular theoretical positions.
- Digital archaeology is not simply a new age.
- There is a mythos about digital archaeology that one needs to forget or de-emphasize.
- Digital archaeology has both enabled archaeological theory and correlates with particular types of theory. From data organization and statistics, through modelling and simulation, to individual visualization and GIS there has been an increasingly greater resolution on the individual in archaeological theory that has been generally matched by increasing smaller but more powerful processors in hardware and a greater specificity of computer languages.
- Post-processual archaeology requires computing to be ancillary and focused on the process of doing archaeology in the field, for digital archaeology cannot inform on interpreting the mind of the prehistoric native. Thus post-processual archaeology will by its nature de-emphasize digital archaeology but will emphasize the public participation in the digitalization process. Cognitive archaeology suggests that artificial intelligence can imitate human thought and thus holds out the opportunity to model and understand the individual and makes digital archaeology more primary in its tool set.
- There will be an increased emphasis on the variety of different types of spatial, geometric and temporal systems as the digital archaeology increases its reach into more and more prehistoric problems using methods such as GIS.
- Increased use of digital visualizations and communication systems will change the nature of archaeology requiring the fusion of different types of realities while broadening participation.

In short, digital archaeology uses future technology to understand past behaviour and thus, perhaps the words of George Orwell, the prophet on time and culture, are most appropriate: 'He who controls the past commands the future. Who commands the future conquers the past' (Orwell 1961).

Notes

1 Veblen (1857–1929) was the first to coin the term 'technological determinism' but it was only a point in the developmental line of understanding the importance of technological change for theory and methodology. Earlier was Bacon's (1561–1626) conception of technology as a mechanism for control. During the next century (1596–1716) it gets transformed by Descartes, Leibniz and Pascal from being a mechanism of control with others into suggesting that the entire world is controlled by technological principles. Emmanuel Kant (1724–1804) spans the eighteenth century like a colossus but retreats by arguing that the technological knowledge is limited to only one sphere – the phenomenal – which is separate from the noumena. Kapp (1808–1896) both expands and contracts its import-ance, suggesting that technology determines conceptions of space and time thus limiting what one may conceive and what one may control. Friedrich Dessauer (1881–1963), facing the inroads of romanticism and increasing awareness of the importance of psychology, argues that technology is not about control but about experience, and it has become the new way for human beings to experience. It is a type of religious experience – and religious experiences take on technological meanings. Marshall McLuhan (1911–1980) takes Kapp a further step suggesting that technology abolishes space and time.
2 My children – grown adults – were horrified when they discovered old copies of my dissertation and my Master's thesis. They exist only on 'onion skin'. It had to be explained that in those 'ancient' times prior to Xerox, carbon paper was one of the few ways to make multiple copies.
3 Recently, a group that I directed were concerned with developing new sets of mathematical tools to determine cultural 'hot spots' in a discontinuous environment. In other words how does environmental patchiness interact with cultural patchiness? Hot spots are the ultimate in patchiness. The innovation was to define two types of clustering that could be calculated independently and that would interact with each other. The first type of clustering was a clustering using some-what standard clustering techniques on the 'data layers'. In other words, one wished to see if there were clusters of attributes, clusters of non-spatial variables and if so, project how the data that makes up these clusters appear spatially. The second type of clustering is the inverse. It is clustering the spatial coordinates – in other words, clustering on the spatial layer and projecting those onto the material and environmental attributes. One could examine spatial clusters for content and content clusters for spatial location. Do they co-occur or not? In addition, one may consider cultural and environmental patchiness on both a global and local level.
4 This is similar to the Heisenberg uncertainty principle.

References

Allen, K. M. S., S. W. Green and E. B. W. Zubrow (eds) (1990) *Interpreting space: GIS and archaeology*. London; New York: Taylor & Francis.

Bacon, F. (1787) *The essays of Francis Bacon . . . on civil, moral, literary and polit-ical subjects. Together with the life of that celebrated writer*. London, Printed at the Logographic Press by J. Walter and sold by J. Robson [etc.].

Bacon, F. and B. Montagu (1825) *Works*. London: Pickering.

Carey, J. (1992) *Communication as culture: essays on media and society*. New York: Routledge.

Costopoulos, A. (2001) 'Evaluating the impact of increasing memory on agent behaviour: Adaptive patterns in an agent-based simulation of subsistence.' *Journal of Artificial Societies and Social Simulation* 4(4) <http://www.soc.surrey.ac.uk/JASSS/4/4/7.html>

Costopoulos, A. (2002) 'Playful agents, inexorable process: elements of a coherent theory of iteration in anthropological simulation.' *Archeologia e Calcolatori* 13: 259–65.

Costopoulos, A. (2004) Personal Communication. Society of American Archaeology Meetings, Montreal, Canada April 1.

Crane, N. (2003) *Mercator: the man who mapped the planet.* New York: H. Holt.

Deetz, J. J. F. (1971) *Man's imprint from the past; readings in the methods of archaeology. Selected by James Deetz.* Boston: Little, Brown.

Deetz, J. J. F. (1977) *In small things forgotten: the archaeology of early American life.* Garden City, NY: Anchor Press/Doubleday.

Deetz, J., A. E. Yentsch and M. Beandry (eds) (1992) *The art and mystery of historical archaeology: essays in honor of James Deetz.* Boca Raton: CRC Press.

Dunnell, R. C. and E. S. Hall (eds) (1978) *Archaeological essays in honor of Irving B. Rouse.* The Hague; New York: Mouton.

Ellen, R. F. and K. Fukui (1996) *Redefining nature: ecology, culture and domestication.* Oxford, UK; Washington, DC: Berg.

Eos (2003) *PhotoModeler Pro: archaeology measurement and modeling software.*

Florman, S. (1976) *The existential pleasures of engineering.* New York: St Martin's.

Frake, C. O. and A. S. Dil (1980) *Language and cultural description: essays.* Stanford, CA: Stanford University Press.

Furht, B. (2000) *Handbook of internet computing.* Boca Raton, FL: CRC Press.

Gaffney, V. L. and Z. Stančič (1991) *GIS approaches to regional analysis: a case study of the island of Hvar.* Ljubljana: Znanstveni inštitut Filozofske fakultete.

Gattiker, U. E. (2001) *The internet as a diverse community: cultural, organizational, and political issues.* Mahwah, NJ: Lawrence Erlbaum.

Gillings, M. and A. Wise (1990) *GIS guide to good practice.* Oxford, UK: Oxbow.

Graham, G. (1999) *The internet: a philosophical inquiry.* London; New York: Routledge.

Hacker, S. (1989) *Pleasure, power and technology: some tales of gender, engineering, and the cooperative workplace.* Boston: Unwin.

Hacker, S. (1990) *Doing it the hard way: investigations of gender and technology.* Boston: Unwin.

Heisenberg, W. (1958) *The physicist's conception of nature.* New York: Harcourt Brace.

Hill J. N. and J. Gunn (1977) *The individual in prehistory: studies of variability in style in prehistoric technologies.* New York: Academic Press.

Hodder, I. (1992) *Theory and practice in archaeology.* London; New York: Routledge.

Hodder, I. (1995) *Interpreting archaeology: finding meaning in the past.* London; New York: Routledge.

Hodder, I. (2001) *Archaeological theory today.* Cambridge, UK; Malden, MA: Polity Press; Blackwell Publishers.

Kapp, E. (1978) *Grundlinien einer Philosophie der Technik.* Düsseldorf: Stern-Verlag Janssen.

Kuhn, T. S. (1970) *The structure of scientific revolutions.* Chicago, IL: University of Chicago.

Lenntorp, B. (1976) *Paths in space-time environments: a time-geographic study of movement possibilities of individuals.* Lund: LiberLäromedel/Gleerup.

Lenntorp, B. (1978) 'The time-compact society and its representation.' *Series: Rapporter och notiser/Institutionen för kulturgeografi och ekonomisk geografi vid Lunds universitet* 49: 21.

Lightman, A. P. (1993) *Einstein's dreams.* New York: Pantheon Books.

Lock, G. R. and J. Moffett (eds) (1992) *Computer applications and quantitative methods in archaeology,* BAR Int. Series 577. Oxford: Tempus Raparatum.

Lock, G. R. and Z. Stančič (1995) *Archaeology and geographical information systems: a European perspective.* London; Bristol, PA: Taylor & Francis.

Longacre, W. A. (1970) *Archaeology as anthropology: a case study.* Tucson: University of Arizona Press.

Martin, P. S. (1962a) *Chapters in the prehistory of eastern Arizona.* Chicago, Il: Chicago Natural History Museum.

Martin, P. S. (1962b) *Indians before Columbus; twenty thousand years of North American history revealed by archeology [by] Paul S. Martin, George I. Quimby [and] Donald Collier.* Chicago, Il: University of Chicago Press.

Martin, P. S. and F. Plog (1973) *The archaeology of Arizona; a study of the southwest region [by] Paul S. Martin [and] Fred Plog.* Garden City, NY: Published for the American Museum of Natural History [by] Doubleday/Natural History Press.

McCarthy, J. (2000) *The future of logic based AI.* http://www-formal.stanford.edu/jmc/reviews/dreyfus/node2.html#SECTION00020000000000000000

Nevada: Legislative Tax Study Group and R. A. Zubrow (1960) *Financing state and local government in Nevada.* Carson City.

Ong, W. J. (1982) *Orality & Literacy: The Technologizing of the Word.* London: Routledge.

Orwell, G. (1961) *1984, a novel.* New York: New American Library.

Petrie, L. (1995) *GIS in archaeology: an annotated bibliography.* Sydney: Archaeological Computing Laboratory University of Sydney.

Piaget, J. (1997) *The child's conception of space/Jean Piaget and Bärbel Inhelder.* London; New York: Routledge.

Price, W. C. and S. S. Chissick (eds) (1977) *The uncertainty principle and foundations of quantum mechanics: a fifty years' survey.* New York: Wiley.

Renfrew, C. and E. B. W. Zubrow (1994) *The ancient mind: elements of cognitive archaeology.* Cambridge; New York: Cambridge University Press.

Rhodes, J. D. (2001) *Videoconferencing for the real world: implementing effective visual communication systems.* Boston: Focal Press.

Riley, R. (2001) 'The three C's of database usage at Dust Cave.' 58th annual meeting of the Southeastern Archaeological, Chattanooga.

Roberts, J. C. and N. Ryan (2001) 'Alternative archaeological representations within virtual worlds', in Richard Bowden (ed.) *Proceedings of the 4th UK Virtual Reality Specialist Interest Group Conference – Brunel University*, pp. 179–88, Uxbridge, Middlesex, November 1997.

Russell, B. (1917/1963) On the notion of cause. *Mysticism and logic and other essays.* London: Unwin.

Schaphorst, R. and NetLibrary Inc. (1999) *Videoconferencing and videotelephony technology and standards*. Boston: Artech House.

Schwartz, D. G., M. Divitini, and T. BraseyLvik (eds) (2000) *Internet-based organizational memory and knowledge management*. Hershey, PA: Idea Group Pub.

Sherwood, S. C. (1998) 'Geoarchaeological structure and interim management of the Dust Cave relational database.' 55th annual meeting of the Southeastern Archaeological Conference, Greenville, South Carolina.

Smith, Q. and A. Jokić (2003) *Consciousness: new philosophical perspectives*. Oxford; New York: Clarendon Press; Oxford University Press.

Summers, G. and S. Branting (2003) Kerkenes Dag.

Taylor, W. W. (1967) *A study of archeology*. Carbondale: Southern Ilinois University Press.

Turner, F. J. (1985) *The frontier in American history*. Malabar, FL: Robert E. Krieger.

Van Andel, T. H. and N. J. Shackleton (2002) The Stage 3 Project.

Vote, D. M. Acevedo, S. Joukowky and D. Laidlan (2000) 'ARCHAVE – A Three Dimensional GIS for a CAVE Environment'. *CAA 2000: Computing Archaeology for Understanding the Past*, Ljubljana, Slovenia: BAR International Series Archaeopress.

Wescott, K. and R. J. Brandon (2000) *Practical applications of GIS for archaeologists: a predictive modeling toolkit*. London; Philadelphia: Taylor & Francis.

Wheatley, D. and M. Gillings (2002) *Spatial technology and archaeology: the archaeological applications of GIS*. London; New York: Taylor & Francis.

Whitley, D. S. (1998) *Reader in archaeological theory: post-processual and cognitive approaches*. London; New York: Routledge.

Wilford, J. N. (2000) *The mapmakers*. New York: A.A. Knopf.

Wormington, H. M. and R. H. Lister (1956) *Archaeological investigations on the Uncompahgre Plateau in West Central Colorado*. Denver, CO: Denver Museum of Natural History.

Yasuda, Y. and Y. Miyatsuka (2003) 'Archaeological 3D visualization for Chinese fortress sites.' *International Archives of Photogrammetry and Remote Sensing* 34 (5/W1): 87–90.

Young, G. (1998) *The Internet*. New York: H.W. Wilson.

Zubrow, E., Nunez, M., Daly, P., Frachetti, M., Trella, P., Chestnut, D., Mitchell, P., Niskanen, K., Rajala, A., and Thurston, E. (1999) 'Archaeological survey of the Finnish-Russian Border and the Oulanka River Valley.' *Oulanka Reports* 20.

Part II

DATA COLLECTION

2

ARCHAEOLOGICAL SURVEY IN A DIGITAL WORLD

Matt Bradley

One of the most dramatic influences digital techniques have had within archaeology is their impact upon archaeological recording. One aspect of this is the spatial recording of sites using 'real-time' survey software combined with surveying equipment, such as the Total Station Theodolite (TST), Global Positioning Systems (GPS) and laser scanners.

This chapter examines the use of such 'real-time' techniques in recording archaeological sites. It does not examine the high-end or cutting edge aspects of such work because, such techniques, although innovative, are expensive, and their worth for archaeological recording unproven. Instead, it looks at the practical application of digital techniques to real archaeological cases. Two quite different archaeological sites are examined, Dorchester Abbey – a historic complex of ecclesiastical buildings, and the Ferrybridge Chariot – an Iron Age inhumation placed within a square barrow. Each of these investigations faced very different problems, but produced generally similar solutions that have helped to develop practical survey techniques for the twenty-first century.

The use of these techniques has important implications for archaeological survey. It adds a new dimension to the debate about the subjective versus objective nature of field recording. The industry standards for conventional planning have long been widely accepted, and most archaeologists with relevant experience know implicitly what the potentially subjective elements of such techniques are. The use of digital technology can be misleading, because while it is easy to focus upon the levels of precision available, and the potential efficiency with regards to time spent in the field, the simple use of the word 'digital' often implies a degree of scientific objectivity, as well as accuracy and precision, that may not be there in reality. The basic principles of field survey which determine the outcome of any type of survey are the same, regardless of the techniques used, and basic issues like resolution and definition are largely determined by a combination of time pressure, resources available, and personal decisions and preferences. This does not change when using even the most sophisticated of 'digital' techniques.

However, there are clear benefits to the use of digital techniques. First, because the survey team has an instant view of the data being captured: real time survey techniques allow a greater degree of interpretation on site. Second, as we have done with the Ferrybridge Chariot, the use of real time survey techniques allows the data to be processed very quickly and supplied to the public domain, allowing interested parties the opportunity to share in the process of excavating an important site almost as it is happening. Real time dissemination of results is useful as a community service. It involves local communities in important scientific discoveries and processes occurring around them, that more standard techniques of excavation, survey and publishing, with the extensive time lapses that are part of this process, would have excluded them from.

Dorchester Abbey

Introduction

The Abbey of St Peter and St Paul, Dorchester, Oxfordshire, represents one of the earliest shrines of Christianity. The site became a missionary centre after the land was given to St Birinus in 634. In 1170 the site became an Augustinian Abbey and the existing church was built. Almost all of the monastic buildings were destroyed in the Dissolution of 1536, except the Abbey church, which was purchased by Richard Beauforest who then gave it to the parish. Since the monastic records were destroyed in the sixteenth century, the history of the building previous to this has to rely on structural evidence. The picture is further complicated by major alterations in the seventeenth century and subsequent renovation (Sherwood and Pevsner 1970).

A limited survey of the church was conducted as part of a recording programme being carried out by Oxford Archaeology during the most recent stage of renovation work. A range of paper and digital techniques had been used already to record parts of the abbey revealed during its renovation, and the purpose of the survey was to tie these together as a cohesive whole, as well as recording new data.

The survey consisted of recording selective internal elevations of the abbey tied into an existing digital plan. A survey company (Sterling Surveys) had already surveyed a plan of the abbey at 1:100, so a good control network of survey stations had already been established. The survey had two main objectives: to record the position of wall paintings uncovered during renovation of the interior of the abbey, and to tie in hand drawn material recorded during stripping and re-plastering of certain areas of the abbey to put them in their general context.

Recording techniques available

From the start it was decided to use a reflectorless TST utilising 'real-time' survey techniques as the basis for recording the elevations. However, a brief summary of other possibilities is given below and why they were not used.

Traditional techniques of recording an elevation consist of setting up a datum line and measuring off this with a tape measure with the aid of a plumb bob. The sheer size of the elevations at Dorchester Abbey precluded using just this method. Although scaffolding was in place at one time or another, covering all of the area eventually surveyed, maintaining an effective control between different areas of the elevation, and over a long time period would have been extremely difficult, not to mention tedious. Supplementing this technique by either using a dumpy level or traditional theodolite would have speeded up the process and made maintaining control easier, but considerable time and effort can be saved using the technique that was eventually used.

More intricate techniques than that used include photogrammetry and laser scanning. Neither of these was seriously considered, however. This was not a matter of these techniques being any less effective, but the fact that the level of detail recorded by these techniques would have been greater than that necessary for the job, particularly considering their relative expense.

TSTs have been in archaeology long enough now for most people to be familiar to some extent with what they do. Essentially it is an electronic theodolite with distance measuring capabilities using Electromagnetic Distance Measurement (EDM). This works by measuring the length of time an infra-red beam takes to travel between the TST and a special reflecting prism. A reflectorless TST uses a more powerful infrared beam, or laser, so that a prism is unnecessary and measurements can be taken directly off a surface, with a slight fall in accuracy, the amount of which depends on the type of TST used and the surface the measurement is taken off. This has obvious advantages for recording an elevation; it negates the need for triangulating points from two positions as with a traditional theodolite and greatly speeds up the recording process.

The usefulness of using a TST, and especially a reflectorless one, is increased exponentially if the survey can be done using 'real-time' techniques. Ordinarily a TST records points to an internal memory with a code (either point, line, etc., or, more often, a more interpretative code, e.g. stringcourse, corbel, etc.). When downloaded this can be converted into a layer in a CAD drawing. The disadvantage of this method is you can only be sure that you have covered everything, and your data is any good, after the survey when you have downloaded your data and checked it. In practice a certain amount of post-processing is necessary to make sense of the data, and the more complicated the entity you are recording the more processing is required. A way around this is to use 'real-time' survey. This involves connecting a laptop, husky, tablet or other portable computer to the TST, and, using appropriate software, controlling what you record from the screen. This has the major advantage of being able to see 'real-time' what you are recording. Any problems can be sorted out on the spot and you can ensure you have included all the detail required. The data can then be easily put into a CAD package (indeed some kinds of this software work as an AutoCAD plug-in) with much less editing and post-processing).

Methodology

It was decided in this case to record two-dimensional elevations rather than recording the required areas of the abbey in three dimensions. The amount of recording necessary to get a convincing 3-D model of a building is much greater than for just recording in 2-D, and was unnecessary for the level of detail required. Creating a 3-D model would not have added substantially to the interpretation or understanding of the parts of the abbey recorded in this case.

The basic method for dealing with the paintings was to take square-on photos of each area of wall painting, using 35 mm black and white and slide film, as well as with a digital camera. Each photo taken had a minimum of four targets in the picture. The position of these targets was fixed using the TST;[1] they could then be used to rectify the photos at a later stage onto the elevation.

Once the position of the wall paintings had been established, an outline survey was conducted of each internal elevation where these occurred. Other internal elevations were then surveyed where previous hand-drawn recording had taken place. Once a basic outline of each required elevation had been recorded, salient points of detail were added. Key points were identified and surveyed in, and photographs taken of these areas, using a similar technique as that described above. These photos were later rectified using the key points as a reference. This greatly speeds up the recording of detail, especially as with the type of reflectorless TST used, measurements were not always reliable unless the surface being measured was completely flat, or if the measurement taken was at too oblique an angle. The infra-red beam is approximately 10 mm in diameter, although the further away it gets from its base point the more dispersed it becomes. So any detail of less diameter than this can be difficult to record. The beam also disperses the more oblique the angle between the target in relation to the base point. Differences of up to 0.5 metres were observed in measurements of the same point taken obliquely and square on. To supplement the photos taken brief measured sketches were also used of certain, more complex, details.

A selective approach was used when deciding which detail to record: for example, where the detail of a window was found to be the same as for another window this was not recorded separately. It was not the point of the survey to record every slight difference in building structure, but to give the wall paintings and areas previously recorded some general context. A fine balance had therefore to be kept to ensure an appropriate level of recording necessary for the job: too much detail would take too long and swamp the data that was the focus of the survey; too little and the data would not have enough context.

Once the survey was complete the data was exported from Penmap as a DXF file and then opened in AutoCAD. The data was then split into individual two-dimensional elevations. Additional detail was added from the rectified photos and sketch drawings. Onto these were rectified the photos of the wall painting. The photos were then trimmed so they just showed the areas of wall painting. Hand-drawn, measured detail was added by scanning in the paper copies, geo-referencing the scans in the CAD drawing and digitising them. Some of the results are shown in Figures 2.1 to 2.3.

Ferrybridge Chariot burial

In the autumn of 2003, while conducting archaeological investigations preceding a road scheme, Oxford Archaeology unearthed the remains of a most unusual inhumation – what is colloquially known as a 'chariot burial' that had been placed intact within the remains of a square-barrow enclosure ditch. Such chariot burials are extremely rare in British Archaeology, and this example was only the twenty-first of its kind recovered. They date to the Iron Age and are generally associated with what is known as the Arras Culture, a regionally related burial tradition defined by the presence of square barrows and focused on the Yorkshire Wolds. The Ferrybridge burial, while still in Yorkshire, lay far to the west of the normal range of the Arras Culture, but located within a square ditch enclosure, bore all the earmarks of this tradition.[2] What is more, the enclosure ditch, which surrounded this inhumation, was packed with disarticulated animal remains, mostly bovine.

Perhaps the most important element surrounding the significance of chariot burials lay in their continental connections, for with the exception of the single chariot found in Edinburgh, the closest culturally similar rites to those practised by the Arras Culture, are those found in the Champagne region of north-eastern France. The continental tradition of two-wheeled vehicle burials dates to between approximately 530 BC and 200 BC and shares several traits with the rites of Yorkshire, including the placement of two-wheeled vehicles within the burials and the use of square and rectilinear ditch enclosures around a central grave pit. Yet despite the correlation between these two burial cultures pointed out by Stead (1965, 1959), several significant differences are also known. Key among these is the positioning of the skeletons, with human remains generally being placed in

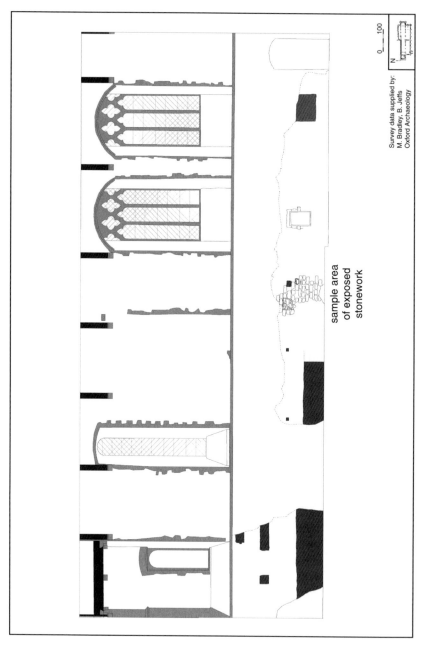

Survey data supplied by:
M. Bradley, B. Jeffs
Oxford Archaeology

sample area
of exposed
stonework

0 ___ 100

Figure 2.1 Internal north elevation nave, Dorchester Abbey.

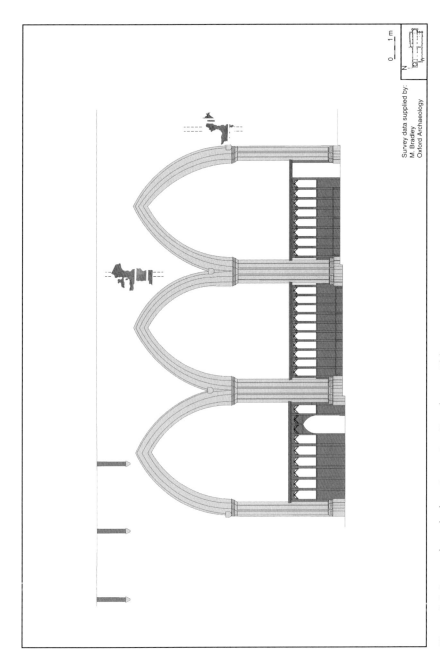

Figure 2.2 Internal north elevation quire, Dorchester Abbey.

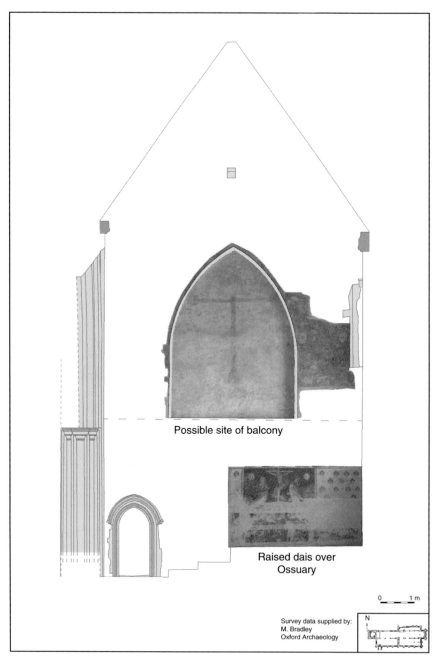

Possible site of balcony

Raised dais over
Ossuary

0   1 m

Survey data supplied by:
M. Bradley
Oxford Archaeology

N

Figure 2.3 Internal east elevation People's Chapel, Dorchester Abbey.

crouched positions on their sides in Yorkshire, but normally placed in fully extended dorsal positions in Champagne. An additional significant difference in the two rites was that while the Yorkshire chariots have tended to be recovered disarticulated, with the wheels having been removed from the main body of the vehicle, the French burials are more frequently found fully constructed, with the wheels in upright positions upon the axle. It is in both of these elements that the Ferrybridge burial took on immediate significance, for even before excavation had begun, it seemed likely that the vehicle had been buried fully articulated and intact, in a rite more similar to those of France. What is more, as was discovered throughout the excavation, the skeleton was recovered laid on his back, with his arms fully extended, and his legs crouched and laid to the left side. Thus, this excavation posed the possibility of addressing issues of both British and European importance.

Additional importance was placed upon this find because of the early identification of the burial as containing a chariot. Of the other 20 two-wheeled vehicles uncovered in Britain, most had been found before the advantage of modern surveying techniques, and very few had been recognised as containing two-wheeled vehicles until the excavation was well underway. In this instance, however the careful initial investigation by Paul Murray, combined with the upstanding wheels of the intact vehicle, allowed Oxford Archaeology the foreknowledge that other excavations had lacked.

These varying elements of significance, care and fortune allowed Oxford Archaeology to construct a methodology that would allow the greatest amount of information about the chariot to be recorded. It was hoped that through the proper use of technology, enough information could be gleaned to be able to reconstruct the chariot, and preserve, if possible not only the excavated remains, but elements of the excavation itself that would enable others to reconstruct how Oxford Archaeology deconstructed the burial. To this end, a variety of 'real-time' and traditional recording techniques were combined to gather as much information as possible about the burial during the excavation process.

The excavation of the site was managed and directed by Angela Boyle, with the assistance of Paul Murray. The survey and spatial recording of the site were conducted by Christopher Breedon using the methodology developed by Thomas Evans. While there were many elements of this excavation that used new and innovative techniques, the bulk of the work was performed through the application of standard techniques and a remarkably good collaboration of specialists from Oxford Archaeology, Bradford University and the British Museum. These elements of the excavation, while well worth noting, were not digitally oriented and as such are not addressed in this forum. The digital survey and spatial recording of the site, however, were based upon the practical application of digital techniques and as such are addressed herein.

Recording techniques available and equipment used

After an initial examination of the varying techniques available, it was decided that the best results would be gained by using a technique similar to that used upon standing structures such as Dorchester Abbey. Though there was a brief investigation into the possible use of laser scanning, it was determined that the actual gains of the use of this technology would have been very limited in this case. Additionally, the potential significance of the site caused all elements of the excavation and survey team to err on the side of caution and avoid the use of 'new fangled gadgets' where no clear benefits would be gained. To this end it was decided to use a reflectorless TST and 'real-time' survey techniques to record the burial and its surrounding enclosure ditch, as it was unearthed. Due to the potential importance of the site, it was also decided to take a series of rectified photographs of each phase of the excavation that would allow both illustrative reconstruction and later digitising of any remains that appeared. These two digital techniques were then combined with more traditional hand drawings of the site that allowed for perceptual elements of the excavation to be captured.

Due to the nature of the site, and the need for 'real-time' mapping to provide predicative solutions, it was determined that the survey would be conducted using 3-D approaches throughout. This technique, while very useful, does have some drawbacks. Perhaps key among these is that the placement of objects within 3-D space can occasionally be tricky, and the surveyors need to be aware of how the images are forming as the results are being produced.

Methodology

The basic method of spatial recording and survey utilised was to combine 'real-time' survey with rectified digital photography and hand-drawn plans to ensure the greatest amount of data could be recovered. The survey itself was performed using a combination of reflectorless recording of each of the elements of the work, and the more standard detail prism technique familiar to most archaeologists.[3] Combined, these techniques allowed for a three-dimensional survey to be produced that included both surface and line detail of the artefact remains and soil staining from the chariot. The advantages of 'real-time' survey as a CAD plug-in became apparent as by having two or three 'viewports' open, each one presenting a different perspective (normally top plan, side elevation, and 3-D isometric), it is immediately obvious if one of the three co-ordinates is incorrect.

Although it had been originally intended to record the general outline of each animal bone using 'real-time' techniques, this approach was immediately abandoned upon the first sight of the enclosure ditch. At the time of excavation, it was estimated that the remains of at least 250 different cattle alone were included in the ditch. The sheer volume of animal bones would have made the practical application of such a method impossible – especially considering the concerns regarding the security and integrity of the site itself. As a result, it was decided that the position of each bone would be recorded, and that their actual outline would be captured through the use of the digitally rectified photography.

The use of digital photography on site was limited to those used for rectified photography, and general 'working shots' that recorded the process of excavation rather than the archaeology. Additional archive quality film based photography was also conducted as part of the normal excavation process. The rectified digital photographs had a minimum of four targets in the picture. The position of these targets was fixed using the TST, they could then be used to rectify the photos at a later stage into the drawing. An initial plan for the creation of a standardised approach to rectifying the photographs had been created to speed the rectification process. It involved use of a simple photographic frame that could be readily repositioned to create photos that were taken from a consistent height. Though the theory behind this approach proved sound, the application of it proved impossible since the weight of the frame which was large enough to span across the site was too great, and promised to damage the archaeological remains. As a result, the more pragmatic approach of holding the camera and levelling the photographs with a line level was adopted.

Each day, the data being recorded was backed up, and in the case of the work conducted in TPSCAD, it was transferred first into AutoCAD r14, and then into later versions of Autodesk Map. The digital photographs were downloaded onto the computer at the end of each day and rectified during the process of the excavation. Daily backups were essential and these copies being kept off site. Additional copies of the data were sent back to Oxford at least once a week for backup and further work upon the more powerful processing machines of the central office.

Once the survey was completed the data was compiled, and at the time of writing is being processed for review and analysis. However, due to the manner in which the survey was being conducted, a series of images were able to be constructed during the process of excavation, and released both to the press and on the Oxford Archaeology website. As the post-excavation and analytical stages of the project continue, more elaborate models of the work will be produced. These will include 3-D reconstructions of both the chariot and the burial ground. Yet perhaps more significantly, the careful digital recording of spatial information will allow us to compare this burial and its use of space to other vehicle burials in Britain and Europe. Using spatially oriented programs such as GIS, and statistical comparisons of the placement of artefacts within the grave contexts, we will be able to note the similarities and differences between the sets of two burial rites and compare results.

Findings

As shown in Figures 2.4 to 2.7 the effort taken in recording this burial proved worthwhile. The careful recording of the soil staining has revealed a great deal of construction detail about the chariot. Both wheels can eventually be digitally reconstructed, as indeed can the yoke, pole and axle – information that had never before been captured in a British two-wheeled vehicle. By itself, this information adds a great deal to our understanding of Iron Age burial rites and construction techniques.

Yet perhaps more importantly, the skeletal remains found at this site were unlike the other vehicle burials recovered from Yorkshire. They consisted of a male, between 30 and 40 years of age, buried on its back, with its upper body extended and its legs in a crouched position and turned to the left. Also within the central burial pit, to the left of the skeleton, was found the hindquarters of a pig, and to the left of his shoulder the remains of what appears to be a spearhead.

It is, of course, immediately tempting to call the body positioning and the use of grave space a hybrid between the continental rites and those of Britain – but to do so would be highly inappropriate. Analysis is still underway, and a great deal more investigation into the details of this burial are necessary before any real interpretations can be made. However, because of the nature of the recording used in this excavation, and because of the analytical techniques which can be applied, we may be able to note the degree of similarities and differences between this burial and those of

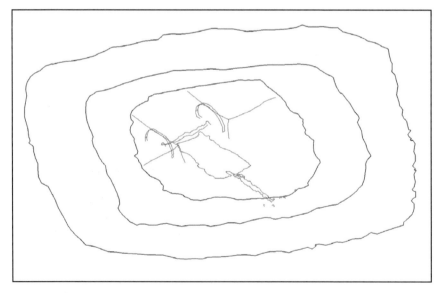

Figure 2.4 Simplified version of real-time CAD based line drawing of Ferrybridge Chariot.

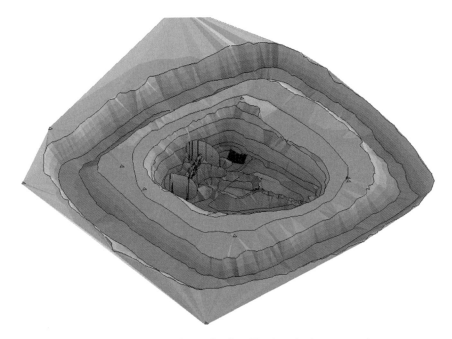

Figure 2.5 GIS contour model of Ferrybridge Chariot, during excavation.

both Yorkshire the Champagne. This may in itself assist us in discovering more about the strange relationship between the cultures of these two regions.

Conclusions

These projects show quite different applications of digital surveying techniques. The Dorchester Abbey survey is a good example of using a mixture of digital and traditional techniques to get a high-quality record cost effectively and quickly, while the Ferrybridge Chariot shows the maximal approach to data recording. Digital methods have not yet reached the stage when they can wholly supplant the intelligently executed measured sketch, but for larger areas, and when strict measured control is rigorously enforced, they can make recording both easier and quicker. The technology does have limitations, but these are becoming less and less of a problem. Reflectorless TSTs are now available more cheaply than ever and technology has moved on even from the relatively new equipment used for these surveys, which is only a couple of years old. The latest machines are more accurate and cheaper. The use of these technologies has allowed for a number of important advances. As well as speeding up data collection it allows the survey team greater interaction with the data as they collect it, and the rapid dissemination of important results to a public audience.

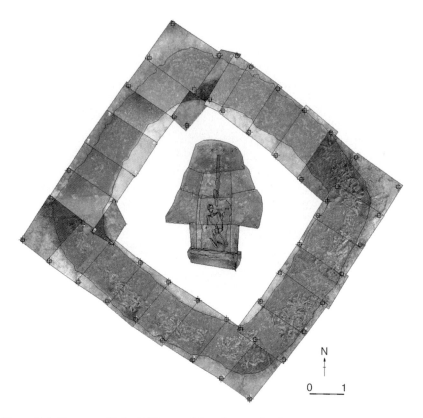

Figure 2.6 Photorectified CAD model of Ferrybridge Chariot, used during excavation.

The key to implementing this kind of technology is to scale it to the needs of the project you are doing. It will not be appropriate for all kinds of survey, or even all kinds of building survey, and it doesn't necessarily have to mean recording every last detail if it is used. In order to be effective use of the technology must fit the precision and accuracy required and there is no need to do more than is necessary just because we can. Digital techniques should be used to supplement rather than supplant more traditional methods of recording.

Notes

1 The TST used in this case was a Leica TCR 705 with a reflectorless infra-red laser of maximum range 30 metres dependent on conditions (in practice about 15 metres because of problems with oblique measurements). Into this was connected a 486 50 Mhz Fujitsu laptop with 16 MB RAM running Penmap 2.3 software. It

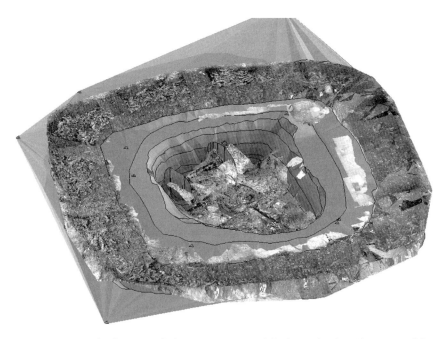

Figure 2.7 Simple photorectified GIS contour model of Ferrybridge Chariot used for
    initial post-excavation phase.

    should be noted that the laptop and software used is hardly 'state of the art' and
in fact was seven years old when the survey was conducted, and is still in use !

2 Only one other chariot has ever been recovered from Britain as far outside the
Wolds as the Ferrybridge example. The Newbridge chariot was recovered in the
outskirts of Edinburgh and, like the Ferrybridge burial, it was also found intact
and articulated.

3 A Leica 400 TCR series reflectorless TST was used in combination with a state-of-
the-art pen computer. The availability of an on-site generator allowed us the luxury of using such a high-end solution, without fear of battery drain. The software
used was a combination of Leica's now defunct TPSCAD, and Latimer CAD's
TheoLT. Both of these allow survey directly into AutoCAD, as mentioned above.
Because of the limits of the older version of Penmap available newer software
with greater flexibility in 3-D was used. All three software packages can be used to
produce 3-D results that are immediately visible on the screen, however, and each
has its own advantages and disadvantages.

References

Sherwood, J. and Pevsner, N. (1970) *The Buildings of England: Oxfordshire.*
Harmondsworth: Penguin.

Stead, I.M. (1959) 'A chariot burial on Pexton Moor, North Riding', *Antiquity* 33:
214–16.

Stead, I.M. (1965) *The La Tene Cultures of Eastern Yorkshire.* York: Yorkshire
Philosophical Society.

3

DROWNING IN DATA?

Digital data in a British contracting unit

Paul Backhouse

In the beginning there was rescue archaeology financed through public funding; then came the advent of the contracting unit funded by developers. Throughout these different periods we have recorded archaeology in minute detail, and with each passing year more data is captured and added to the record. During this period of unbridled growth and expansion in the archaeological world, technologies available to the archaeologist have also undergone similar growth and expansion. So how has the advent of the microchip helped or hindered the archaeological process? From field to post-excavation computers are now endemic, but in what ways are they really useful, or are they just poorly understood and improperly used tools that can actually cause more damage to the archaeological record than we currently realise? This paper examines how technology has spread through contracting units based on a combination of my own experience and the observations of others across the field.

Adoption of technology – good or bad?

During the last ten years I have seen the spread of computers from items of status to 'one on every desk' – the dissemination of IT has been unplanned and *ad hoc*, with some areas that would clearly benefit from computerisation being left till last due to inactive or technologically illiterate managers. Contract and rescue archaeology are reactionary in their nature. Lead times are tight, preparation can be limited and long-term planning can be nigh on impossible. A turn-around time of two weeks between receiving a contract and deploying diggers in the field is pure luxury. As a result of this particular set of circumstances, the first elements of the business to be forgotten are forward planning and investment in training. This has meant that it is usually faster, and always safer, to rely on old methods rather than invest in what, in the long term, would be a more rapid and efficient method. It is only due to the presence of early adopters, those few individuals with both the understanding to see the value of computers and the capacity to buy them, that contract archaeology has adopted technology at all.

The adoption of technology has generally been undertaken in a reactionary and sporadic way: *we have a problem, this may be a solution*. The problem with this approach is that the introduction of technology within one process of archaeology always has a knock-on effect on the processes after it. Both the adoption of CAD in the field affects elements of post-excavation through to publication, and the use of GIS in the analysis requires different information to be collected in the field, often using different techniques, standards and categories. The adoption of any technological approach causes a ripple, or a tsunami affecting the rest of the organisation. Put simply, it is not just a case of using a computer to do a task that had previously been done in a different way; a degree of conceptual change is required on multiple levels to successfully incorporate new technology in ways that are not only effective and useful, but also expand the range of what is possible within the parameters of contract archaeology. This includes not only better 'real time' integration of data analysis and field work, but also increased research potential and information dissemination.

Computing has been used in the field and in the post-excavation process as a means to an end without really realising its implications. Normally, it is not until the data is evaluated months or years down the line that we discover that key elements of the record are missing that prevent us from using the technology as intended. The adoption of programs or hardware inappropriate to the tasks in hand has also meant a vast waste of resources with work having to be redone over and over again. Changes of technology and/or access to different digital approaches have also occurred, rendering obsolete processes that were previously completely acceptable. To be fair, however, it is not surprising projects that can last over ten years have to port their data from one application to another over and over again as technology and use changes. The problem is generally lack of forethought as to what is going to be done with the data, and how the information moves through the entire unit. Understanding this is the first step to creating a better solution.

Understanding data flow in a contracting unit

If we look at a typical contracting unit operating in British archaeology now, we are likely to see a patchwork of technological landscapes used throughout its organisation. Some portions of the unit use technology that was available in the early 1900s, while others use technology that is at the present-day cutting edge – at least in archaeological terms. Yet before we can move our situation forward, we need to examine how information moves across the patchwork landscape, and how technology is, can and should be used.

The field

Unless you are working on a truly exceptional site – and I don't mean that the site is a rare example of a fourth-century Roman villa, but rather a site where the project manager has invested in technology – it is likely that very little digital data capture occurs. If digital data is being captured it is very much undertaken in a patchwork model; a bit of survey here, digital photography there. Most records are still paper based, and in this area standard data gathering techniques have not changed since the creation of contracting units. There are cases where this is changing, but only very slowly. CAD maps from initial surveys and site layouts are now common, but their use in the field is sporadic at best. Total station survey of features as they arise is more common, but usually this requires a 'survey specialist' to operate the machine. Database analysis or GIS is only very rarely used on sites.

Instead, information is written on context sheets. Plans are normally drawn by hand, with survey points shot in later by a survey team. While almost all sites use levels, most spatial data is gathered off a site grid. All this data is then shipped off site and entered on to computers at the office.

This is beginning to change, and even since the time that this chapter was first proposed we have seen some innovation in this process. Yet even so, the normal practice remains that most sites are recorded by traditional techniques, the results written on paper, and the data then moved to a central location for digitising and data entry.

There are reasons for this. For years I have been predicting pocket computers on site, recording data via touch screens producing databases of context sheets. I have been involved into research and development on the feasibility of on-site recording as far back as 1995. It was obvious even then that computer technology made or will make this kind of recording feasible. So eight years down the line, apart from small forays into portable computing, as far as I am aware not one contract unit has invested in a large number of portable computers. Is it the cost? Partly, but more significantly it is the ruggedness of the machine that causes problems. One example comes to mind. On one occasion a new portable computer was sent to site to aid in surveying and data logging. It was on site for less than three days before returned to the head office with a broken screen.

> Cost new: £1,500
> Cost to repair: £800
> Life in field: 3 days

The machine was then given to a senior member of staff who used it rarely in the field, but it was kept in good condition for a number of years.

It is a well-known truism that any equipment that goes to site ends up broken. Digital cameras are dropped in buckets of water, mobile phones are buried in trial trenches, EDMs fall off cliffs. Archaeologists, it seems, cannot be trusted with equipment that use batteries without breaking something – electronic casualty rates in the field are very high. Contracting units have now become very wary of investiture in technology for the field given its short operating life, and it is unlikely that contracting units will invest in technology now, unless it can be shown clearly that the investment would reap rewards in saving both time and money, and this is generally a good thing. However, this fact has greatly delayed elements of digital data capture in the field, and has resulted in both inaccuracies and inefficiencies being added down the line.

Post-excavation

Since the nature of fieldwork requires that data collection is normally paper based, it is at the post-excavation stage that digital data normally begins. What affects the decision as to what data is 'digitised' is the availability of resources, the relative experience of the post-excavation staff, and the access to given technology (primarily software). The main driver behind these decisions, however, is the understanding of the archaeologist leading the project. This person will either drive the project forward into a digitised form, or not. Sometimes this digital data capture results in all site plans being digitised or just the creation of a context database. Sometimes a specific site deserves more, sometimes far less. It is all based on the needs and knowledge of the manager of that specific project.

Yet, it is here where we see the strengths in using and capturing digital data from day one on site, and indeed, perhaps before one ever gets to the site. The translation of data in post-excavation from analogue to digital costs time, and increases the inaccuracy of the data. It removes the data one more step away from the individual who made the observations in the first place. An interpretation on site recorded on paper is reinterpreted in post-excavation, introducing data irrelevance and data inaccuracy. This is then passed down the line to analysis where interpretations are added to potentially dubious data and erroneous conclusions can be drawn.

Publication

With the advent of digital data and the increase in the creation of archaeological data, publication and storage of the archaeological evidence have become more of a contentious problem. As the amount of data collected and analysed has grown, there has been increasing recognition in the archaeological community that the printing of vast tomes of data serves and informs very few people. Archaeological publications in general may be very worthy, but they cost a fortune to create and have a very small readership. What is more, limited print runs and poor circulation restrict access to those tomes, further reducing their value even to those who wish to read and analyse them.

Since all archaeological sites need to be recorded and archived for perpetuity in the county museums and in the site and monument offices, why in this day and age do we also need to publish such vast monographs? With the omnipresence of the home PC market and the general accessibility to computers, a growing number of publications have tried to combine the traditional books with the introduction of CDs. This has generally been in an effort to shorten the book, increase its educational value and to avoid publishing material interesting only to a limited audience. Unfortunately, when this has been taken forward there is either poor or no integration within the book.

Despite approaches to digital publishing such as those discussed by Julian Richards within this volume, the CD or DVD is usually an afterthought. Such a format is still not normally considered at the stage of writing the book; a fault that I am as guilty as anyone. But changes are occurring and being accepted. The recent publication by Oxford Archaeology *Gathering the People, Settling the Land* was created to address a particular set of circumstances. The site consisted of a larger number of distinct features only associated by their date. To explore the site, it was decided to create a digital map to which the user could click on each feature and drill down the various levels of the site resulting in the ability to view section illustrations. The book that accompanied the CD is a synthetic look at the site, it avoids publishing the tedious specialist reports and tables allowing them to be placed on the CD instead. Even so, the book and CD are not integrated, and while interesting, the publication would have been better if such ideas had been synthesised.

The biggest problem with archaeology in the contract sector is to a certain extent the sector itself – archaeologists' work for clients who want the archaeology removed so their development can continue as quickly as possible. The client doesn't care about the post-excavation. Indeed they have little reason to: a site may be excavated in six months, but the results appear six years later in a 600-page book that a maximum of 500 people will read.

Archiving

The archive system is well founded in British archaeology and paper copies of the archaeological record are stored safely. Digital data is a different story, and it is here that the true problem with digital archaeology in contracting units shows its ugly head. Generally, digital data from any completed project is either left on a computer and abandoned, or archived on tape and preserved for the future. There are times, however, when it would probably be better for the archaeology if the digital data was either lost or deleted and never seen again. The reason I argue this is that this digital data, which at the moment sits on any number of hard drives across any number of archaeological units, generally has no contextual information with it. Digital data, much like archaeological data, must have attached relevance to be useful, but normally it does not. It sits as a simple file within a folder with an obscure name that perhaps meant something to someone at some-time. Countless hard drives and external storage devices are populated with little 'white elephants' that no one wants or even knows how to deal with!

As an example, you might want to try the following experiment. Open an area of your computer or network where files are stored but which you do not use every day. Now go down four directories into the folder structure and ask yourself – do I know what is in these files without opening them? If I opened them would it help? In most cases you will probably find that these folders are filled with different versions of the same text sitting right next to each other. Perhaps instead you will find five different versions of the same image appear in the same folder, or better yet in five different folders. Chances are another folder sits on another machine with the same data in it. Or is that data slightly different? This is the real problem with digital data, not that we are collecting enough or we are collecting a patchwork of data, but that we are failing contextualising it from its point of origin. We are not creating metadata, and without metadata, digital data will eventually lose its meaning. As a result, it is easy to end up with a mountain of millions of bits of meaningless nothing. This nothing is then sent off to be stored.

The insistence of digital archiving bodies, such as the Archaeological Data Service (ADS), on the proper use and control of metadata is a saving grace, but the process of assigning metadata also frequently highlights some of the greatest weaknesses of digital data. Metadata forces you to look at the data which is to be deposited and describe it in meaningful ways. Unfortunately, this metadata process is not initiated until the archiving stage of the project, by which point the context of the data is missing and its meaning has been lost. This then adds cost to the digital archiving process, a cost that the developers seldom wish to pay.

This brings us to the issues of the ever-increasing cost of digital archiving, for with the eternally increasing amount of digital files that are created, there is an ever-increasing amount of economic cost in turning them into a digital resource. One case in point is the Eynsham Abbey project (http://ads.ahds.ac.uk/project/userinfo/charging2.html). Eynsham Abbey was dug from 1989 to 1992 and the post-excavation was undertaken by Oxford Archaeology using funding provided by English Heritage. The digital part of the project was archived at a cost of £6,484 or 1.2 per cent of the budget – a very reasonable proportion. The project was, however, largely completed using traditional, non-digitally oriented techniques. As a result comparatively little digital data was created and deposited. If Eynsham Abbey were undertaken today I would estimate that ten times the amount of digital data would be created (not an unreasonable assumption, as the illustrations for the book associated with the project totalled over six gigabytes alone). Therefore if Eynsham were deposited today the cost is more likely to be 10–12 per cent of the budget or £64,000. However, the budget to perform the work is highly unlikely to increase by the same percentage, meaning the project would cost the organisation money to undertake.

A solution?

So we are facing a situation where the data we are collecting is 'dirty' and inaccurate, it's being replicated, copied and edited before being left on a floppy disk or hard drive without context so that someone in two years' time will have no idea what the files are and if they are important. The solution for contracting units does not lie merely in creating and maintaining repositories for digital information, but rather in something more fundamental: in understanding and joining digital resources, and using them appropriately. The solution can be introduced by considering what one is doing and why, by appropriately weeding and managing the data as it is produced, and by then keeping that data as though it were precious, which of course it is.

One major step in the right direction to solving these issues was taken by the creation of Framework Archaeology, the joint venture by Oxford Archaeology and Wessex Archaeological Trust when they began operations for the British Airport Authority. This joint effort perhaps gives an idea of where archaeology and the intelligent use of computing in the future may lie – not simply because of its uses of technology, but because of the way it uses it (see Beck 2000 for an overview).

Even before Framework started, the excavation process was given great consideration: the way it was undertaken, its goals, its use of personnel and the nature of the problems that exist. Out of this process came a decision to look at the archaeological site in a different way. Efforts were made to understand the whole archaeological system, and with this knowledge, different technologies were considered where they might enhance the excavation process.

Framework first adopted a series of key ideals on which to undertake the excavation. First, the decision was made to try to undertake a lot of the excavation analysis on site, front-loading much of the post-excavation process to be conducted at location, and in time to inform the excavation process. Steps were made to ensure facilities were available to process the finds and environmental remains. Even flint and pottery analysis was undertaken on site. Second, all staff on site were encouraged and trained to consider not only the area they were working, but the site as a whole. It was realised that if the whole archaeological landscape was considered and understood, it would be easier to decide which areas of the site were less important and which needed to be explored further.

Running through all of this was an information system designed to allow all the data collected on site to be analysed on site in a relatively short period of time. To achieve this, Framework archaeology has created a truly exceptional series of databases and a unified GIS – which can be used to query and analyse the data across the different project locations as the excavation progresses. These are updated constantly so that the information on the network is as close to real-time as practical. Excavators are encouraged to consider and interpret what they find, and that information is added to the database as well. The information is reviewed, and data is cleaned, leaving the excavator's interpretations, and from that point, better-informed decisions can be made as the excavation progresses.

What is perhaps more important, the goals for the use of each technology are understood, and the data produced by the project is reviewed and given meaning as it is being taken. This helps to alleviate the issue of redundant and meaningless data, and provides a better understanding of what can be kept and what can be deleted. It requires a significant degree of administration, but this returns significance to the data that is held. It also reduces the time and effort spent in the weeding-out process when it comes to the archiving of the digital records.

The model adopted by Framework combines technology with an overall data collection strategy. It allows decisions to be made in the field based on greater understanding, it highlights the voice of the excavator, allowing them to think about the greater picture, and allows the team to better remove false or inaccurate data on site before it even progresses into the post-excavation phase. This should be the true use of digital archaeology: increasing the accuracy and understanding of the archaeology on site and at the same time increasing the quality of the data gathered for analysis and archiving.

Considering the future

Throughout this chapter I have shown and tracked the sporadic growth of the use of computing in contract archaeology and how by trial and error processing power has been applied to the problem of archaeology. I have discussed the problems we are facing and shown how through the adoption of a more cohesive approach one can begin to better use the technology available. The adoption of a forward thinking approach to the use of technology can not only solve the issues created by that technology, but also add to the value one can get from it. If you ask me, digital archaeology is not about using computers, rather it is about using technology well – with forethought and with planning. Failure to do this will mean that we lose the good data as we drown in sheer volume of the bad.

Reference

Beck, A. (2000) 'Intellectual excavation and dynamic information management systems', in G. Lock and K. Brown (eds) *On the Theory and Practice of Archaeological Computing*. Oxford: Oxford University Committee for Archaeology Monograph, pp. 73–88.

Part III

QUANTIFICATION
MADE EASY

4

YOU, ME AND IT

The application of simple quantitative
techniques in the examination of gender,
identity and social reproduction in the Early
to Middle Iron Age of north-eastern France

Thomas L. Evans

Introduction

Over the past 20 years, the wide-ranging use of databases has greatly
increased the ease with which data can be gathered, stored, summarised and
reviewed. Combined with the ever-increasing accessibility of statistical
software packages, this has greatly increased the ability for even the lone
archaeologist to apply complex quantitative techniques to their data. Yet
while there is an ever-widening array of statistical tools by which data can
be examined, it is not the development of new techniques that has had the
greatest impact upon archaeology. Rather, it is the relative speed and ease
with which existing statistical techniques can be applied, to the point where
almost anyone can examine exceptionally large data sets with relative ease
using complex techniques.

However, while access to 'number-crunching' approaches is growing,
there remains a general fear of, and miscomprehension about, the application of quantitative methods to archaeological questions. Despite the fact
that statistical approaches have become commonplace in the description of
artefact assemblages, they seldom are used to investigate any questions
beyond the descriptive. This chapter, unlike most of the works in this volume, does not demonstrate the application of a new technique. While the
search for new approaches is clearly worthwhile, this volume is not the
forum for the discussion of the complex and admittedly dry mathematical
discussion that such a paper would necessitate. Rather, the chapter
addresses the application of common quantitative approaches, facilitated by
information technology, to a broadly theoretical question: the question of
identity. It does this to illustrate that the growing amount of data and our
growing capacity to analyse it in manners that expand our own perceptive
capacities provides us with additional means by which we can develop

archaeological theory. Yet to do this, we must first form meaningful questions about our theories that can be addressed in a meaningful way – the first step of which is, of course, to attempt to understand the theories themselves.

Identity and social reproduction

Identity is not digital. It is an abstract term used to describe a complex series of inter-related personal concepts and societal ideologies that form not only our view of ourselves, but also how others define us. To this end, identity can be seen as a continuum of social and personal definitions that are undergoing constant redefinition. It is through identity that we create boundaries between the *self* and the *other*, while it simultaneously also serves as a unifying factor that can define the concept of *us*. It allows both individuality and conformity, and as such creates an interwoven network of apparently contradictory ideas that allow us to define who we are and how we relate to each other. This may indeed be one reason why despite the fact that there is a plethora of archaeological writings on the topic, very few archaeologists actually try to define what we mean when we use the term identity, and such definitions are left to philosophers (Thomas 1996). Nevertheless, concepts of identity are innately tied to our forms of social reproduction. They define not only whom we interact with, but also how we interact with them. These forms of interaction change based upon the circumstances of the specific interaction we are engaged in, and so do the identities of the individuals in question.

Yet the human psyche makes it difficult, if not impossible to understand concepts unless we define them and break them down into more readily understandable categories. The key to this is neither to attempt to examine a culture's concept of identity as a whole, nor to forget that one is studying an element that is part of a larger concept. Instead, one needs to break the subject into those parts of it that are comprehensible. We must identify those elements that might be reflected in the archaeological record while remembering they are only one part of a larger image. In effect, one needs to 'digitise' the elements of identity that can be addressed through the archaeo-logical record. Just as when digitising an image, one needs to understand what it needs to be digitised for. Similarly, in breaking down and categoris-ing identity, one is only seeing a small part of the cultural picture, but by beginning to examine the constituent parts, one may gain insights and clues that will allow one to interpolate what those aspects of identity and/or culture that are missing from the image may be.

Mean identities in the Upper Seine Basin

An approach to examining identity and social reproduction through the use of simple quantitative techniques

The case presented is an investigation of the cemetery burials in the Upper Seine Basin in north-eastern France (see Figure 4.1) dating between the Hallstatt Finale (approximately 600 BC) and the La Tène Moyenne (approximately 130 BC). The focus of this work is on two specific and inter-related aspects of identity: social status and gender. The work has been performed in a systematic manner using a combination of simple descriptive statistics and more complex exploratory multivariate techniques, particularly correspondence analysis. The results of these quantitative examinations were then investigated to determine if any new patterns could be noted in the data. Though the use of correspondence analysis was essential in the determination of the validity of the comparison of the cemeteries from the different regions, the results of those tests primarily indicated that overwhelmingly similar patterns in the use of artefacts and space within the burial rites were present (Evans 2004). Additionally while it would have been possible to discuss how elements of identity might be detected through the use of correspondence analysis, that method's application and uses have been clearly demonstrated in other volumes dedicated to its application (Madsen 1988), and its application is now frequently used in archaeological analysis (Shennan 1997: 308–52; Baxter 1996: 110–18). Instead, this chapter's goal is to demonstrate that exploratory quantitative techniques can be used to address more theoretically oriented questions. The application of several basic techniques, mean frequency and the associated standard errors, are presented here.

To this end, the bulk of the work discussed here was conducted through the comparison of the mean frequency of the artefact assemblage of three separate categories that reflect the ways in which we presently address issues of both gender and social status within Iron Age studies. This comparison was conducted using a simple spreadsheet program available to almost every individual armed with a computer using no greater than a 486 processor. Indeed, one of the key reasons why such a study was not attempted before was bound to the amount of data that needed to be gathered and processed, and the capacity for computers to do so before 1995.

In fairness, however, the more sophisticated elements of this study, particularly the examination of rationality and ongoing investigation of the relationship between landscape and space usage within the cemetery, do require more sophisticated understanding of statistics and access to more powerful soft and hardware. Regardless, despite the use of high-end solutions, the most interesting results have derived from the simple comparison of mean frequencies – those that result from trying to identify the 'normal'

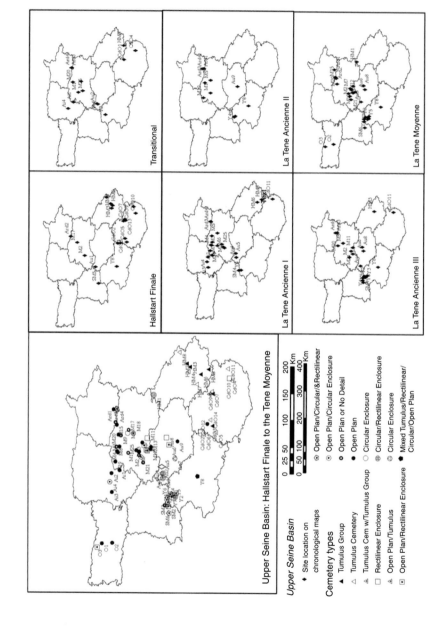

Figure 4.1 Geographic situation of sites.

ways in which individuals portrayed themselves and/or their cultural rites within the burial rites, and how that changed over time.

The problems with gender, status and identity in the Upper Seine Basin 600 to 130 BC

Excavations in north-east France have produced thousands of Iron Age graves that have been the focus of study for almost 200 years. Many of these burials, such as the '*Princess of Vix*' and the warrior and chariot burial of *Somme-Bionne*, have almost come to define our understanding of burial rites and social reproduction during the Iron Age, despite the fact that such burials represent only a fraction of the burials identified to the varying periods. Even so, these burials have raised some key issues tied to both identity and our understanding of Iron Age exchange systems that, until recently, have not been adequately addressed due to the sheer volume of data. The most fundamental of these questions are tied to issues of gender and social status, two elements of identity that in this case are intrinsically inter-related and integral to how we understand social reproduction in the period. Yet our own modern Western definitions of these two elements, particularly gender, in many ways bias our ways of interpreting the remains. To this end, we view gender and status in Iron Age France as being in someway similar to our own social models, but the evidence we have to support such an interpretation is limited.

The Hallstatt Finale (600–530 BC) and the subsequent Transitional Period (530–470 BC, defined as the Hallstatt Finale II period by Hatt and Roualet 1977) has been defined by the existence of high prestige female burials found with four-wheeled 'wagons', such as *les Locheres* (the Princess of Vix). During the Transitional Period this began to change until in the La Tène Ancienne I (470–400 BC) prestige burials tended to be associated with 'wealthy' male warriors, occasionally found with two-wheeled 'chariots'. This change in the association of status from female burials found with little evidence of warfare to male burials whose defining characteristic is the presence of a warrior assemblage, has fed a great amount of debate about the role of gender and of social status. Yet, despite their obvious and compelling nature, such elite burials from any of the periods are extremely rare, and there have been very few attempts to understand such issues in burial rites as a whole. As a result, we understand only the outlying examples of the burials, not the norm. However, even here there are problems – for our definitions of genders are based upon a nineteenth-century definition of the concept that we have inherited.

Traditionally speaking, one of the key elements to defining biological sex in the region has been tied to the presence or absence of the warrior assemblage and/or torcs, which although frequently associated with both male and female individuals in classical art and literature, have been used as female identifiers since 1886. At that time, August Nicaise identified the apparent mutual exclusivity between warrior burials and burials with torcs (Nicaise 1886: 80). To Nicaise and his contemporaries, warrior burials, which contained spears, swords, shields and/or helmets, were clearly male inhumations. By default, they concluded that the individuals with torcs must have been female. To examine this hypothesis they conducted a limited series of osteological examinations, which supported the female prevalence of torc bearing.

There are, however, some obvious problems with this interpretation. To begin with, even assuming Nicaise's osteological and statistical examinations were unbiased, there was no osteological examination of the burials with warrior assemblages: it was so obvious that warriors must be male that this examination was not conducted. Additionally, even today there remains the problem of the biasing of the examination of the skeletons by expected results. This is particularly valid due to the nature of how osteological tests are conducted in France.

Osteological tests of burials are now routine, and they do tend to support Nicaise's findings. However, due to the very valid concerns of bone conditions the burials are normally examined *in situ* and such examinations clearly can bias the osteologist due to the presence of an engendering artefact assemblage. This is the nature of osteological work, especially when undertaken in the field. The biological sexing of individuals is frequently male biased, with estimates indicating that blind osteological testing produces a 12 per cent pro-male bias (Wiess 1972: 239–50; Parker Pearson 1999: 95–7). Additionally, elevated amounts of osteological androgens can be caused in children through strenuous exercise. This results in women developing narrow, masculine appearing pelvises (Taylor 1996; Parker Pearson 1999: 97–8). Thus women who were trained in warfare from an early age would be much more likely to be osteologically identified as a male. Human remains specialists are very clear about such biases, but frequently other archaeologists over-emphasise the sexing evidence and give a male or female designation to a burial when all that exists is a percentage chance of sexing. When one examines a burial with objects which are used to engender the skeleton, the 12 per cent bias would no doubt be increased. Yet even with such instances of bias, there have been a number of cases where skeletons of one sex have been buried with objects that should belong to the opposite gender, and at least two individuals with both warrior assemblages and wearing torcs.

What is perhaps more important, however, is that there are a series of burials that appear to contradict Nicaise's rule. At Tinqueux Tomb 12, one burial found with a sword was osteologically identified as female aged 17 to 25 due to the gracile nature of the long bones (Flouest et Stead 1981: 151–76).[1] In the case of Tomb 19 in the cemetery known as 'Croyats' or 'la Justice' at Montigny-Lencoup in the Seine-et-Marne, an individual, identified as male, was uncovered in direct context with an item identified as a *'torque'* (Guillaumet 1977: 2: 38–44). Unfortunately, this excavation was conducted in 1894–1895, and there were not many details given, though the identification of the individual as a male obviously post-dates Nicaise's argument of torcs being an exclusively feminine grave good. More problematic, perhaps, is the case of Tomb 25 in the site at Vrigny in the Marne (Chossenot *et al.* 1981: 131–50). This is the La Tène Ancienne Ia inhumation of a pre-to-early adolescent with two spearheads by the right side of the head (one spearhead being quite small and probably representing a javelin), and bearing a bronze torc. However, because of the nature of the skeleton, it is difficult to determine if the individual was actually wearing it.

The excavations at the site of les Terres du Coer in Perrogney-les-Fontaines, in the Haute-Marne produced even more interesting results (Balliot 1900: 33–9). Dug by Balliot in 1900, the site consisted of some 23 burials dating to the La Tène Ancienne. One of those burials, dating to the La Tène Ancienne I, contained an individual with a boar's tusk on the central right thorax, two fibula on the chest (presumably at the clavicles), a bracelet on the left wrist, an 'applique' just above the crest of the skull, wearing a *torc* and with a *spear* next to and aligned with the right lower leg (point to the foot of the tomb) and a *sword* in the mirrored position by the left lower leg (hilts at foot, points towards the head of the tomb and by the mid thigh).

Then there is the case of Tomb 8 at Champ Dolent near Cernay-les-Reims. This reasonably well-recorded two-wheeled vehicle burial[2] contained a single individual placed centrally in a two-wheeled vehicle tomb in a normal extended dorsal position, along the normal central line of the grave. The individual is laid out with a torc upon its neck, a bracelet upon each forearm and with a spear and sword placed in clear and direct association with the individual. The spear is located in a normal position to the left of the skeleton at the level of the head, and the sword is placed to the side of the individual, slightly away from the body. There is no evidence for a double inhumation nor was an intrusive burial recorded. Indeed, all evidence indicates that this was a single, intact tomb with the body and all grave goods remaining *in situ*. It is clearly a case of an individual buried with weapons, but wearing a torc and bracelets. It is, in short, a single burial with both male and female grave goods.

These cases are clearly problematic, but it is not simply a case of Nicaise's categories being wrong. The frequency of both torcs and warrior related items in a grave is extremely rare, and though there is increased bias in osteological sexing of burials due to the presence of grave goods, there is clearly some validity to Nicaise's conclusions or else the osteologists would have identified such issues long ago. Clearly torcs are more frequently found with females, and weapons more frequently found with males, but also clearly the simple and bi-polar model of Nicaise is not the whole picture. It is clear that while the two groups appear to be *normally* exclusive, they are not *always* so. Some individuals bore both torcs and sword. The question is, how frequent was this overlap.

The assemblages do appear to be linked in some way with the individual's biological sex, but the degree to which they formed sexually discriminate sets is unclear since the methods of sexing the skeletons is not completely reliable. In order to understand and address these issues, and the degree to which these burial categories are actually mutually exclusive, it is essential to examine the nature of these groups. Through such a comparison of normal practices some insights into the level of social and/or biological exclusivity that these categories had may be gained. This in turn helps us to begin trying to uncover the gender roles of the Iron Age inhabitants of the region, rather than merely viewing them through the cultural biases of the nineteenth century.

Yet this issue is not tied to gender alone. Since the very items most frequently used to identify gender, the torcs and warrior assemblage, are also generally thought to be tied to social rank and thus prestige, clearly other elements of identity, those tied to social status, are also involved. The presence or absence of both torcs and weaponry has been frequently used to identify individuals' social rank, and when viewed on a cemetery wide level, the relative prestige of the community as a whole. Yet leaving aside our own sense of aesthetic, and the general sense that individuals with engendering items also tend to have a higher frequency of other items in the grave, no substantial examination had been carried out to examine the validity of this statement.

Furthermore, there is some evidence that the energy expenditure involved in burial rites can also be used to indicate status within a given society. Tainter, for example, uses ethnographic evidence to suggest that the amount of labour expended in a mortuary ritual is directly related to the social rank of the deceased (1977: 332). Such examinations are, however, quite limited, tending to indicate only the very highest and lowest status levels of a society when other elements of social differentiation are removed (Wason 1994: 77). An analysis such as this one which divides burials into rigid categories is far more likely to note the existence of distinctive castes rather than cultural mobility regardless of whether such clear-cut social divisions existed. This is an 'artefact' of the analysis process, a side effect of the 'digitisation' of the cultural divisions into neat categories that one must be aware of while examining social status.

Determining the validity of the association of status and prestige items

Before one can assume that there is indeed a prestige value associated with a particular artefact type, one should examine the other evidence generally associated with it. In this instance, in order to understand whether there was any differentiation in prestige associated with the gender related items, a simple comparison between the mean frequency of items in each of the three categories was performed. If those graves with the engendering torcs or weapons had a significantly higher frequency of items within their grave assemblage than those Neuter graves that did not have engendering grave goods, then a degree of validity in the association between prestige and torcs and/or weapons could be established. If no such clearly defined differentiation between overall artefact frequency and the presence of engendering grave goods was found, then one would not be able to establish such an association between status and the torc bearing or warrior assemblages (though clearly it would by no means disprove such an association with prestige).

This then was one of the key questions that needed to be established, and due to the nature of the relationship archaeologists have created between these engendering items and social status, it is clear that each of these questions is related directly to one another and must be addressed together. This is done for individuals whose graves did not include such items to those whose graves did to see if there was any significant or even substantial differentiation between the overall frequency of items within the graves.

Examining the gender categories

Similarly, an examination of the types of artefacts included in those graves identified as male or female through both osteological and artefactual methods was made. This allows one to note the differences and similarities in the non-engendering artefacts included in the grave, and determine the differences and similarities in each gender group's artefact assemblages. The differences in these results could then be compared across the different periods of examination, and patterns in the changes between groups over time could be identified and interpreted. Through this, it was hoped that a better understanding of the relationship between the so-called Masculine and Feminine categories of graves could be determined. If the two groups were found to have been mutually exclusive in a range of grave goods other than those that were used to define their gender, then some greater validity could be seen in the interpretation that the grave represented two distinct gender groups. The failure to identify any such variation would, however, lead to the conclusion that a different form of gender model was in place, one that could either have represented the existence of multiple genders within the society, or one that represented that the society had flexible gender roles in which biological sexing was not necessarily definitive to one's role in society.

Digitising the self

Methods of examining gender, status and social reproduction

In order to begin quantifying the data and examining the results a standard-ised methodology was produced. Data was gathered from 80 cemeteries from the Upper Seine Basin that were chosen based upon the following criteria:

1   The site was available in a published form by 1997.
2   The site was excavated and presented to acceptable professional stand-ards, including the presence of adequate plans and/or descriptions of the burial contexts.
3   A minimum of five burials were included in the description of the site. This was done in order to avoid the over-emphasis of individual cases which could skew the statistical analysis. Sites without this number may have been considered in the interpretations (i.e. *les Locheres* at Vix), but were not included in the statistical analysis.

This process eliminated a large number of the potential sites, including many of the best-known ones (such as the Magny-Lambert complex and Somme-Bionne), but was necessary in order to ensure that the dataset could be meaningfully analysed. The list of cemeteries is produced in Table 4.1.

Each burial in each cemetery was entered into a database, noting the position of the skeleton, and the position of the artefacts both in relation to the grave cut and to the body. This created a two-level interactive data-base that could note the relative positions of the artefacts both to the body and the grave regardless of the positioning of the body itself, allowing for similarities and differences to thus be noted. This process was conducted in order to allow for the use of exploratory multivariate techniques that allowed me to determine whether or not a single culture was being observed, or if indeed there were different cultural traditions being represented in the burial rites. The results of that study clearly showed that while differences were identified, the burial rites of each of the cemeteries were effectively uniform for each period of the study – though obvious differences existed across the temporal divisions (Evans 2004).

In addition to the indications of the multivariate examinations, the over-all similarity in the graves can be noted by the ways in which the bodies were placed. Of the 1,150 burials compared in this study, 1,107 were inhumations of one form or another. Of these inhumations 1,028 were posi-tioned on their backs with their limbs primarily extended (a vast number of subtle variations in this positioning were identified, and this is presently being assessed for further analysis, but these differences did not seem to reflect any regional patterning). The remaining 79 burials were placed in other positions. No clear patterns of placement could be identified within the 43 burials included in the study. Therefore, it can be noted that the vast majority (89.39 per cent) of the population that could be examined were placed in extended dorsal position. This, and indeed the lack of any clear-cut differentiation in artefact assemblages or its placement within the grave, points to a fairly clear degree of cultural uniformity in burial rites across the different periods.

This is not to say that there were no elements of variation that could be identified in this study, but rather that those elements that were found were relatively minor, and tended to represent frequency of items normally associated with prestige. As such, they appeared to represent some reflection of aspects of community related social reproduction through concepts of prestation. This is addressed elsewhere (Evans 2004), and generally suggest a tendency towards patterns of cultural cores or centres being formed through prestige exchange networks being represented in the burial rites. Though complicated, the results can be summed up as generally indicating, but by no means proving, that a series of centres for prestige and cultural influence appear to have existed in the Côtes-d'Or and Haute-Marne in the Hallstatt Finale (600–530 BC) and Transitional (530–470 BC) periods and moved to the Aisne and Marne regions in the La Tène Ancienne I (470–400 BC). During the La Tène Ancienne II (410–320 BC) no clear pattern could be identified due to the significant decrease in the population (see Figures 4.2 and 4.3). Any such core-periphery based system that might have been postulated

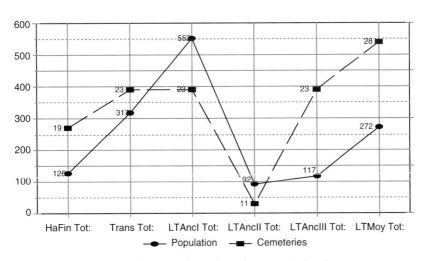

Figure 4.2 Cemetery population and number of cemeteries by phase.

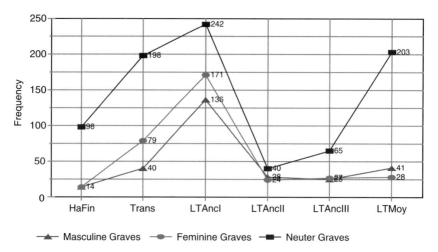

Figure 4.3 Comparison of USB populations by gender category.

Note: The difference in population in the LTAncI noted in Figures and is due to the presence of the three individuals that could be associated specifically to this period that have elements of both masculine and feminine categories.

for the region, however, would appear to have fragmented by the La Tène Ancienne III (320–220 BC), leaving no clear centre for cultural practice nor for prestige exchange 'wealth' by the La Tène Moyenne (220–120 BC). Even so, though such a moving central location of cultural practices may be indicated by those results, the high degree of uniformity of artefact styles, assemblages and placement of both body and grave goods within the burial suggest a single cultural group existed within the region over all the periods investigated.

These results therefore indicated that an examination of gender and social status that included all of the cemeteries could be performed in a holistic manner and would provide meaningful results. Yet, in order to make a comparative examination over time of the nature of gender and status, the burials had to be divided into three categories that reflect our understanding of the archaeological remains: Masculine, Feminine and Neuter.[3] These categories were used in part to test both existing gender and status models, and if they proved valid, to examine changes in patterns of social reproduction over time. It should be noted that due to the extended period over which the cemeteries were excavated, and nature by which even the osteologically sexed burials were identified, attempting to separate the biologically identified burials from those identified through artefact assemblages proved implausible. It was therefore determined that for this initial survey, these more general categories would be utilised.

The *Masculine* category consisted of all burials that were biologically identified as male, and/or had warrior grave goods (which have traditionally been utilised to identify burials as male by French archaeologists) associated with the burials. The *Feminine* category consisted of all biologically determined female and/or torc-bearing burials. The final category consisted of the *Neuter* burials: those burials that could neither be osteologically identified, nor had any gender identifying objects placed within them. As the engendering items were also frequently associated with prestige and social status, these three categories in part served to identify both the potential gender groups within the society, and the status groups. It should be noted, however, that at no point was it assumed that the Neuter group represented a third gender identity, nor is there any indication that this should be seen as the case. Rather, the Neuter category was merely defined as having a lack of osteological or artefact defining characteristics. The creation and comparison of this category was indeed crucial to the study since both masculine and feminine engendering artefacts are also interpreted as prestige items and the validity of this definition needed to be questioned. Additionally, since individuals within this category would also have included both males and females, it could be used in the identification of elements associated with gender.

This then was part of the purpose of this investigation: to test if there were any significant differences in the frequency of any artefacts types (excluding the engendering artefacts) between these categories, noting how the presence or absence of such prestige related items related to the overall frequency of other items in the grave. For example, if individuals who were buried with torcs were also found to have a higher frequency of all other items within the grave, then this would further the argument that torcs really were prestige related items buried with social elites. Lack of correlation between so-called prestige items and overall frequency would not disprove such a theory, but would raise additional questions as to the validity of our definition of social status within that society. Comparative frequencies between the masculine and feminine groups were also examined in order to understand the validity of such categories. If these categories were shown to hold some validity, this form of investigation also held the potential of examining how the relation between these social/gender groups changed over time – thus investigating how social interaction altered between the Early to Middle Iron Ages.

For those not familiar with statistical examinations, a simple description of how to interpret the results should be presented. The graphs presented here (Figures 4.2 to 4.12) show the *mean frequency*[4] for each artefact type or combination of types (such as warrior assemblages, which consist of swords, spears, and/or shields) as they occur within each social/gender category. These results are usually identified by use of a solid line as indicated on the varying legends for each figure. When possible to place them without confusion, the actual mean frequency value for each social/gender category is presented to the left of each result.[5]

Many of the graphs that were produced to indicate two degrees of maximum and minimum *standard error* for each frequency value were also projected upon the graves.[6] These are usually in the form of a dotted line as indicated on each figure's legend. In this instance, the importance of the standard error lies not only in the confidence levels noting where the actual mean value is likely to lie, but also in the indication that 95 per cent of the population of each category has a mean value that falls within that range. As a result, one can identify the extent as the *normal* range into which such values fall and how much overlap normally exists between the categories. Results with no overlap (e.g. the results for LTAncI shown in Figure 4.4) show distinct and differentiated results, while those with complete overlap or the inclusion of the maximum and minimum range within other results show that there is no significance to the differences between groups (e.g. Figure 4.4 HaFin results for Neuter and Masculine values, and LTAncIII Masculine and Feminine values). Such clearly overlapping results may, in fact, indicate that the results appeared to have an overall similarity, but additional statistical tests are needed to validate the significance of such a finding. Finally, those results in which the maximum standard error overlaps the minimum standard error of another category (e.g. Figure 4.4 LTAncII Masculine and Feminine results) again show that there is no clearly significant difference between the groups. Such results may also be indicative of a hierarchical relationship where the artefact type is present in both categories, but that the results are generally more closely related to one category than another. However, again this is a matter of interpretation, and additional statistical tests need to be carried out to

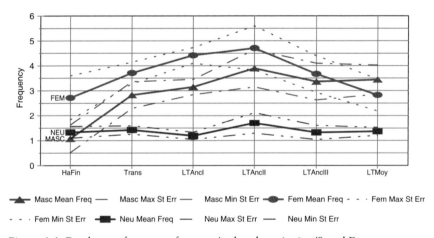

Figure 4.4 Gender artefact mean frequencies by phase (str) w/Stand Err.

determine the significance of such findings. It is also possible to interpret an overlap of this type as an indication that the 'poorest' members of one category are effectively similar to the richest members of the other category. This would suggest a lack of clear differentiation between the comparative groups. All of this therefore means that the range of results indicated by the standard error are generally at least as important as the mean frequencies.

Quantified identities and social reproduction of the Upper Seine Basin

Results and initial findings

Before we can examine the results related solely to the gender and status related aspects of identity, one must first examine the more general results and how they impact the study. Examination of Figures 4.2 and 4.3 indicate that very clear changes occurred over the period of study within the population of the cemeteries within the region. Figure 4.2 shows the population of individuals that were interred within the cemeteries over the different periods as compared to the number of cemeteries that have been identified for these periods. These results show a steady increase in the population for each cemetery over time until the La Tène Ancienne II, when there is a marked decrease both in the number of burials and in the number of cemeteries. This is followed by a marked increase in the number of cemeteries found in the La Tène Ancienne III, but a much more gradual increase in the number of burials associated with each cemetery.

These results are comparatively significant. They indicate an important change in overall population being interred during that period, and perhaps a drastic decrease in the population inhabiting the region at the time. It should be noted that there is in fact correlation between the dates for the La Tène Ancienne II and the so-called 'Great Celtic Migrations' (Moscati et al. 1991) that are associated with the sacking of Rome and the assaults upon Greece (Livy 1960: 32–55; Polybius, II: 14–35), and could be used to support many of the present interpretations of the period (Kruta 1991a; Cunliffe 1997: 68–90). Yet regardless of such associations with historic events, one thing it clearly denotes is an important alteration in society as reflected by the burial remains.

Social status

Comparing the different total artefact frequencies of the social/gender categories begins to reveal patterns in the relationship of the categories (Figures 4.4 and 4.5), the most readily examined of which are those related to status. Even a cursory examination of these figures shows that there is a

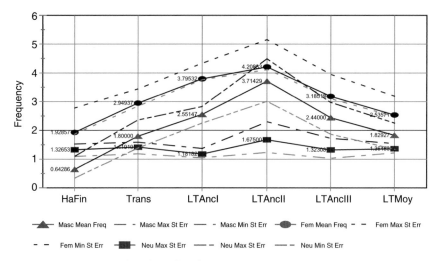

Figure 4.5 Non-engendered artefact frequency.

clear association between the presence of engendered grave goods and the frequency of other artefacts. Comparison of Figures 4.4 and 4.5 shows that the burials in the Masculine and Feminine categories have a higher frequency of all grave goods over most periods than Neuter burials, indicating that regardless of the gender related associations of these burial categories, there is a clear indication that an association exists between the presence of gender identifying grave goods and general 'burial wealth'. If this is examined in association with the comparative populations of each group (Figure 4.3), then even without defining any cultural values to specific artefact categories, one can see that the general association between societal prestige and the presence of torcs and/or weaponry has some validity. Changes in the general shape and level of difference can be argued to represent some form of change in the social relationship between these categories, which will be discussed later.

Yet while an indicative overall pattern does exist, it is important to note that in the results for the Hallstatt Finale the Masculine burials have both a lower total artefact frequency (Figure 4.4) and a lower frequency of non-gender associated artefacts (Figure 4.5) than the Neuter burials. One should also note that the standard errors of each category have a considerable range of overlap in both figures. Figure 4.5 additionally shows that this overlap also exists for the non-engendered items during the Transitional and the La Tène Moyenne periods. This indicates a lack of significance in the difference in the results for those periods, but that some degree of significance can be associated with the difference in the frequency of non-engendered artefacts between the Masculine and Neuter results noted in the other periods.

Interestingly, there is no overlap in the total frequency of artefacts between the Feminine burials and those identified as Neuter for any period. In the instance of non-engendered grave goods, only the Hallstatt Finale shows any overlap between these two categories. Since the examination of non-engendered items does, however, remove a series of components (torcs and weaponry) from the artefact assemblages of the engendered categories (Masculine and Feminine), a reduction in the overall frequency of items is to be expected. After all, even if all the grave goods have the same relative prestige value, which is of course unlikely, removing any subset of them will reduce the overall frequency of the whole. As a result, it can be said with a degree of confidence that Feminine burials clearly had a higher frequency of artefacts within the graves than Neuter burials. What is more, for all periods except the Hallstatt Finale, a similar confidence can be placed upon the frequency by which artefacts were placed in Masculine burials.

This overall pattern for both the Masculine and Feminine burials to have a higher artefact frequency therefore generally supports the association between social prestige and the presence of torcs and/or the warrior assemblage within the graves for all periods except perhaps the Hallstatt Finale. This is further suggested by the comparatively higher frequency of even the non-engendered artefacts even when a sample of the population of artefacts (those that are used to denote gender) is removed.

This does not, however, support the conclusion that Masculine burials held the same status as Neuter burials during the Hallstatt Finale. Considering the overall pattern in the frequency with which artefacts are included in the engendering categories, it seems likely that the warrior assemblage was associated with prestige even during the Hallstatt Finale. If one then bears in mind the comparative energy expended in the manufacture of the torcs and warfare related items, then the association of all engendered items and prestige is persuasive. If said interpretation is correct, the overlap of the artefact frequency in the Masculine and Neuter graves may not indicate an accurate degree of comparative social status between the two groups. Rather it would merely reflect that the Masculine associated burials had no less prestige than those in the Neuter category, and that additional prestige may have been being reflected in the warrior assemblage. Regardless, this evidence, when considered in combination with existing theories, clearly supports the hypothesis that torcs and weaponry were generally associated with prestige and status within the burial rites.

Indeed, examination of the general shape of the Masculine and Feminine categories shows that the overall frequency of artefacts within each group more or less parallels one another. This suggests, but by no mean proves, that regardless of whatever other social groups these two categories may represent, the comparative amount of 'grave wealth' interred with each seems to be related to one another. This is particularly pronounced in Figure 4.5 where the presence of the gender related objects is removed from the comparison. Such a correlation in general artefact frequencies could be interpreted as suggesting that the Masculine and Feminine categories represent related status groups within the society.

There are differences in the patterns that can be identified, however, and need to be considered. Figures 4.4 and 4.5 show that while the Neuter burials maintain a more or less constant frequency of grave goods for the entire period of study, the Masculine and Feminine burials show an overall increase in all grave goods up until the La Tène Ancienne II. In Figure 4.5 one will note that after that period, both Masculine and Feminine burials show a steady decrease in non-engendered items, thus maintaining a more or less parallel relationship through all periods. In Figure 4.4, however, during the La Tène Ancienne III, Feminine burials begin to show a steady decrease in the overall artefact frequency, while the frequency of items in the Masculine graves remains more or less level, dropping slightly in the La Tène Ancienne II, and rising slightly in the La Tène Ancienne III and La Tène Moyenne. This suggests a change in the relationship in how prestige was being represented in the burial rites over time. Such a change is likely to represent a change in the nature of status in these two populations that is related to the ratio of the category defining artefacts themselves.

Gender

The change in this pattern of artefact frequency of the gender defining grave goods suggests that changes in the relationship between the torc bearing and warrior assemblages do not only reflect transformations in the representation societal prestige, but in the nature of gender roles within the culture. A comparison of the relative shape of the Masculine and Feminine categories in Figure 4.4 shows that they maintain a similarity in their overall relative frequencies for all periods except the finale two. As previously noted, those periods show that the total artefact frequency of the Feminine burials continues to reduce while that of the Masculine burials more or less levels out (Figure 4.4). This is not the case with the frequency of the non-engendered items, however, where the relationship between the Masculine and Feminine results remain stable. This is particularly interesting since it indicates a change in the stability of the relative artefact frequency of the very items that are used to engender the graves themselves. Indeed, the significance of this change can be seen when comparing the frequency with which Masculine and Feminine defining artefacts are being included in their respective graves types.

Examination of these two categories of engendering artefact assemblages is illustrated in Figure 4.6, which shows the frequency of torcs in relation to the frequency of the warrior assemblage (swords, spears, and/or shields). These results show that despite the similarity in the frequency of the overall artefact assemblages between the Masculine and Feminine burials, the

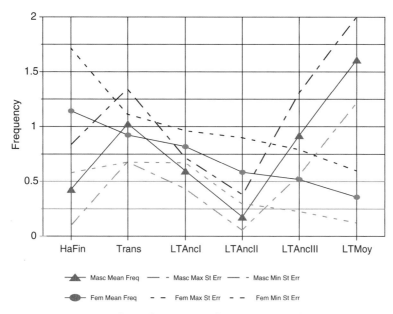

Figure 4.6 Comparison of USB frequencies of warrior to torc bearing assemblage.

frequency in which the engendering artefacts occurs bears little resemblance. The frequency of torcs in the graves undertakes a steady decrease over time, from the Hallstatt Finale to the La Tène Moyenne, while the frequency of the warrior assemblage shows marked changes over the different periods. An initial increase in the frequency of the warrior assemblage in the Masculine graves between the Hallstatt Finale and the Transitional periods is followed by the marked decrease in the frequency of the items that continues until the La Tène Ancienne II. This is followed by a notable increase in the frequency of warrior related grave goods until end of the study in the La Tène Moyenne. It is at that period that a significant difference between the frequency of the warrior assemblage can be noted when compared to the frequency of torcs.

Clearly an important change in the dynamic of these two burial categories is being noted, and if the association between the warrior and torc bearing assemblages and gender is indeed valid, these results could suggest a very distinct alteration in the role of gender and social reproduction in the society. Yet such an association has not yet been demonstrated, and in the lack of the ability to reliably re-sex the burials or conduct genetic tests upon the skeletal remains, this must be done through a comparative examination of the other, non-engendering items in the Masculine and Feminine burial assemblages. Such an examination must identify if there are other artefact types that are mutually exclusive to each group, or other patterns within the burial record that indicate exclusivity. If identified, they will help to support the idea that the Masculine and Feminine categories are exclusive to one another and that two biologically determined gender sets existed in the Iron Age. Failure to find such exclusivity would help to erode such a bi-polar gender model when faced with the problem set of burials including the apparent dual and cross-gender burials that have already been identified.

It is therefore perhaps best to begin with the examination of some of the individual items that made up the grave assemblages as a whole. Between the Hallstatt Finale and the La Tène Moyenne, the most commonly occurring grave good in any category were ceramic vases. Figure 4.7 shows the frequency of ceramic vessel in all categories, while Figure 4.8 compares masculine to feminine categories only. Examination of these figures shows that the overall frequency of results is the same for all periods except the La Tène Ancienne II where the Masculine ceramics frequency becomes distinctly (though not significantly) higher than the other categories. One will also note that while the Neuter values are generally lower for each of the different periods, in the Hallstatt Finale it is marginally higher than the Masculine ceramic frequency, and in the La Tène Moyenne it is higher than both of the engendered categories. These results indicate that the frequency of items other than vases gives the engendered items their higher overall frequencies. Additionally, when comparing the Masculine to Feminine ceramics frequency, there is no period in which a significant difference occurs.

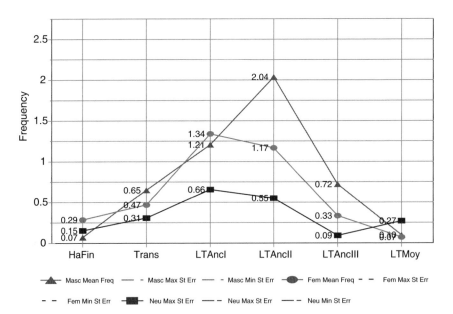

Figure 4.7 Ceramics in all categories.

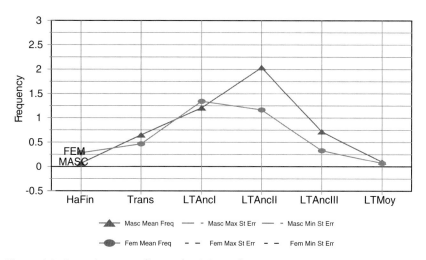

Figure 4.8 Ceramics: masculine to feminine only.

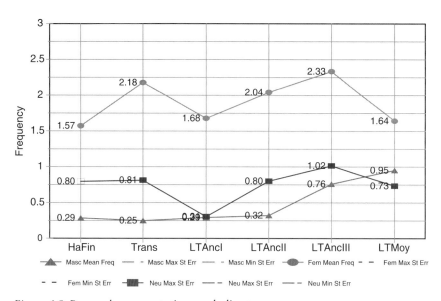

Figure 4.9 Personal ornamentation, excluding torcs.

Thus, one can say that there is no clearly defined difference in the frequency with which ceramics occurs in the Masculine and Feminine graves.

Figure 4.9 illustrates the frequency of objects of personal ornamentation included in the assemblages. These objects include bracelets, fibula, earrings, finger rings, beads pendants, buckles and ring belts, but exclude torcs since this would clearly have skewed the results of those burials defined by

81

their presence. These results are in many ways the most revealing of all the summary statistics examined in this study. Unlike the other items, the frequency of objects of personal ornamentation are always most common in Feminine burials, but also have higher frequency in the Neuter burials than they do in the Masculine burials for all periods except the La Tène Moyenne (though there is a notable correlation in the frequency of these two categories in the La Tène Ancienne I). Figure 4.10 shows that fibula occur most frequently within the Feminine category for all periods. The Masculine and Neuter burials, however, show a more or less parallel set of results with an indeterminate but apparently relative relationship between their frequencies. This then is curious, but not particularly revealing.

If, however, one looks specifically at the frequency of bracelets (Figure 4.11), one notes that in all periods, except the La Tène Moyenne, the Neuter burials have a higher frequency of bracelets than the Masculine burials, and the Feminine burials have a higher frequency than either of the other two groups. This is revealing, primarily because regardless of the criteria that defines the other two categories, the Neuter burials are presumably made up of a combination of both male and female individuals. As a result, if bracelets were associated with some form of feminine gender association, they would be found most frequently in the Feminine burials, and more frequently in the Neuter burials than in Masculine graves. This suggests that bracelets do have some association with the gender of the

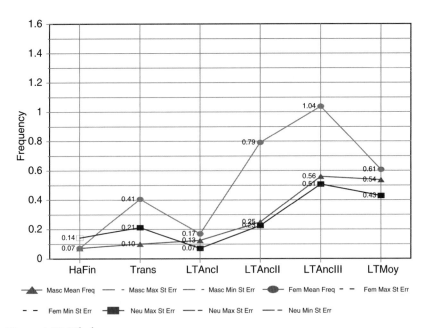

Figure 4.10 Fibula.

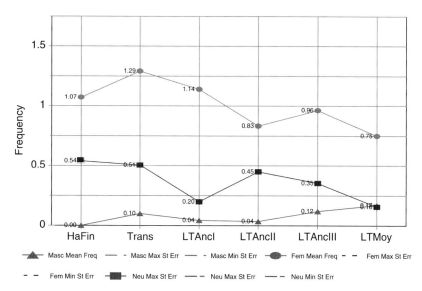

Figure 4.11 Bracelets.

interred. Yet while this is revealing, what is most interesting is that they are clearly not gender identifiers, or they would not be found in the Masculine graves. In every period except the Hallstatt Finale, the Masculine category shows the presence of bracelets, and there is some suggestion that this occurs with greater frequency after the La Tène Ancienne II.

Thus, bracelets, while more frequently associated with the Feminine category, are clearly not definitively feminine artefacts. Indeed, with the exception of the artefacts used to sex the graves, the only artefact types identified with only one of the categories are razors (Evans 2004: 178). Yet, the definition of razors and the identification of the osteological sex of the burials based on their presence suffer the same problems as the engendering artefacts. Within this study, only four razors were found in Masculine graves, and an equal number were found in Neuter graves. As a result, no definitive variation in their frequency based on gender can be applied.

The lack of any clear-cut differentiation between the artefact assemblages (excluding those objects used to define the categories) associated with the Masculine and Feminine burials re-emphasises the doubts regarding the nature of these two categories raised by the existence of burials where the sex of the individual in question appears to be of a sex opposite to that suggested by the grave assemblage. The mutual exclusivity of the two engendered categories is clearly not reliable. Cases such as the 'torc bearing warriors' of Terres du Couer and Champs Dolent draw even greater suspicion upon the existence of a bi-polar gender divide.

Despite this, there remains the fact that in most cases most individuals buried with torcs do not have weapons and visa versa. Additionally, though intrinsically biased, the osteological tests do show that most individuals buried with torcs are female, and most buried with a warrior assemblage are male. Clearly, if there were serious faults in the biological sexing of these two categories, osteologists would have identified the problem by now. There can be little doubt that there is a greater tendency for torcs and bracelets to be found with biological females and for weapons to be found with biological males. Instead, what we appear to be seeing is a completely different set of gender roles.

While these categories were dominated by one sex or the other, they may still have been open to members of the other sex. Examples of flexible gender definitions can be seen throughout the world. The *backward men* of the Lakota Sioux are biological males who dress and act in a manner normally associated with women. They are in no way seen as female, but rather exist as a category of their own (Fire 1973). Other cultures, such as the Hua of Papua New Guinea, note that the degree of an individual's masculinity or femininity can change over time based upon the amount of contact they have with the opposite sex (Parker Pearson 1999: 95–123). Tacitus notes that the Britons '. . . recognise no distinction of sex among their rulers . . .' (*Agricola*: 16) and describes Bouddica as beginning her speech with the comment that '. . . this is not the first time that the Britons have been led to battle by a woman' (*Annals*: Book XIV).

While one should be careful to avoid reading too much into such cross-temporal and spatial analogies, the point remains that many cultures do have a more complex set of gender roles within their society than those of nineteenth century France. The results of this examination suggest such may also have been the case for the population of the Upper Seine Basin in the Early to Middle Iron Ages. It is impossible to say if these results represent the existence of multiple gender roles such as found among the Lakota, flexible gender roles such as we are beginning to find in modern Europe and the US, or some completely different form of gender differentiation. All that this suggests is that the Iron Age identities of that region do not appear to have consisted of a simple bi-polar definition of Masculine or Feminine.

Additionally, it would appear that these aspects of gender related burials also seem to be in some way tied to the nature of social reproduction and status within the funerary rites. The correlation between the presence of these items in the grave context and the presence of other items is clear for all phases except the Hallstatt Finale. Even there, one would be relatively safe in assuming that some additional prestige existed. What is particularly interesting is that this pattern changes over time, with the prestige related 'engender' burials showing more and more marked differentiation from the Neuter burials until the La Tène Ancienne III. During that period, one sees a decrease in the frequency of all artefacts in the two engendered groups except in those Masculine-defining items associated with warfare. The fact that this influences the overall frequency of grave goods in the Masculine burials enough to maintain an overall artefact frequency that is more or less stable despite the reduction of other items indicates that these changes are fairly clearly related to the nature of those male-dominated aspects of society being represented through the presence of warrior related items.

Regardless of whether the individuals interred with such items were warriors themselves or were merely using the weaponry as symbolic representations of power, the increased use of these items clearly shows an increase in the importance of representing warfare in the burial rites. The increase in the use of these symbols, and the steady decrease in the prestige related to the feminine associated torcs burials, shows changes in the manners in which the deceased's identity was being represented. It suggests an increase in the association of the prestige of the masculine dominated warrior role, and may be a gradual decrease in the association with the prestige of the feminine dominated torc wearing population. That this occurs in the phase immediately following the massive depopulation of the cemetery may in fact give a clue as to nature of these changes.

Figure 4.12 shows the overall artefact frequency as compared to the overall population of each period. It reveals that both the population and the frequency of grave goods for the region continued to increase up to and including the La Tène Ancienne I. However, where there was a dramatic drop in the buried population in the La Tène Ancienne II, the overall artefact frequency continued to grow at the same rate as previously observed. It was not until the following period that the artefact frequency for the population as a whole began to drop. Comparison of this to the results indicated by Figures 4.4 and 4.6 notes that the changes in the relationship between the different gender categories also occurred at this time. It was in fact during the La Tene Ancienne III that the frequency of the warrior assemblage increased remarkably, impacting the overall frequency of grave goods

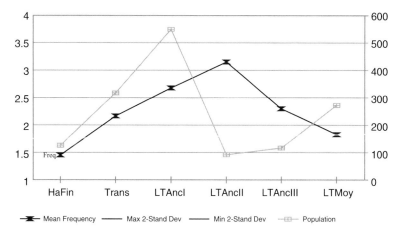

Figure 4.12 Total artefact frequency and population.

in the Masculine category as a whole. Such a change in these masculine and warfare related items in particular suggest a change in the gender and prestige related modes of social reproduction. This is revealing by itself, but there is an additional aspect that needs to be remembered: the warrior assemblage is related to war.

Whatever was occurring during these periods, it was in some way related to the way in which both gender and status related elements of the social identities were being reflected within the burial rites. A great deal more study needs to be undertaken before this is truly understood. Elements of placement of the graves within the cemeteries and of the cemeteries within the landscape must be studied, and a broader examination of the burials of the period must be undertaken. These initial results, however, do indicate the potential of such lines of investigation for Iron Age studies.

Conclusions

This use of simple statistical methods applied to a regionally wide data set has by no means proven any hypothetical or theoretical concepts. Rather, by merely examining the data as a whole, it has added to the questions related to the period, and raised issues regarding our understanding of the roles of how gender, status and overall aspects of identity may have influenced and been influenced by other modes of social reproduction. In this case, the results of the study have suggested that while there is some validity to the presence of prestige items within the grave contexts, the Iron Age in the Upper Seine Basin saw a much more complicated definition of gender than is presently considered. The results indicate that while certain objects were found more frequently with males and others more frequently associated with females, there is no clear definition between the two categories in the funerary context even in the instances of grave goods that are considered gender defining by the archaeologists. This implies that either there was flexibility in the gender roles of the society, or that more than two socially recognised genders existed within it. Either way, though there were certainly gender associations found with the grave goods, it would not appear that the gender roles were the clear bi-polar definitions we generally use in our interpretations.

The statistical and landscape related approaches used by this project as a whole have been used to explore elements of the information gathered by over a century of investigation through the use of techniques that expand our ability to perceive meaning. It represents one example of how access to both statistical packages and general computing has truly influenced our ability to conduct archaeological research. Data sets that previously were so large that they could not be comprehended can now be examined in a manner that allows us to perceive patterns that might otherwise have escaped us. To this end, the most significant element of modern quantitative methodology that has impacted archaeology is not the application of the newest techniques but rather the ability for anyone to apply even the oldest techniques to their study.

However, with this comes the need for care to be utilised. The inappropriate use of quantitative methods may appear to give results when indeed all they show is nonsense, and indeed in this study there were numerous times where the apparent mathematical relationship between results could have led to a meaningful association of numbers. If one is not careful, the mystical allure of numbers can allow one to readily see patterns where none exist, or worse yet, where the patterns are caused by a mathematical and not the cultural relationship. One must also use techniques that are appropriate to one's question and not use whatever method is handy to address one's questions or data. After all, computers do not think, and statistical applications will produce results whether or not the methods used are appropriate to the data. One must always be aware of the proper use of differing techniques and apply them appropriately. In this sense, as we begin to assimilate both the power of computers and of quantitative methods into our own identities as archaeologists, we must become more and more aware of exactly what that means and how it impacts our understanding of both archaeology and ourselves.

Table 4.1 List of examined sites in the Upper Seine Basin

Site code	Site name	Reference
AISNE		
Ai1	«La Muette»à Dravegny (Aisne)	Massy and Thirion, 1980
Ai2	«Le Desssus de Prugny»à Chassemy (Aisne)	Fercoq du Leslay, 1984
Ai3	Pernant	Lobjois, 1969
Ai4	Bucy-Le-Long	Lobjois, 1974a; Lobjois, 1974b; Ancien and Lobjois, 1981; Desenne and Guichard, 1992; Desenne, Ilett and Guichard, 1993; Constantin, Gransear, Guichard, Pion and Pommepuy, 1993
ARDENNES		
Ard1	«La Hourgnotte» à Liry (Ardennes)	Duval, 1971; Duval, 1972
Ard2	«La Motelle» à Hauvine	Simonnet, 1938; Simonnet, 1939; Roualet, Rapoin, Fluzin and Uran, 1985

Continued overleaf

87

Table 4.1 continued

Site code	Site name	Reference
Ard3	Mont-Trote à Manre (Ardennes)	Rozoy, 1986/7?
Ard4	Rouliers (Ardennes)	Rozoy, 1986/7?
AUBE		
Au1	«le Crepin» ferme de Frecul, Barbuise-Courtavant (Aube)	Brisson and Lemoine, 1962
Au2	«Les Greves de Fecul» à Barbuise-Courtavant (Aube)	Lemoine, Gardien and Wabrave, 1964
Au3	«Les Greves de Courtavant» 1 at Courtavant, in the commune de Barbuise (Aube)	Revailler, 1968; Piette, 1979: 26–28
Au4	«Les Greves de Courtavant» 2 or «Necropole 2» at Courtavant/Barbuise Aube	Piette, 1979: 20–39
Au5	«Les Greves de la Villeneuve»	Piette, 1971: 8–40; Piette, 1972: 5–18; Peitte, 1979: 20–39; Piette, 1984: 135–151
Au6	«La Perriere» à Saint-Benoit-sur-Seine (Aube)	Bienaime, 1989; Biename, 1984
Au7	«La Cotes d'Ervaux» Estissac (Aube)	Deffressigne and Villes, 1997; Brun and Chaume, 1997: 347–353;
Au8	«Les Vermillonnes» à Luyers	Guillier, 1991
Au9	«La Chevre» at Isle-Aumont (or Isle-au-Mont, or Butte d'Ilse-Aumont etc.), Aube	Carrard de Breban, 1849
COTES-D'OR		
CdO1	Minot(Cotes D'Or) «Crais de Charme»	Henry, 1949–1950: 26–28
CdO2	Le Grand Tumulus de Larrey	Joffroy, 1964–1965
Cdo3	Les Tumulus de Fontaine-en-Duesmois	Ratel, 1969
CdO4	Quetinieres à Longvic (Cotes d'Or)	Barral and Depierre, 1993
CdO5	Le Grand Tumulus de Lantilly (Cotes-d'Or)	Corot, 1905
CdO6	Toucheboeuf à Laignes (Cotes-d'Or)	Joly, 1950
CdO7	Vendues at Fraignot (Cotes-d'Or)	Joffroy, 1957
CdO8	«Chamberceau» – la Foret de Champberceau à Commune de Vernois-les-Vesvres (Cotes-d'Or)	Henry, 1932; Corot, 1900; Ratel, 1979
CdO9	Le Clausets et les 3 tumuli des Breuil à Minot	Corot, 1891–1892
CdO10	Rente-Neuve à Couchey	Ratel, 1961
CdO11	Bressy-sur-Tille (Cotes-d'Or)	Roger Ratel, 1977
CdO12	Nod-Sur-Seine (Cotes-d'Or)	Dr Brulard, 1905

CdO13	les Tumulus de Larcon (Cotes-d'Or) called «le tumulus Bourrachot» and «le tumulus Ramaget»	Ratel, 1967
CdO14	Tumulus de la Meusse (Cotes-d'Or)	Henry, 1932
HAUTE-MARNE		
HM1	Hoericourt I at Hoericourt (Haute-Marne) in vicinity of Saint-Dizier	Flouest, 1974
HM2	Essey-les-Eaux	Balliot, 1901; Bailliot, 1902; Thevenard, Villes and Neiss, 1996: 202–203
HM3	«Chatelet» à Vitry-les-Nogents (Haute-Marne)	Ballet, 1952
HM4	Marsois (N11) à Nogent-en-Bas (Haute-Marne)	Thomas and Thomas, 1989
HM5	Montsaugeon «Tumlus I et II» and «de la Croix» (Tumulus I only)	Royer, Royer and Flouest, 1888; Thevenard, Villes and Neiss, 1996: 259–263
HM6	«les Terres du Coer» Perogney-les-Fontaines	Balliot, 1900; Thevenard, Villes and Neiss, 1996: 277–279
HM7	«le Tumulus de Moulin-Brule» à Courcelles-sur-Aujon, HM	Trin, 1905; Thevenard, Villes and Neiss, 1996: 180–181
HM8	La Mottet de Nijon	Lepage, 1984b; Lepage, 1985; Thevenard, Villes and Neiss, 1996: 264–266
MARNE		
M1	Jogasses (Marne)	Hatt and Roualet, 1976; Favret, 1927
M2	Vert-la-Gravelle (Marne)	Charpy, 1986; Lepage, 1966; Brisson, Loppin and Cherriere, 1956
M3	Vrigny (Marne)	Chossenot, Neiss, and Sauget, 1981: 131–150
M4	Tinqueux (Marne)	Flouest and Stead, 1981b
M5	Le Chemin de Dats near St Memmie (Marne)	Chossenot, Charpy, and Fischer, 1990; Charpy and Chossenots, 1989; Favret, 1924
M6	Le Mont-Saint-Bernard/Beau-Regard à Etrechy (Marne)	Roualet, 1981
M7	Barbiere à Villesenuex (Marne)	Roualet and Kruta, 1980; Favret, 1950

Continued overleaf

Table 4.1 continued

Site code	Site name	Reference
M8	Champ Dolent à Cernay-les-Reims (Marne)	Guillaume, 1970: 40–47
M9	Marquis à Prunay (Marne)	Guillaume, 1970: 65–67
M10	Fin d'Ecrury à Fere-Champenoise (Marne)	Brisson and Hatt, 1960; Brisson, 1935
M11	Le Mont la Pierre à Sommesous (Marne)	Guillier and Villes, 1995
M12	Saint-Mard à Gourgacon (Marne)	Brisson and Loppin, 1938c
M13	Les Poplainnaux à Gourgancon (Marne)	Brisson and Loppin, 1938b
M14	La Corbillere à Gourgancon (Marne)	Brisson and Loppin, 1938a
M15	«Le Fer-a-Cheval» à Betheniville (Marne)	Dupis, 1932
M16	«Terres de Monsieur» commune de Bergeres-les-Vertus (Marne)	Brisson and Duval, 1934
M17	«La Noue du Moulin» à Fagnieres (near Chalons-sur-Marne) (Marne)	Chossenot and Chossenot, 1981
M18	«Les Cotes-en-Marne» à Ecury-sur-Coole (Marne)	Therot, (1931a); Therot, (1931b)
M19	Jonchery-sur-Vestle (Marne)	Legros, 1975
M20	Argentelle à Beine (Marne)	Morgen and Roualet, 1975; Morgen and Roualet, 1976
M21	«Cour» à Villevenard	Roland and Hu, 1931
M22	Puisieulx-Taissy (also just Puisieulx) à Marne	Chance, 1910; Bretz-Mahler, 1971; Joffroy and Bretz-Mahler, 1959
M23	«la Tempete» à Normee (Marne)	Brisson and Hatt, 1969; Bretz-Mahler, 1971; Joffroy and Bretz-Mahler, 1959
M24	Fere Champenoise «Au dessus du Faubourg de Connantre»	Brisson, Hatt and Roualet, 1970
M25	Mont Gravet à Villenueve-Renneville (Marne)	Brisson, Roualet and Hatt, 1971; Brisson, Roualet and Hatt 1972; Bretz-Mahler and Brisson, 1958
OISE		
O1	Mory-Montcruz «Sous-les-Vignes-d'en-Haut» (canton Breteuil-sur-Noye, arrondissement Clermont) Oise	Blanchet, 1983

O2	Breuil-le-Sec (Oise)	Degenne and Duval, 1983; Degenne, 1978; Massy, Mantel, Meniel and Rapis, 1986
O3	Tartigny called «Moulin de Tartigny», Chemin des Moulins, and La Petite Couture	
SEINE-ET-MARNE		
SM1	Montigny-Lencoup (Seine-et-Marne) called «Croyats» and «La Justice»	Guillaumet, 1977; Buisson, 1901
SM2		Gours-aux-Lions a Marolles-sur-Seine (Seine et Marne) Mordant, 1970: 11–12, 89–125
SM3	Gobillons à Chatenay-sur-Seine (Seine et Marne)	Bontillot, Mordant, Mordant and Paris, 1975
SM4	Gravon (Seine-et-Marne)	Scherer and Mordant, 1972; Mordant, 1966
SM5	«Montapot» à Salins (Seine-et-Marne)	E. Chouquet, 1877
SM6	Cannes-Ecluse (Seine-et-Marne)	R. Baron, 1964
YONNE		
Y1	«Beajeu» à Pont-sur-Yonne (Yonne): also called «Volteuse»	Prampart, 1989; Prampart, 1970
Y2	Soucy/Mocques Bouteilles (Yonne)	Baray, Desffressigne, Leroyer and Villemeur, 1994: 83–173
Y3	«La Longue Raie» at Michery (Yonne)	Baray, Desffressigne, Leroyer and Villemeur, 1994: 57–82
Y4	«la Creole» at Serbonnes (Yonne)	Baray, Desffressigne, Leroyer and Villemeur, 1994: 15–56
Y5	Renardieres à Pont Sur Yonne	Prampart, 1981
Y6	Gringalet à Sergines (Yonne)	Parruzot and Delinon, 1979
Y7	Villeperrot (Yonne)	Prampart, 1979
Y8	«La Picardie» in Gurgy (Yonne)	Dolar and Pellet, 1980

Notes

1 Because neither the pelvis nor the cranium survived, this biological sexing was always somewhat suspect, but still notes an example of the uncertainty of mutual exclusivity of the masculine and feminine assemblages.

2 Excavated on 14 July 1910 by H. Gillet and J. Orblix, the report holds reasonable written records and site plans which, though crudely drawn, give quite adequate representation of body and artefact placement. These records are well presented in Guillaume (1970: 40–7). Unfortunately, there is no indication of whether or not an osteological examination of the site was conducted. Considering the date of discovery, however, it seems unlikely.

3 A fourth category of 'Both' was also created that contained those burials that included either individuals who were osteologically sexed as one sex but included items from the 'opposite' gender, or that contained elements of both of the engendered categories. Since this group was exceptionally small and primarily made up of 'problem' cases, it was determined that use or comparison of these individuals was inappropriate to the purposes of this study.

4 The mean frequency is the mean average for the category which represents the total number of artefacts found in the relative category divided by the number of individuals in that category.

5 In the case of most Period level investigation these results were rounded off at two decimal places.

6 The standard error of the mean can be said to represent one way of determining the degree of confidence we have in our estimate of the mean of the population (in this case population representing the case we are studying, not the demographic population of the region). Standard error is determined by dividing an estimate of the population's standard deviation by the square root of the number of observations noted in the sample. Assuming a normal distribution, a single degree of standard error will contain 68.2 per cent of the means of the population. A value of 1.96 standard errors, or two degrees, represents the range into which 95 per cent of the means will fall. Within archaeology, this is said to represent a degree of *significance*. For a more comprehensive description see Shennan, 1997: 77–9.

List of abbreviations

AFEAF   Association français pour l'étude de l'age du Fer
BSAC   *Bulletin de la Société archéologique champenoise*
MSACSAM *Mémoires de la Société d'Agriculture, Commerce, Sciences et Arts du département de la Marne*
RAE   *Revue archéologiques de l'Est et du Centre–Est*

Bibliography

Ancien, A.-M. and Lobjois, G. (1981) 'Neuf enclos circulaire dans la Valee du L'Ainse'. *Cahiers Archaeologique de Picardie* 8: 43–64.

Balliot, L. (1900) 'Les Tumulus de Perrogny', in *Annales de la Société d'Histoire, D'archéologie, et des Beaux-Arts de Chaumont. T.2 1900–1905*. Chaumont: Société d'Histoire, D'archéologie, et des Beaux-Arts de Chaumont.

Baxter, M. J. (1996) *Exploratory Multivariate Analysis in Archaeology*. Edinburgh: Edinburgh University Press.

Buchsenshutz, O. (1984) *Structures d'Habitats et Fortifications de l'Âge du Fer en France Septentrionale: Memories de la Société Prehistorique Française, t. 18*. Paris: Maison des Sciences de l'Homme.

Chosssenot, D., Neiss, R. and Sauget, J. M. (1981) 'Fouille de sauvetage d'une nécrople de La Tene I à Vrigny (Marne)' in *L'Age du Fer en France Septentrionale – Mémoires de la Société Archéologiquge Champenoise – 2*. p. 131. Société Archéologiquge Champenoise.

Cunliffe, B. W. (1997) *The Ancient Celts*. Oxford: Oxford University Press.

Evans, T. L. (2004) *Quantified Identities: A Statistical Summary and Analysis of Iron*

Age Cemeteries in North-Eastern France 600–130 BC. BAR International series 1226. Oxford: Archaeopress.

Fire, J. (1973) *Lame Deer, Souix Medicine Man.* London: Simon & Schuster.

Flouest, J.-L. and Stead, I. M. (1981) 'Fouille de sauvetage a Tinquex (Marne), 1974', in *Mémoires de la Société Archéologique Champenoise – 2,* pp. 151–76. Société Archéologiguque Champenoise.

Guillaume P. (1970) 'Les Notes de Fouille d'Henri Gillet (1890–1947) – Notices par Commune'. *Cahiers Archéologue du Nort-Est. t. XIII fasc 1 et 2,* 40–7.

Guillaumet, J. P. (1977) 'La necropolis gauloise de Montigny-Lencoup (Seine-et-Marne)' 'Etude descriptive'. *Bulletin de Société Archaéologique de Sens. Fasc 21: Les Senones: Avant la Conquête a la Lumière de Denrienres Découvertes: Habitat, Commerce, Sépulture: Actes du Colloque de La Tène tenu a Sens 15 Mai 1877. Vol 21,* pp. 38–44. Sens: Société Archaéologique de Sens.

Hatt, J. J. and Roualet, P. (1977) 'La chronologie de La Tène en Champagne'. *RAE, t. XXXII, fasc. 1–2,* 7–36.

Kruta, V. (1991a) 'The first Celtic expansion: Prehistory to history', in S. Moscati *et al.* (eds) *The Celts.* Milan: Rizzoli Publications, pp. 195–213.

Kruta, V. (1991b) 'La céramique peinte de la Champagne dans le contexte de l'art celtique de IVe siècle avant J-C', in *La céramique peinte celtique dans son contexte européen. Actes du symposium international d'Hautevillers, 1987 Mémoires de la Société archéologique champenoise, no 5.* La Société archéologique champenoise, pp. 143–57.

Livy, Titus (1960) *The Early History of Rome: Books I–V of The History of Rome from its Foundation.* Trans. A. de Sélincourt. London: Penguin.

Madsen, T. (1988) 'Multivariate statistics and archaeology', in *Multivariate Archaeology: Numerical Approaches in Scandinavian Archaeology. Jutland Archaeological Society Publication XXI,* Moesgård: Aarhus University Press.

Moscati, S., Frey, O. H., Kruta V, Rafferty, B. and Szaró, M. (1991) *The Celts.* London: Rizzoli Publications.

Nicaise, A. (1886) *Le Port Féminin di Torque dans la region de l'Est de la Gaule. MSACSAM, vol 78, 1884–1885,* pp. 75–89.

Parker Pearson, M. (1999) *The Archaeology of Death and Burial.* Thrupp, UK: Sutton Publishing Ltd.

Polybius (1979) *The Rise of the Roman Empire.* Trans. I. Scott-Kilver. London: Penguin.

Shennan, S. (1997) *Quantifying Archaeology.* Edinburgh: Edinburgh University Press.

Tainter, J. (1977) 'Modeling change in Prehistoric Social systems', in Binford L. *For Theory Building in Archaeology.* New York: Academic Press, pp. 327–52.

Taylor, T. (1996) *The Prehistory of Sex: four million years of sexual character.* London: Bantam Books.

Thomas, J. (1996) *Time, Culture & Identity.* London: Routledge.

Wason, P. K. (1994) *The Archaeology of Rank.* Cambridge: Cambridge University Press.

Wiess, K. M. (1972) 'On systematic bias in skeletal sexing'. *American Journal of Physical Anthropology 37:* 239–50.

Part IV

MODELLING THE PAST

5

JOUMA'S TENT
Bedouin and digital archaeology

Carol Palmer and Patrick Daly

Introduction

The survey outlined in this chapter is part of a study of pastoralists living in the Wadi Faynan area in southern Jordan. In this study, the location of bedouin campsites in the landscape is identified, as is the distribution of artefacts around them, using a variety of field techniques and the data analysed using Geographic Information Systems (GIS). This work bridges two distinct but related scales of human behaviour and data. To understand the relationships that nomadic pastoralists have with their landscape it is necessary to address social practices enacted at a large 'regional' scale, such as movement, land use, and campsite location. Within such broader patterns of activity, this study also looks at more intimate social practices related to individual sites and families. Digital techniques provide a useful means to examine different scales within the same overall methodological framework, exploring multiple scales simultaneously, and allowing each to feed into the other.

The full range of analysis conducted as part of our research in the Wadi Faynan far exceeds the limits of what can be included in this chapter, so we have selected two discrete aspects that demonstrate how our theoretical and practical approaches to the study of pastoralists have been further enhanced by the use of digital techniques. In particular, the use of databases and GIS in our research pulls together information collected in the field as part of more 'standard' landscape archaeological methods, as well as information collected from inhabitants of the region in the present day using ethnographic methods. Using digital techniques we have amalgamated anthropological and archaeological data enabling us to consider both wider patterns of land use and localised discard practices at individual camp sites. The ultimate aim of our research is to provide a better understanding of the nature of contemporary bedouin land use, as well as to equip archaeologists working in the region to better discern the residue of modern pastoralists and separate this material from relics of earlier periods that are often indistinguishable even to a trained eye.

One of the main questions that face all who study pastoral societies, especially those who retain a significant amount of 'traditional' social practices and material culture, is how much such societies are affected by the political, social, and economic climate of the region where they reside. The bedouin that are central to our work are in a period characterised by transition and a negotiation between traditional and non-traditional ways of life, partly in response to external factors, and partly brought about by internal decisions. Our main interest, for the purpose of this chapter, is to apply digital techniques to see how non-traditional influences have altered different aspects of traditional bedouin social practices. We approach this by looking at two distinct aspects of life. First, we focus upon wider landscape use in the Wadi Faynan and how this has shifted in recent memory.

The bedouin have long used different elements of the landscape, largely to support the herding activities that are the traditional backbone of bedouin economy. The major factors that regulate movement though the landscape and location of campsites are largely environmentally determined, as bedouin living in very marginal conditions typically seek to exploit suitable environmental niches that best facilitate their needs. This includes access to water and suitable grazing for their goats, as well as protection from the elements. This is moderated by social considerations that arise from the complex organisation and sets of social relationships that are prevalent in bedouin society. As a result, it is usual for camp location to be influenced by family and tribal affiliation. Our research, as presented here, incorporates information from both archaeological and ethnographic surveys to show how land use in the Wadi Faynan is organised in response to both social and environmental considerations, with particular interest in how land use has been influenced by less traditional factors in recent years.

The second element of the study, one also potentially affected by the encroachment of different ways of life and the accoutrements associated with them, is related to the use of material culture at the campsite level. We are particularly interested in investigating site formation processes. This is done to see how the increased availability of different forms of material culture, in particular more durable forms such as metal and plastics, impact upon discard activity and thus site formation processes. This study provides useful information not just about what different forms of material culture the bedouin in the Wadi Faynan are using and how this reflects changing conditions of life, but also how this contributes to the archaeological residue in the area. This leads to the second goal of our research, which is to better understand and recognise the signature of bedouin pastoral campsites so that they can be more clearly distinguished from the mass of ancient sites in the same landscape, and to evaluate how they have changed as a result of the availability of more durable forms of material culture.

Both of these lines of inquiry have been studied using a variety of field-based methods, including detailed archaeological survey of abandoned camp sites, ethnographic inquiry of bedouin currently residing in Wadi Faynan, and geoarchaeological analysis of camp-site floor surfaces. All of this work has been facilitated by the extensive use of digital techniques, most specifically GIS, which has been employed in both scales of analysis. While a number of other studies of bedouin campsites have used various mapping techniques to display the distribution of different aspects of material culture, this study is the first example of the use of GIS in the management and analysis of ethnographic and ethnoarchaeological data. After a brief overview of the case study area, some selected results are presented.

The Bedouin Camp Survey

The Wadi Faynan landscape survey

The Wadi Faynan (Feinan) is situated about 40 km northwest of the World Heritage site of Petra, the ancient capital of the Nabatean Kingdom, and 70 km southeast of the Dead Sea (Figure 5.1). The Wadi Faynan is between 100 and 200 m above sea level, but, to the east, over the course of just *c.* 15 km, the land quickly rises to *c.* 1,400 m above sea level to the plateau above the picturesque village of Dana. At Wadi Faynan, although winters are mild, the summers are hot with daytime temperatures regularly topping 40°C. Rainfall is low; at Ghor al-Safi, just south of the Dead Sea, annual precipitation is only 80 mm, although on the plateau it is approximately 300 mm (Swenne 1995). There is a high degree of variability in rainfall from year to year and rain usually causes powerful flash-flooding, a pattern that has shaped the landscape, forming and re-forming wadis over millennia. All of these factors play a role in decision-making of the bedouin residents about movement and camp location at different times of the year.

The study of bedouin camps in the Wadi Faynan is part of the Wadi Faynan Landscape Survey (WFLS), directed by Professor Graeme Barker (Barker 2000). This is a multi-disciplinary project with archaeologists, geographers and environmental biologists working together to understand the evolution of what is today an arid and relatively sparsely inhabited landscape. By contrast, the area is rich in archaeological remains, from villages associated with early farming (Najjar *et al.* 1990; Finlayson *et al.* 2000; Simmons and Najjar 1996) to major settlements of the Nabatean, Roman and Byzantine periods and, in particular, the massive mound of masonry and copper slag that is Khirbet Faynan ('the ruin of Faynan'). The WFLS has performed a particularly detailed study of the relic field systems associated with major periods of occupation (Barker *et al.* 1997, 1998, 1999), as well as performed a broader survey of the area beyond them (Barker *et al.* 2000). Recent excavations and survey work in nearby Wadi Fidan (Levy *et al.* 2002) attest to the importance of this region in the Early

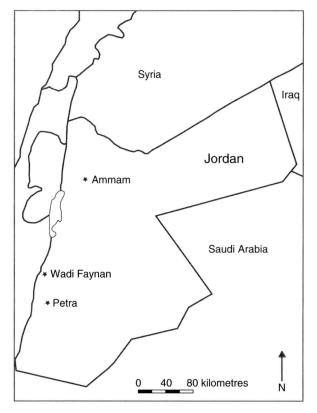

Figure 5.1 The Wadi Faynan study area.

Bronze and Iron Ages as one of the largest sources of copper ore in the southern Levant. Pollution from ancient mining and smelting in the Wadi Faynan appears to have had a devastating impact on the landscape (Barker *et al.* 1999; Pyatt *et al.* 2000) and, even today, has an impact on the bedouin living in the area (Grattan *et al.* 2003). The material remains left by the bedouin have added to the already dense collection of residue from previous periods of human activity.

Contemporary and recent land-use

Though earlier periods were known to have wetter climates, the present landscape is arid and sparsely occupied. Traditionally, Wadi Faynan formed part of a seasonal round where local bedouin and semi-nomadic villagers from Dana camped with their animals in the wadi during the winter and moved to the uplands in the summer (see also Lancaster and Lancaster 1999: 119–20). As well as mild winter conditions, Wadi Faynan has good access to water; there are springs in the lower Wadi Dana and Wadi Ghuwayr. By April or May at the latest, however, temperatures in the area rise considerably and local grazing areas quickly become exhausted.

In the recent past, there has been year-round settlement around Faynan, in addition to seasonal occupation. In 1993, the Wadi Faynan became the southern border of the Dana Nature Reserve, managed by Jordan's Royal Society for the Conservation of Nature (RSCN) (Chatty 2002; Rowe 1997; Swenne 1995). The RSCN's local base in the Wadi Faynan area is a camp at the foot of the Wadi Dana, originally established by the Natural Resources Authority (NRA) as a base from which to undertake mineral prospection. The same RSCN camp became a joint research facility with the Council for British Research in the Levant (CBRL) during the time of WFLS fieldwork (1996–2000). Regular and occasional work from organisations associated with the camp means it is an important focal point for the local people and visitors to the area. The first school in Wadi Faynan was based at this camp, but was replaced in 1992 by the present primary school located along the track that leads to the camp, about a kilometre away.

The main local bedouin tribes are the 'Amārīn, Sa'idiyin, Rashaydah, and the much smaller Manaja'. The most numerous group camping in and around the Wadi Faynan are the 'Azāzma bedouin who came to the area from the Negev following the formation of the State of Israel in 1948. The 'Azāzma originate from Beersheba and had previously been sheep and camel herders (see Bailey 1991: 4–5), though today the main livestock maintained by all of the bedouin are goats. Year-round habitation in the area is facilitated by the use of supplementary fodder, which until 1997, was heavily subsidised (Rowe 1997). Modern bedouin no longer shift camp using camels; they have trucks (Chatty 1986).

Influenced by governmental settlement schemes, economic imperatives and, increasingly, by their own choice, bedouin are becoming more settled. In the 1970s the nearby village of Gregora and its associated irrigation scheme was founded, principally by members of the 'Amārīn and Sa'idiyin (Lancaster and Lancaster 1999: 154–5; Swenne 1995). Today, the nearest secondary schools, clinic, and shops are there. In the late 1990s, the 'Azāzma were given land in the Wadi Ghuweibe, north of the Wadi Faynan, to start their own village. In part due to increased activity in the Wadi Faynan, the Rashaydah tribe, who were growing vegetables for the commercial market in the Wadi Faynan for a brief period during the 1990s (Lancaster and Lancaster 1999: 122–3),[1] have most recently begun building their own village west of the ancient field system. Our research at the wider landscape level investigates the location of campsites to see how the influx of facilities and infrastructure associated with sedentary forms of living affects location decision-making.

Analysis of modern land-use

The Bedouin Camp Survey took place during the springs of 1999 and 2000. During 1999, a general survey was conducted to examine the location of tents in the landscape, to document main tent characteristics, including durable and non-durable architectural features, and to observe activities occurring around them.

In 1999, 83 tent sites were visited and recorded. Most of them had been occupied very recently, and in 75 cases it was possible to find out exactly who had lived in each and for how long. This number includes 18 tents that were occupied when they were recorded. The occupants provided invaluable information about tent life that was then applied to abandoned sites. All the sites were visited with Jouma from the ʻAzāzma tribal group, our main informant and an experienced archaeologist. This survey does not pretend to represent a study of all the campsites in the Wadi Faynan area, rather it focuses on detailed consideration of particular concentrations in the east and south of the survey area. Recently abandoned bedouin camp-sites are relatively easy to identify due to the spreads of animal dung and discarded modern refuse left behind. Older sites are more difficult to detect because they appear as isolated stone platforms, single lines of stones or stone-lined hearths, alone or in combination. Some of the stone platforms are superficially similar to other ancient features, including graves of Bronze Age date, and so defining the characteristics of each was an important part of understanding not just more recent bedouin activity, but also prehistoric material remains.

In the Bedouin Camp Survey, the position of each tent site was recorded according to a hand-held GPS reading, and the tent orientation noted where identifiable. All sites were sketched and the spatial organisation of the tent recorded where it could be determined. Outside the tent itself, supplementary features such as goat and kid pens, chicken coops, outside hearths, and a variety of features associated with storage of materials were recorded. Where possible, general details were also taken on the inhabitants, their tribal affiliation, the number of family members living in the tent, estimated numbers of livestock held, and any family relationships between tents inhabited by a group were noted.

The analysis of the sites in the wider landscape was undertaken as part of the framework established for the whole Wadi Faynan study area. On the basis of aerial photography, a photogrametric plan of the study area was constructed (Barker *et al.* 1997). This plan served as the foundation of a digital terrain model made in Arc-View 3.2 using the Spatial Analyst extension. During the survey of sites in the study area, GPS was used to locate all sites recorded, including bedouin camps. This database was converted into an 'event theme' in Arc-View, which created an array of points based upon UTM co-ordinates (one for each site) that were placed within the background landscape model. Each of the points was linked with related databases containing information on the sites, principally the material culture but for the bedouin sites information on tribal affiliations, tent form and orientation. At a wider landscape scale, it is possible to investigate patterns of settlement location, how sites are situated both within the environment and in reference to other sites and other people operating in the same space. An example of this is demonstrated and discussed below.

Results

Figure 5.2 is a depiction of the tents included in the Bedouin Camp Survey, their location and the tribal affiliation of the occupiers. There are obvious clusters of tribal groupings, making it clear that the inhabitants of Wadi Faynan strongly identify themselves with their 'tribe'. The figure also shows the numerical dominance of the 'Azāzma, who camp at the lower Wadi Dana and in the Wadi Shayqar. Between the RSCN camp and the school, along the main track, there is a cluster of 'Amārīn tents, which represent a group of close-relatives. One influential member of this group has been employed as an NRA camp guard for approximately 25 years, which, in part, explains the preference for this location. Another camp guard, from the Sa'idiyin, camps year-round just east of the RSCN camp. The Rashaydah

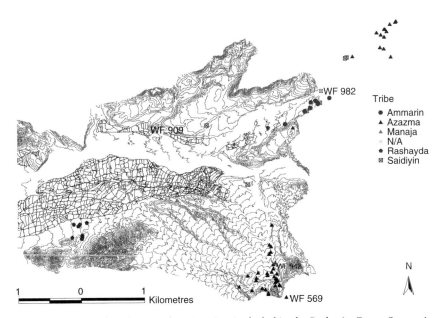

Figure 5.2 Map of study area showing sites included in the Bedouin Camp Survey in 1999, coded by tribal affiliation. These locations were not all inhabited at the same time but represent habitations over a period of years.

camp away from all these groups, more centrally in the Wadi Faynan. One of the Rashaydah is an archaeological guard for the CBRL, and some of his family tend to camp in areas where he can best perform his duties – that is, near to archaeological sites (for example, WF915–917) – which are close to the excavations at WF100 (Wright *et al.* 1998). A small Manaja' encampment (one family, but with two wives and, therefore, two tents) also exists in this larger area.

The entire area has good access to water, one of the main reasons for its popularity as a camping ground. In the lower Wadi Dana, water is now piped, via the RSCN camp, to the school, and people camping here are able draw off water from taps along the pipeline. People camping elsewhere have to transport their water, either by truck or on donkey-back. All the campsites are relatively close to tracks negotiable by a vehicle, and access is clearly an important consideration in their location.

The Wadi Faynan has long been a favourite winter camping ground and the main period of occupation continues to be the winter. Only eight of the tent sites surveyed were said to be exclusively summer sites, with one more inhabited year round. Where men have year-round employment, usually by association with the RSCN camp, their family does not necessarily stay with them during the summer. The family may move up the mountain to cooler and better grazing territory with the main tent. In contrast with the low number of summer tent sites, 57 were known to be occupied during the winter and early spring. Our findings show that these sites are all situated in relatively protected locations, on lower terraces beside wadi bottoms, which agrees with the literature (see also Avni 1992: 245; Banning and Köhler-Rollefson 1992: 187–9). Here, tents are protected from winter storms, have a measure of privacy, and the nearby wadi bottom provides a convenient place to discard waste from primary butchery, which is often performed there, as well as providing discrete toilet facilities. Winter flash floods in the wadis flush out all unsavoury debris. Summer camping sites are situated on ridge tops and in locations where every advantage may be taken of summer breezes (see also Banning and Köhler-Rollefson 1992: 189). Whether a winter or summer camp, most tents face broadly east, that is 57 out of 73 where this could be determined, which is commonly noted for the positioning of tents in northern Arabia, in general (Avni 1992: 245; Dickson 1959: 79; Jabbur 1995: 255). This positioning is said to give most protection from the prevailing wind, a characteristic particularly important in winter.

Houses of hair

Material culture of a mobile way of life

The archaeological visibility of nomadic pastoralists has long been debated. Early on, Childe (1951: 70) famously stated that 'Pastoralists are not likely to leave many vestiges by which the archaeologist could recognise their presence' (see also Cribb 1991a: 65; Finkelstein 1995: 23). Pastoral camp-sites are indeed ephemeral, but there is evidence from recent studies that nomadic pastoralists do leave visible traces in the form of fixed campsite 'architecture' and durable artefactual and environmental remains (Avni 1992; Banning and Köhler-Rollefson 1983, 1986, 1992; Cribb 1991a, 1991b; Hole 1979; Palmer and Smith in Barker *et al.* 2000; Simms 1988; Simms and Russell 1996). The debate on the visibility of pastoral campsites in the longer term continues to be a lively one (Finkelstein 1995; Rosen 1992), with an apparent absence of settlements or a reduced number of settlement sites often interpreted as evidence of an increasing pastoral element (LaBianca 1990; Finkelstein 1992).

The black tent is a 'pillar' of bedouin life (Jabbur 1995: 241–56), a defin-ing feature of the arid Near East (Figure 5.3). In Arabic the black tent is called, *bayt al-sha'r*, or 'house of hair', due to the black goat hair used to weave its fabric. The main components of the tent are its roof, sides (or 'walls'), and poles, all held upright with ropes (for more detailed description of tent components see Dalman 1964: 12–44, and Weir 1990: 13–18). Within the rectangular area covered by the tent, space is organised by activity, gender and, during the winter, it can separate animals and people in some groups. Transverse screens divide the tent into different

Figure 5.3 A black tent, *bayt al-sha'r*, in the Wadi Faynan (photograph C. Palmer).

105

compartments, which vary according to season, family requirements and occasion.

Thus, bedouin tents are made from fabric and wooden components that are not normally preserved in the archaeological record. The only pieces in use today that might have greater durability are metal rods, which secure guy ropes, and nails that attach the sides to the roof of the tent. There are, however, durable architectural features of bedouin camps that do remain after people have moved on (Palmer and Smith in Barker *et al.* 2000; and see also Banning and Köhler-Rollefson 1983, 1986, 1992). Stones are used to construct various types of platforms for storing household items, such as bedding. Stone platforms are also important in milk processing. Larger installations used as beds consist of an outline of stones usually with an infill of sediment; so-called sleeping platforms. Stone kid pens outside the tent protect very young animals from cold and rain during the winter. Clusters of large rocks used to secure guy ropes are often visible, as noted above, and alignments of stones often indicate the position of tent walls or internal screens. Gullies are dug to direct winter rain water away from living areas. Hearths appear to be one of the most durable aspects of campsites, and the arrangement of stones, or their absence around these hearths, usually indicate whether these served for the reception of guests in the men's area or, rather, when found in a three-stone configuration, accommodated the griddle, *sāj*, for bread-making in the women's area. Certain tribal groups may even be identified by the arrangement of the hearth in the hospitality area of the tent; the Rashaydah build large stone-lined rectangular hearths to resemble those of the greatest *sheikh*.

During the late nineteenth and early twentieth centuries, travellers and ethnographers noted the relative paucity of bedouin material culture compared with their rich heritage of poetry and complex codes of conduct (e.g. Musil 1928). Tent furnishings and equipment are described in some detail by Dalman (1964: 44–52) and Musil (1928: 64–72). Certain items are more strongly associated with either the men's or women's sections. Many items are highly perishable. For example, there is a rich, highly decorative tradition of weaving performed by women (Weir 1990), and the beauty of the screen between the men's and women's portions of the tent contributes greatly to the status of the inhabitants of the bedouin 'house'. All the furnishing and equipment are portable. In the past, these were carried from encampment to encampment and discarded only if beyond repair, reuse, or recycling into some other object. Broken, lost, or discarded objects like these may be also expected on sites.

Survey and analysis

In 2000, we studied four abandoned campsites in great detail; an artefact distribution study was undertaken, samples were taken for environmental and geo-archaeological analysis, and the sites were mapped intensively. The sites were chosen because they had been left abandoned for variable periods of time; from as little as a few months (WF942) to three to four years (WF869), to approximately 15 years previously (WF982). In addition, one site (WF909) was occupied beyond living memory. Based on eastings and northings, each site was planned and a large grid superimposed over the area. Using a 1 m planning frame, artefacts lying on the surface, as well as major features associated with the overall site plan, were recorded on a metre-by-metre basis. Artefacts were recorded according to material (e.g. glass, metal, bone) and size classes (<2 cm, 2–5 cm, and >5 cm). The team also recorded known function or a description of less specifically identified items (e.g. a sardine can or a food can). In both 1999 and 2000, recording in the field was made on paper with the data later transferred to a computerised spreadsheet. Individual site grids and plans were linked into the overall Wadi Faynan grid using GPS readings.

In the site orientated analysis, a detailed digital model was made of each of the sites for which data were collected. This was done by digitising the paper plans in AutoCAD, which provided a base template over which the artefact distributions were displayed. As the data were collected using a system of regular 1-metre square grids, the analysis was based upon this scale, using digitised grid squares that were geo-referenced. The CAD files were then imported into Arc-Info where they were converted into polygon coverages. These were then exported as shapefiles and were imported into Arc-View. These shapefiles (based upon the 1-metre grid that was used to collect the data) served as the basis through which the artefact data were displayed visually; each grid square was given a unique ID and linked with the underlying database that contained all of the data related to the individual grid square. This enabled queries to be made of the data and displayed on the grids, which were layered over a base map of the site showing all structural remains. On the individual site scale, it is possible to show very detailed distributions of different artefact types, and relate this with patterns of human activity. Furthermore, by comparing the results of the four different camps, it is possible to show differences between material culture discard based upon seasonality, as well as how post-discard processes modify the material culture assemblages over time. Selected results are demonstrated and discussed below.

Artefacts and activities around tent sites

It is evident from the results that most of the materials discarded around tents are disposable modern consumables. This includes food wrappings and containers, detergent packets, personal hygiene and beauty products, and medicine packaging. The discarded items demonstrate that the bedouin in Wadi Faynan have access to a good range of convenience foods – from sardines to cheese triangles (foil) – to modern cleaning and beauty products, and other items such as music cassettes, moulded plastic toys for children, torches and batteries. Nails, used to pin the sides of a tent to its roof are also discarded frequently. Otherwise, useful items seem to have been removed immediately, unless they are broken, as is indeed the case with the pieces of paraffin lamp, mirror fragments, shears, and discarded spinning whorl identified. Occasionally, useful items may be stashed – even tents themselves – to be collected later, but this practice was not evident at these particular campsites. The bedouin are highly resourceful and will reuse discarded items wherever possible. Children make toys from household refuse; sardine cans are frequently adapted with a few pieces of wire, cut out pieces of plastic or paper into little vehicles.

The results of the GIS analysis, Figure 5.4a–c, show the distribution of items, including bone and plant remains (chiefly large charcoal fragments) around the sites. There is a clear decline in artefact density through time (Table 5.1) WF942 represents the most recently abandoned, just a few months before the survey, while WF869 was abandoned three years previously. WF982 was abandoned approximately 15 years ago. For all the sites,

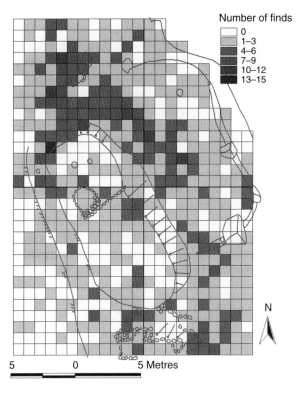

Number of finds

- 0
- 1–3
- 4–6
- 7–9
- 10–12
- 13–15

5   0   5 Metres

N

(a) WF942

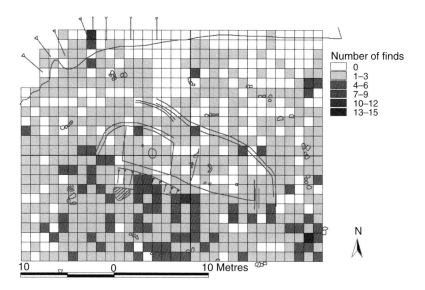

(b) WF869

(c) WF982

Figure 5.4 Distribution of all finds for sites (a) WF942, (b) WF869 and (c) WF982.

Table 5.1 Density of items recovered from the campsites

Site No.	WF942	WF869	WF982
items (excl. charcoal) per m^2	1.94	1.38	0.39
m^2 mapped	612	752	592
minimum no. items per m^2	0	0	0
maximum no. items per m^2	15	14	15
median no. items per m^2	1	1	0
standard deviation	2.18	1.62	1.12

there are low densities of material associated with the former site of the tent, or tent platform, with accumulations immediately outside. These will be discussed in turn, with results from the GIS analysis shown in turn for each site.

Site WF942

WF942 is situated on a narrow ledge in the Wadi Shayqar (Figure 5.5) and is one of a group of tent sites, WF936–944, used by the 'Azāzma. As the most recently abandoned campsite, WF942 had the densest spread of debris. Across the 612 m^2 surveyed, average artefact density is 1.94 per square metre, but it was not evenly distributed (see Table 5.1). Debris was particularly concentrated towards the north and west of the human living quarters, and the ash dump from daily cleaning of the hearth was also here. In the human living area, there were abandoned shoes, a broken handbag handle, and other items that were discarded during removal of the tent. Beyond the tent platform was refuse representing food waste and discarded parts of the tent – mostly pieces of rope and fragments of material used for repairs. This site contained the highest density of tent fabric and sacking fragments, as well as pieces of rope and twine. Figure 5.6a shows the common use of plastic items at this site. The lowest density of plastic was associated with the goat area of the tent and the densest areas were to the north and west, which mostly represented discarded food containers. The plastic debris to the south of WF942, probably dates to the time WF940, immediately to the south, was occupied. The distribution of food cans, Figure 5.6b, further suggests that most of the debris to the north and east of the site represents food consumption.

This campsite had evidence of primary butchery – principally goat lower limbs that are not meat-bearing. Figure 5.6c shows the distribution of goat bone around the site. Beyond the wall in the wadi bottom was further evidence of primary butchery, including lower goat limbs and skins (Figure 5.7). There was also a decaying donkey carcass, left there after the site was abandoned. One member of the family who had lived there had said they had camped here for a relatively short period of approximately one month.

Figure 5.5 View of WF942 looking south-east. The dark dung-covered area, representing the goat section of the tent, is to the right and the family living
area to the left, with a recently used hearth and rough stone sleeping
platform. To its left is WF941 and a rubble wall marking the edge of the
wadi (photograph C. Palmer).

Site 869

WF869 was occupied by Jouma, our principle informant, and his family
who are from the 'Azāzma. There is a lower density of artefacts at this site
than at WF942, the more recently abandoned campsite, with 1.38 artefacts
per m² over the 752 m² surveyed (see Table 5.2). Most of the finds were
glass, plastic and cans associated with food packaging. These were mostly
concentrated to the rear of the tent, immediately down slope from the tent
platform. The ash dump was also located here, towards the end where the
family lived. Figure 5.8a shows how food cans were concentrated to the
back of the site. Plastic items, Figure 5.8b, were also more common here,
although also relatively widely distributed across the whole site. Again,
there were relatively low concentrations of bone. Figure 5.8c shows the
distribution of goat bone including horn fragments. Almost all bone fragments were relatively large lower limb bones, indicating primary butchery.
Jouma said that he had held a relatively large *mansaf*, the traditional
celebratory meal, here when his brother, an Imam, visited. A large hearth in
the goat section of the tent had been used to cook the meat.

111

(a) WF942 – all plastic finds

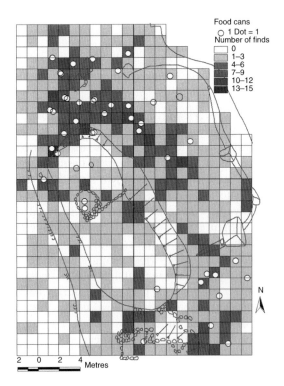

(b) WF942 – all food cans

(c) WF942 – bone

Figure 5.6 Distribution of all finds at WF942, with overlay of find spots of (a) all plastic, (b) all food cans and (c) bone.

Figure 5.7 Discarded articulated left hind limb from primary butchery at WF942 (photograph: C. Palmer).

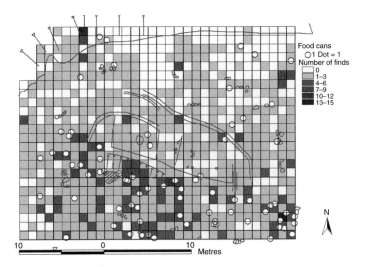

(a) WF869 – all food cans

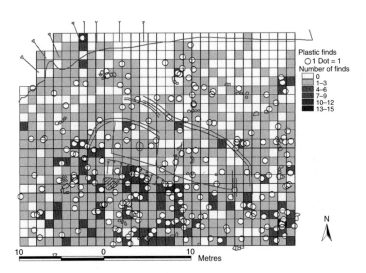

(b) WF869 –all plastic finds

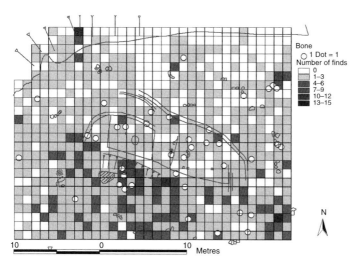

(c) WF869 – bone

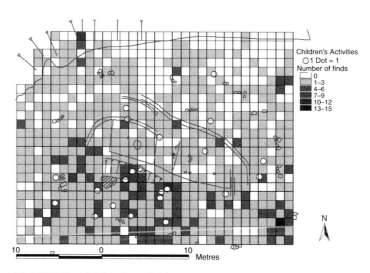

(d) WF869 – children's activities

Figure 5.8 Distribution of all finds at WF869, with overlay of find spots of (a) food cans, (b) all plastic, (c) bone and (d) children's activities.

There were some conspicuous examples of children's play activities at WF869 (Figure 5.8d). Sardine cans had been modified to make small vehicles (Figure 5.9a) and a shepherd's flute made from plastic piping (Figure 5.9b). Abundant sweet wrappers also attested to their presence. Jouma had seven young children at the time it was occupied, and they have a clear presence in the discarded material culture. Although children's activities were also represented at WF942, Jouma's site contained the most elaborate, albeit broken, home-made toys. It is not clear whether children played among the refuse or whether the concentration of toys here reflects their eventual discard once broken.

Jouma said that this area represents an excellent campsite and had been used by other people before his family came to live there. Even the tent platform they had used was an older one he had enhanced. Jouma added that the presence of an old campsite indicates a good place to camp and so makes a location more attractive. In the material culture, there was evidence of older occupation; a fragment from a rotary quern and old metal amulet (which once contained a piece of paper bearing a quotation from the Koran that conferred good fortune on the wearer). Jouma used this campsite for at least two winters, for approximately six weeks each time, but they will no longer camp here in future due to its inaccessibility by vehicle.

WF982

WF982 was said to have been occupied last approximately 15 years ago by a member of the Sa'idiyin and is located very close to the RSCN camp. Artefact density was much lower at this site: 0.39 artefacts per m^2 for the 588 m^2 surveyed (see Table 5.1). WF 982 had a goat track running through it, and some of the debris, especially to the south of the tent platform, appeared to be more recent, such as the glass (Figure 5.10a). Plastic items had a similar distribution following the track (Figure 5.10b). Degraded debris was present, particularly rusted sardine cans, immediately towards the back of the tent platform (Figure 5.10c). A few bone fragments were also present (Figure 5.10d).

WF909

WF909 had not been occupied within living memory. It was virtually free from artefactual remains and the data were not transferred into Arc-View, but drawn as a conventional plan (Figure 5.11). The site contained a number of clear architectural features: platforms, hearths and rope stones. Sleeping platforms were indicated by larger outlines of stones (with no stone infilling) and platforms used to store household goods or in processing milk products. Although the site was examined intensively, only two copper fragments, probably from cooking pots, were found. The use of copper

(a)

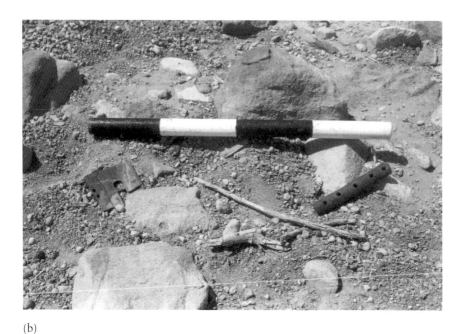

(b)

Figure 5.9 (a) A sardine can modified into a toy and (b) a plastic piping shepherd's flute and broken music cassette (photographs C. Palmer).

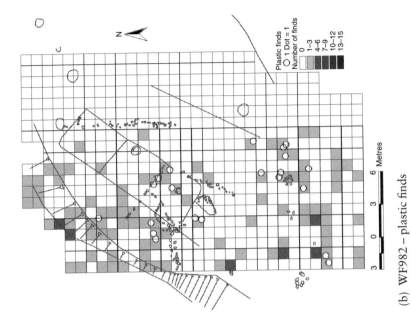

(b) WF982 – plastic finds

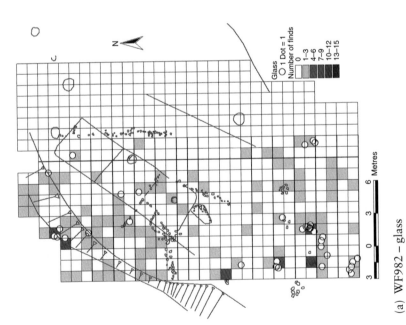

(a) WF982 – glass

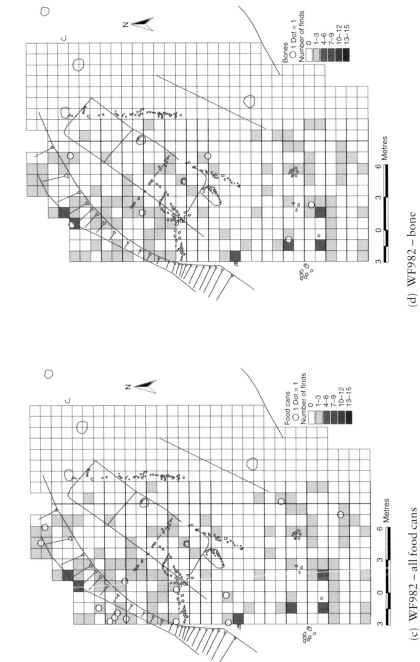

(d) WF982 – bone

(c) WF982 – all food cans

Figure 5.10 Distribution of all finds at WF982, with overlay of find spots of (a) glass, (b) all plastic, (c) all food cans and (d) bone.

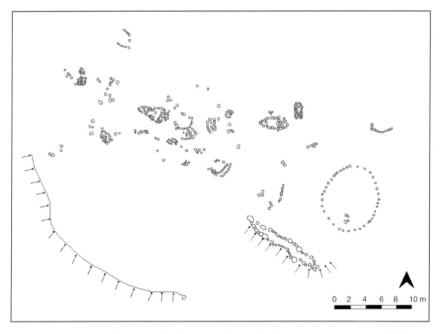

Figure 5.11 WF909 showing platforms and hearths from an encampment. Only two
fragments of copper were found.

utensils suggests that the site dates, at the latest, to the mid-twentieth century. Because it is possible that fine sediment from water or wind activity
may be obscuring artefacts, areas immediately around the hearths were
cleared, revealing hardened surfaces (Figure 5.12). These areas were cleaned
carefully and there were no finds recovered (although no sieving took
place). This lack of finds is perhaps not surprising given that these areas
would have been in the main body of the tent. Excavation across a wider
area may have revealed more. Jouma commented, however, that it was good
that we had cleared the site so neatly because it now made it a much more
attractive place for a camp.

Discussion

The results of the survey demonstrate, above all, changes in the pastoral
way of life in the Wadi Faynan. The area has been affected by political
changes associated with the formation of the State of Israel, the birth and
development of the Hashemite Kingdom of Jordan and influences extending
from widening markets. Bedouin are becoming more sedentary and villagers
more urbanised. Population levels have risen considerably, even in the
relatively sparsely occupied south of Jordan.

Figure 5.12 WF909 after clearing loose soil. There is a hardened surface around the hearth.

Our research shows that current patterns of camp location not only reflect access to water but also to increasing availability of work opportunities and the presence of a primary school. For some families, notably those with the longest tradition of residence in the area, the importance of livestock is diminishing as they take up paid employment. The 'Azāzma are, however, still largely dependent on livestock and their camp location decisions reflect this (Chatty 2002; Rowe 1997): the largest group in the area, they were displaced from the Negev in 1948. The 'Azāzma inhabit some of the most marginal areas of southern Jordan and are, unfortunately, generally disadvantaged. Their ability to graze their animals in better areas is limited by their dispossessed status. Villagers who used to camp in the Wadi Faynan no longer do so due to the availability of better economic options and the areas they formerly camped in have been taken up by the 'Azāzma. The 'Azāzma's relative vulnerability means they practise what might be considered a more 'traditional' bedouin life-way; for example, the women still weave *shigga*, the strips of goat hair cloth that sewn together make the roof of a tent, and they are less likely to use modern appliances.

Aspects of modern life, such as vehicle accessibility, affect specific campsite locations, though the dominant practice of siting winter campsites on protected wadi terraces in the winter and on breezy ridge tops during

summer persists. Wadi terraces are vulnerable to flash-floods that periodic-
ally affect the area and which are likely to remove evidence of occupation.
As in the past, people camping together usually belong to the same tribal
group and are often very closely related.

Modern consumer goods, especially from packaged foods, increase the
visibility of recently abandoned campsites. However, there is a remarkable
fall-off of visibility of these items within a relatively short time, even
though they are more durable. Certainly organic components, goat bone,
fabrics and worked wood, disappear quickly. Surprisingly, though, a site
occupied by Jouma's family some years ago, WF869, has higher quantities
of glass, plastics, food cans and metal. This could be because the site was
occupied by more people, a family of nine compared with a family of five,
or because it was occupied for a longer period (either through single or
multiple episodes). The lower frequency of artefacts recovered from
WF982, occupied some 15 years ago, suggests that the survival of even the
more durable items become much less frequent through time. It should also
be noted, however, that it is possible that fewer disposable consumer goods
were used then. The apparent rapid dispersal of garbage is probably linked
with the flash-flooding and aeolian deposition of sediment during wind
storms (see also Simms and Russell 1996), which can both disperse items or
cover them over.

Artefact distributions are the result of daily routines and practices that
derive from the care and maintenance of animals, family life, such as the
preparation and sharing of food, and economic and social engagement
within and beyond the immediate locality. Although the spatial organisation at recently abandoned tent sites is clear, and readily identified through
the use of contemporary disposable material culture, evidence of activity
quickly disperses over time. The traditional material culture of the region
leaves even fewer traces. Few surface finds may be recovered from open air
pastoral campsites despite the significant increase in the use of more durable
elements of material culture. Campsite architecture features provide the
clearest evidence of recent pastoral activity and artefacts found in association with these features provide good evidence of activity. However, campsites usually represent palimpsests so artefacts may represent several
occupations over the course of many years.

The distribution of artefacts recorded at a Bedūl encampment (*bayt
Qublān*) in the Petra area by Simms (1988) exhibits similar patterns to
those observed here. Living areas have low levels of remains, and refuse is
concentrated to the rear of the tent and particularly around refuse dumps
(also see Cribb 1991b). Refuse location is therefore not an indicator of
activity location (Simms 1988: 207). At the winter sites surveyed at Wadi
Faynan, refuse is discarded closer to the rear of the tent. This patterning
relates to differences in season and length of occupation: Simms' study was
of a summer camp, which was inhabited for a long period, *c.* six months,

whereas the tents studied here were occupied for shorter periods during the winter. In summer inhabitants use a wider area for activities, which are also regularly swept clear of refuse. The degree of sorting due to sweeping activities was also not as clear at the Wadi Faynan sites, a factor which probably relates to length and season of occupation. Where goats are housed within a tent, refuse may be expected within the tent platform too. The concentration of refuse around rope stones, where it is not so easy to sweep, was noted by Simms and occurs at Wadi Faynan, and especially at WF869. Therefore, it is more likely to find materials trapped around durable features of campsite architecture.

Conclusions

For all groups, the growth of state infrastructure, including roads, schools and medical facilities, as well as the opportunity to work for money and buy products – from canned sardines to gas canisters for lighting and cooking – has fundamentally changed local lives. In addition, the impact of modern material culture has had a profound effect on the visibility of recently abandoned bedouin camps, which are today not only distinguished by spreads of animal dung, but also by modern refuse. However, this material is seemingly almost as prone to dispersal over time as more traditional forms of material culture.

Our work has been successful in both documenting and analysing the changing nature of bedouin land use in the Wadi Faynan. We have shown how more recent considerations, such as access for vehicles, work opportunities and infrastructure has impacted upon the location of campsites. However, at the same time, it is noted that a number of more traditional norms have been at least loosely maintained, such as the exploitation of specific environmental niches, and clustering based upon tribal affiliation. Furthermore, we have demonstrated that both material culture use and discard have been influenced by the infusion of various forms of consumer and industrial products that consist of, or produce, more durable material culture, resulting in different site formation dynamics. However, despite this, the standard forms of campsite architecture have been largely maintained and remain the most reliable evidence for identifying abandoned bedouin campsites.

Finally, this work has demonstrated how GIS can be used when dealing with 'living archaeology', in this case the study of still extant but evolving communities of pastoralists who have contributed to the accumulation and alteration of a rich archaeological landscape. This point is particularly important as different interest groups in the Wadi Faynan struggle to find a sustainable balance between preservation of both the natural and cultural heritage of the region, the increasing push for 'development' of the bedouin, and the changes made to the landscape and all in it as a result.

Our results have allowed us to explore the dynamic nature of bedouin ways of life in modern times, as well as to identify signatures that can be used to recognise earlier pastoral campsites and to distinguish them from the much earlier prehistoric features that share the same space. The pastoralists in Wadi Faynan interact with the landscape at a number of different spatial scales, and the presence of their 'archaeological' residue exists on a number of temporal scales. The use of digital techniques was instrumental in allowing us to access and begin to study this in a way that incorporates all of these scales within the same methodological framework. The work presented in this chapter is only an abbreviated example of our research but illustrates the potential of such survey and analysis techniques in the study of pastoral societies that are contending with a full range of non-traditional influences.

Acknowledgements

We are grateful to Professor Graeme Barker for inviting us to join the Wadi Faynan Landscape Survey team and supporting our fieldwork expenses and encouraging this research. The project would not have been possible without the essential support of the staff at the Council for British Research in the Levant in Amman, the Department of Antiquities of Jordan, and the Royal Society for the Conservation of Nature, especially the staff of the Dana Nature Reserve.

The WFLS is supported by the Arts and Humanities Research Board, the Council for British Research in the Levant, the Natural Environment Research Council, the Society of Antiquaries of London and the Universities of Leicester, Bournemouth, Huddersfield and Aberystwyth. Carol Palmer's research was supported by a CBRL Postdoctoral Research Fellowship funded jointly by the CBRL and the University of Leicester.

Without the people of Wadi Faynan and especially Jouma 'Aly Zanoon, this research would not have been possible. Helen Smith's contribution in the field as a co-worker on the Bedouin Camp Survey is gratefully acknowledged. We would also like to thank other members of the WFLS team who assisted in documenting the artefact distributions, and especially Lucy Farr for her drawing skills. Mark Gillings gave invaluable advice on the field method used for recording artefact distributions. Bryan Palmer and Christopher Knüsel patiently helped CP input the artefactual data in the UK. We are grateful to Graeme Barker, Christopher Knüsel and Tom Evans for comments on earlier versions of this paper.

Note

1 This agricultural activity took place within an area of dense historic and prehistoric field systems (mainly late Roman in date) with coherent and well-built

field walls and water management features. In many cases, the structure of the ancient fields were re-used or modified, which dramatically altered their form and that of other evidence of archaeological activity in the area, such as scatters of ancient ceramic material. This is an excellent example of the need to be able to identify the impact of modern land-use on a rich archaeological landscape.

References

Avni, G. (1992) 'Survey of deserted bedouin campsites in the Negev Highlands and its implications for archaeological research', in O. Bar-Yosef and A. Khazanov (eds) *Pastoralism in the Levant: Archaeological Materials in Anthropological Perspectives*, pp. 241–54. Madison: Prehistory Press, Monographs in World Archaeology 10.

Bailey, C. (1991) *Bedouin Poetry from Sinai and the Negev*. Oxford: Clarendon Press.

Banning, E. B. and Köhler-Rollefson, I. (1983) 'Ethnoarchaeological survey in the Beidha area, southern Jordan'. *Annual of the Department of Antiquities of Jordan* 27: 375–83.

Banning, E. B. and Köhler-Rollefson, I. (1986) 'Ethnoarchaeological research in Beidha'. *Zeitschrift des Deutschen Palästina-Vereins* 102: 152–70.

Banning, E. B. and Köhler-Rollefson, I. (1992) 'Ethnographic lessons for the pastoral past: camp locations and material remains near Beidha, southern Jordan', in O. Bar-Yosef and A. Khazanov (eds) *Pastoralism in the Levant: Archaeological Materials in Anthropological Perspectives*, pp. 181–204. Madison: Prehistory Press, Monographs in World Archaeology 10.

Barker, G. (2000) 'Farmers, herders and miners in the Wadi Faynan, southern Jordan: a 10,000-year landscape archaeology', in G. Barker and D. Gilbertson (eds) *The Archaeology of Drylands: Living at the Margin*, pp. 63–85. London: Routledge.

Barker, G., Creighton, O. H., Gilbertson, D. D., Hunt, C. O., Mattingly, D. J., McLaren, S. J. and Thomas, D. C. (1997) 'The Wadi Faynan Project, southern Jordan: a preliminary report on geomorphology and landscape archaeology'. *Levant* 29: 19–40.

Barker, G., Adams, R., Creighton, O. H., Gilbertson, D. D., Grattan, J. P., Hunt, C. O., Mattingly, D. J., McClaren, S. J., Mohammed, H. A., Newson, P., Reynolds, T. E. G. and Thomas, D. C. (1998) 'Environment and land use in the Wadi Faynan, southern Jordan: the second season of geoarchaeology and landscape archaeology (1997)'. *Levant* 30: 5–25.

Barker, G., Adams, R., Creighton, O. H., Crook, D., Gilbertson, D. D., Grattan, J. P., Hunt, C., Mattingly, D. J., McLaren, S. J., Mohammed, H. A., Newson, P., Palmer, C., Pyatt, F. B., Reynolds T. E. G. and Tomber, R. (1999) 'Environment and land use in the Wadi Faynan, southern Jordan: the third season of geoarchaeology and landscape archaeology (1998)'. *Levant* 31: 255–92.

Barker, G., Adams, R., Creighton, O. H., Crook, D., Daly, P., Gilbertson, D. D., Grattan, J. P., Hunt, C. O., Mattingly, D. J., McLaren, S. J., Newson, P., Palmer, C., Pyatt, F. B., Reynolds, T. E. G., Smith, H., Tomber, R. and Truscott, A. J. (2000) 'Environment and land use in the Wadi Faynan, southern Jordan: the fourth season of geoarchaeology and landscape archaeology (1999)'. *Levant* 32: 27–52.

Chatty, D. (1986) *From Camel to Truck: the Bedouin in the Modern World*. New York: Vantage Press.

Chatty, D. (2002) 'Animal reintroduction projects in the Middle East: conservation without a human face', in D. Chatty and M. Colchester (eds) *Conservation and Mobile Indigenous Peoples: Displacement, Forced Settlement, and Sustainable Development*. Studies in Forced Migration, Volume 10. New York: Berghahn Books.

Childe, V. G. (1951[1936]) *Man Makes Himself*. New York: Mentor.

Cribb, R. (1991a) *Nomads in Archaeology*. Cambridge: Cambridge University Press.

Cribb, R. (1991b) 'Mobile villagers: the structure and organisation of nomadic pastoral campsites in the Near East', in G. S. Gamble and W. A. Boismer (eds) *Ethnoarchaeological Approaches to Mobile Campsites. Hunter-gatherer and Pastoralist Case Studies*, pp. 371–93. Ann Arbor: International Monographs in Prehistory.

Dalman, G. (1964[1939]) *Arbeit und Sitte in Palästina*. Band VI: *Zeltleben, Vieh- und Milchwirtschaft, Jagd, Fisfang*. Hildesheim: Georg Olms Verlagsbuchhandlung.

Dickson, H. R. P. (1959 [1949]) *The Arab of the Desert: A Glimpse into Bedawin Life in Kuwait and Sau'di Arabia*. Third Impression. London: George Allen & Unwin.

Finkelstein, I. (1992) 'Invisible nomads: a rejoinder'. *Bulletin of the American Schools of Oriental Research* 287: 87–8.

Finkelstein, I. (1995) *Living on the Fringe: The Archaeology and History of the Negev, Sinai and Neighbouring Regions in the Bronze and Iron Ages*. Sheffield: Sheffield University, Monographs in Mediterranean Archaeology 6.

Finlayson, B., Mithen, S., Carruthers, D., Kennedy, A., Pirie, A. and Tipping, R. (2000) 'The Dana-Faynan-Ghuwayr early prehistory project'. *Levant* 32: 1–26.

Grattan, J., Huxley, S. and Pyatt, F. B. (2003) 'Modern bedouin exposures to copper contamination: an imperial legacy?' *Ecotoxicology and Environmental Safety* 55: 108–15.

Hole, F. (1979) 'Rediscovering the past in the present: ethnoarchaeology in Luristan, Iran', in C. Kramer (eds) *Ethnoarchaeology: Implications of Ethnography for Archaeology*, pp. 192–218. New York: Columbia University Press.

Jabbur, J. S. (1995) *The Bedouins and the Desert: Aspects of Nomadic Life in the Arab East*. New York: State University of New York Press.

LaBianca, Ø. S. (1990) *Sedentarization and Nomadization: Food System Cycles at Hesban and Vicinity in Transjordan*. Berrien Springs, MI: Andrews University Press.

Lancaster, W. and Lancaster, F. (1999) *People, Land and Water in the Arab Middle East: Environments and Landscapes in the Bilād ash-Shām*. Amsterdam: Harwood Academic Publishers.

Levy, T., Adams, R., Hauptmann, A., Prange, M., Schmitt-Strecker, S. and Najjar, M. (2002) 'Early Bronze Age metallurgy: a newly discovered copper manufactory in southern Jordan'. *Antiquity* 76: 425–37.

Musil, A. (1928) *The Manners and Customs of the Rwala Bedouins*. New York: American Geographical Society.

Najjar, M., Abu Dayya, A., Suleiman, E., Weisgerber, G. and Bachmann, H. (1990) 'Tell Wadi Feinan: the first pottery Neolithic Tell in southern Jordan'. *Annual of the Department of Antiquities of Jordan* 34: 27–56.

Pyatt, F. B., Grattan J. P., Hunt, C. O. and McLaren, S. (2000) 'An imperial legacy?

An exploration of the environmental impact of ancient metal mining and smelting in southern Jordan'. *Journal of Archaeological Science* 27: 771–8.

Rosen, S. (1992) Nomads in archaeology: a response to Finkelstein and Perevolotsky. *Bulletin of the American Schools of Oriental Research* 287: 75–85.

Rowe, A. G. (1997) *Pastoralists of the Lower Dana Reserve Area: Attitudes to and Prospects for Integration into the Reserve Management Strategy*. RSCN Report: Amman.

Simmons, A. and Najjar, M. (1996) Test excavations at Ghwair I, a Neolithic settlement in the Wadi Feinan. *ACOR Newsletter* 8(2): 7–8.

Simms, S. R. (1988) 'The archaeological structure of a Bedouin camp'. *Journal of Archaeological Science* 15: 197–211.

Simms, S. R. and Russell, K. W. (1996) 'Ethnoarchaeology of the Bedul Bedouin of Petra, Jordan'. Utah: University of Utah.

Swenne, A. (1995) *Dana Nature Reserve: Rangeland and Livestock Management*. RSCN Report: Amman.

Weir, S. (1990[1976]) *The Bedouin*. London: The British Museum Press.

Wright, K., Najjar, M., Last, J., Moloney, N., Flender, M., Gower, J., Jackson, N., Kennedy, A. and Shafiq, R. (1998) 'The Wadi Faynan Fourth and Third Millennia Project, 1997: report on the first season of test excavations at Wadi Faynan 100'. *Levant* 30: 33–60.

6

DIGITAL ARCHAEOLOGY AND THE SCALAR STRUCTURE OF PASTORAL LANDSCAPES

Modeling mobile societies of prehistoric Central Asia

Michael Frachetti

Digital archaeology and analytical scale

For today's archaeologist, digital tools, such as Geographic Information Systems (GIS), remote sensing, and computer-assisted simulation, can play an equally fundamental role in formulating explanations of the past, as do more traditional archaeological techniques (e.g. excavation or material studies). Digital applications perhaps have made the greatest impact on archaeology by facilitating the analysis of complex matrices of data distributed at various scales. For example, GIS is commonly used to study the spatial relationships of various archaeological elements ranging in scale from ceramic distributions at the site level, to archaeological feature distributions across large regions. In addition, digital technology is frequently used to model social and environmental landscapes, which has enabled archaeologists to better contextualize the places that humans have occupied in the past. This chapter explores how digital techniques can be used to model the social and economic landscapes of mobile pastoralists, and more specifically, addresses how archaeological and ecological data of various conceptual and analytical scales can be correlated in a digital environment to provide a more refined picture of the spatial and temporal patterns of movement for pastoral societies during prehistory. The approach presented in this chapter will help archaeologists to reconcile the inherent gap between the location of archaeological remains within various landscapes and the scales of spatial and temporal variability that brought these landscapes to life in the past.

Since computer aided analysis depends in part upon the quality of input data, the digitally inclined archaeologist must determine the relevant scale of analysis that suits his or her questions; a decision that can make all the

128

difference in producing meaningful analytical output. Accurately selecting the appropriate scale of 'basic analysis units' plays an especially important role in the discovery, collection, documentation, analysis, and interpretation of data retrieved by archaeological survey and excavation. Determining the ideal scale of analysis, of course, depends on one's questions, and as importantly, the extent of the region to be considered in the study. This extent is frequently based on either naturally occurring physical boundaries – such as the geography of a particular valley, drainage system, or island – or by anthropogenic boundaries – like contemporary national boundaries, or expected 'peripheral zones' of major archaeological 'centers.'

Most archaeologists are interested in the locations of human activity – which generally translates into a focus on mark-able places. Survey distribution maps of archaeological features across a territory are now the common first product of contemporary archaeological method. These surveys are often based in a now established trend in 'landscape archaeology,' by which archaeological places are conceptualized in terms of their spatial organization, or in relation to a select set of social, environmental or ecological conditions. Contextualizing archaeological places within a more general sense of spatiality can provide the archaeologist with a clearer picture of settlement patterns over long periods of time – yet short-term dynamic processes remain elusive at this wider scale of analysis. In fact, archaeological survey maps often present the land-use and settlement pattern across a region as a synchronic, generalized slice of time – which itself may represent many centuries or generations of occupation dynamics.

The notion that societies may interact with and construct their landscape at different scales and extents (both in a temporal and spatial sense) can be difficult to conceptualize in graphic or database formats. Even more problematic is producing convincing reconstructions of the choices and variable strategies that individuals (or groups of them) employ within shorter-term periods of time. These issues have a greater impact for archaeologists interested in the construction and use of territory by mobile societies, since their land-use patterns are often more dynamic and variable than those of sedentary populations – given the relative impermanence of nomadic settlements even within short periods of time. In addition to changes in settlement locations, some of the most important activities of mobile societies take place across wide territorial expanses, and are initiated at specific, yet potentially variable times. Therefore, the concept of 'landscape' for mobile societies reflects a wide employment of territory when viewed in terms of 'time-geography' (Ingold 1993; Giddens 1984) or 'human eco-dynamics' (McGlade 1995). Many ethnographic studies have illustrated that nomadic societies use their landscape in largely patterned ways in reaction to a combination of socio-political and ecological conditions, and these patterns are imprinted across their social landscape at a variety of scales (Barth 1964; Barfield 1989; Salzman 1972). For archaeologists, understanding the potential patterns of prehistoric mobile societies presents a challenge, as well as an opportunity to use digital modeling and simulation to recreate prehistoric social and natural landscapes that are not simply defined by archaeological 'places.'

When working in landscapes constructed and occupied by mobile pastoralists, information concerning economic strategies and dynamics of social interaction is more often encoded in the comprehensive layout of the landscape, rather than at particular archaeological 'sites' – making it difficult to decide on the appropriate extent of data collection and analysis. From ethnographic studies of mobile societies, we understand that the primary factors in their use of the landscape are produced through an interplay between spatial and temporal variables – as their investment in particular spaces is often gauged according to seasonal conditions and variable strategies of social interaction (Spooner 1973). In fact, when attempting to document the expanse of a mobile society across a given landscape, one must consider various factors that may have played a role in human experiences at different times and locales. These factors range from ecological dynamics such as seasonality, climate, and terrain, to social and political aspects of specific archaeological feature types. The spatial and temporal extents of ecological and social contexts themselves contribute to the pattern of land-use and landscape production generated by mobile life-ways. This scalar variability makes the selection of a standardized 'basic' unit of analysis (such as the 'site,' or 'feature') problematic.

Underpinning the work presented here is the goal of developing an approach to modeling prehistoric landscapes that accounts for the variability and co-dependence of difference data sources with which we interpret the strategies of mobile societies. Specifically, this means arriving at a better understanding of the specific spatial and temporal constraints to mobile ways of life – including economic activities as well as social and ritual practices. Digital tools are incredibly powerful for simulating past conditions, and enable the exploration and testing of various strategies that would have been employed in the past. The specific aim of this chapter is to illustrate a number of digital approaches and analyses designed to model the economic and cultural landscapes of mobile pastoral societies of the Eastern Eurasian Steppes (Figure 6.1 – inset) during the second millennium BC. First, the scalar qualities of the social contexts of mobile pastoralists are theoretically outlined. Although the environment admittedly plays a major role in the patterned migrations of pastoral societies, for brevity the various scales at which it impacts pastoral strategies will not be theoretically discussed here. A brief overview of the regional ecology and Bronze Age archaeology of eastern Eurasia is provided. Next, a detailed case study using digital modeling of prehistoric pastoralism in the Koksu River Valley is presented and discussed.

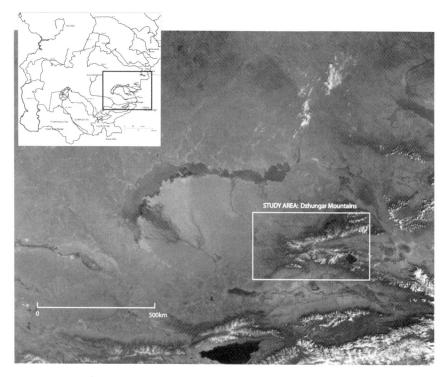

Figure 6.1 Study zone and surrounding region context.

Contextualizing mobile pastoralism

Current archaeological studies of the Eurasian steppes suggest that Bronze Age societies were engaged in a mobile pastoral lifestyle of some form; however, the degree of potential mobility, settlement trends, and regional interaction in both economic and social terms have not been reliably modeled for the region's prehistory. This is partly due to an inherent misalignment in scale that exists between the various forms of archaeological and other data. For example, data recovered from burial locations or settlement features have been used to explain how domestic and ritual spaces were used – yet less frequently does this data provide a view into the wider scale temporal and spatial employment of the landscape, within which domestic and ritual life plays a part. Archaeology and ecology have certainly been discussed in relation to one another, but since burials and settlements reflect a localized scale of landscape use while the ecology acts at a larger scale (discussed in detail below), potential relationships between the two conditions are often overly generalized and reconstructions of mobile pastoral life-ways in prehistory are monolithic, and unconvincing.

Yet using digital technology, it is possible to analyze multiple scales of data and allow them to reflect changes across each other's spatial and temporal boundaries. Using computer simulations, trends in mobility patterns need not simply be linked to seasonal ecology, for example, but can also reflect localized activities that are recovered from settlements, burials, ritual contexts, as well as the changes in the natural environment over the *longue durée*. Each of these contexts impacts the formation of a nomadic population's landscape at a different scale – a topic that I will now explore in detail.

Scale and landscape of mobile pastoralists

In archaeology, the term 'landscape' has come to conceptually describe the contexts created through human interaction with their surroundings, and gives special attention to the correlation between various human experiences and strategies, and the spatial and temporal conditions of both natural and constructed environments (cf. Anshuetz *et al.* 2001). In real life, these spatial and temporal phenomena fall along a scalar continuum, so that human experiences in the 'here and now,' both create and react to conditions that operate at wider scales.

The issue of scale is paramount for archaeologists, because we generally retrieve data on either end of its continuum – be they deposits that reflect momentary events of discard, or long-term accumulations of material that represent activity over centuries or even millennia. Thus for heuristic reasons, archaeologists have divided this continuous scale into levels, which reflect processes that occur on roughly similar spatial and temporal magnitudes. These scalar degrees are simply coined short, middle, and long (or small/medium/large, local/regional/macro-regional, etc.). In order to construct an analytical approach to mobile pastoral societies that accounts for these interwoven scales, archaeological and other data sources must be situated along a continuum of spatial and temporal scale according to how they can be conceptualized as relevant data. The main emphasis in this chapter is upon social factors.

Scales and the social landscape

The social landscape, by definition, refers to the contexts in which societies construct, employ, and experience their natural and social environment. In Landscape Archaeology, 'landscape' conceptually incorporates the constraints and opportunities of the natural setting with socially constructed contexts, and foci of social activity, as they are distributed across space and time. For archaeologists concerned with mobile pastoralism, traces of human activity are distributed across the landscape at large, medium and small-scales. These include herding pathways, pastures, settlements, burials, and institutional locations such as playing fields or ritual sites. These contexts facilitate both the construction and exploitation of the ecology, and condition the manner of interaction between groups and individuals over time. From this perspective the activities of pastoral nomads are conceptualized as different aspects of one social landscape, each pertaining to a different scale of geography and time investment. This framework is specifically useful when applied to mobile societies, in that it contextualizes an array of dynamically changing locales that are activated and deactivated in time, rather than interpolating the activities of mobile groups from discrete archaeological locations.

Large-scale

Mobile pastoralists do not wander aimlessly. For many nomadic societies, the concept of 'territory' takes on a unique definition, in that their movements are almost always confined to an 'orbit' that is regular and repetitive from year to year. This orbit exists as a conceptual space, which may define a large-scale territory, but is experienced incrementally over time as groups pass over it. Therefore, I propose that herding pathways represent a data source at the largest spatial and temporal scale in terms of socially and economically constructed landscapes.

Herding orbits and pathways represent a large-scale data source in that they provide a general spatial extent, over which activities (e.g. migration, camping, rituals) occur on a long-term schedule. An ethnographic example is the Kazakh horse game called *kôkpar*, which entails racing and wrestling for a beheaded goat carcass. This game may take place at any time of the year, but tends to be played during the summer when a number of pastoral groups converge on upland summer pastures. Although the game itself is spatially localized (i.e. a medium-scale event), over the long term, the location and timing of the festival are conditioned by the construction of and adherence to overlapping herding pathways of numerous mobile groups. The repetition of their migration pattern to specific upland pastures annually brings groups together, and over time this pattern creates the institutionalized activity of the game. Therefore, from a temporal perspective, the repetitive use of a particular herding pattern contributes to social interaction on a long-term temporal scale.

At their widest extent, these pathways serve as the arteries through which a network of ecological and social places are connected. The spatial extent, or territory encompassed by pastoral orbits at their widest scale, reflects the boundaries of a broad anthropogenic landscape that serves as the backdrop for the creation of social locations of smaller scales.

Medium-scale

Medium-scale aspects of pastoral social landscapes include settlements, cemeteries, and other group contexts (e.g. playing fields, etc.). These contexts bring together groups of individuals, and demarcate a definable space or territory. For example, Bronze Age burials across Eurasia are often marked with standing stele, or with stone fences that provide a separation between the burials and outside space. In this case, the space of the cemetery rarely extends beyond a radius of 500 meters. For settlements, the activity space around the actual structure is slightly wider, perhaps 1.5 to 2 kilometers (discussed below). In this medium-scale space, social and economic activities that are related to the settlement itself frequently occur. Especially in the case of mobile societies, settlement contexts do not reflect long-term occupation, but rather tend to be occupied seasonally. Although these places may be returned to year after year, the success of a settlement space depends on the availability of localized ecological resources (e.g. water sources) that change from year to year, so that the experience of these places is temporally discrete. Ultimately, medium-scale contexts are created by, and condition social activities. As data sources, they are useful as focal points of constructed space and practices within the wider landscape.

Small-scale

Spatially and temporally small-scale components of the landscape are difficult to recover and model archaeologically. These factors are represented by the kinds of events that archaeologists wish they could demonstrate with material, but more often tend to propose as assumed behavior. However, with the landscapes of Eurasian pastoralists, there is physical archaeological evidence that reflects small-scale events, and that illustrates a social focus on discrete locations, disarticulated from group activity. An example of this type of data is rock-art.

Rock-art is a major element in the assemblage of data available to archaeologists of Eurasia (Mar'yashev 1994). Rock-art is categorized as a small-scale phenomenon *not* because it is rare or disassociated with other contexts, but because it reflects a personal knowledge and attention to the natural and social landscape. Individuals create drawings, and the places they select to carve are at once extremely specific and also set within a broader concept of the landscape (Frachetti and Chippindale 2002). Rock-art reflects the personal investment in the historicity of the landscape, through a reflection of an instantaneous and unrecoverable action. Therefore, the spatial and temporal context of rock-art production reflects an aspect of agentive behavior, where individuals can make their irrevocable mark on their landscape.

Scalar continuity

These scalar phenomena are not separated, but like gears of a clock turn one another over geography and time (Giddens 1984). In real life the experience of large-scale and small-scale phenomena is simultaneous, yet the effects of discrete events may have long-lasting impacts. If we are to understand this complex process in prehistory, our tools for analyzing archaeological data of multiple scales should account for the correlation between these various ecological and social factors.

The remainder of this chapter is devoted to illustrating a digital approach to modeling Bronze Age pastoralism of Eurasia that contextualizes a variety of archaeological data in light of its scalar qualities and role in the creation of pastoral landscapes.

Case study: Bronze Age pastoral patterns in the Dzhungar Mountains

Ecology and prehistory of the Eastern Eurasian Steppe region

The Eastern Eurasian Steppe region is generally located in the modern territories of south/central Russia and eastern Kazakhstan, as well as parts of western Mongolia and northwestern China. The area considered here is bordered by the forest-steppes of southwest Siberia to the north, by the Ishim River to the west, by the Yenisei River and Altai Mountains to the east, and by the Tian Shan Range in the south (Figure 6.1 inset). The specific study region is located within the Koksu River valley, one of the primary conduits of the ancient silk route through the Dzhungar Mountains of eastern Kazakhstan, also known as the 'Dzhungarian Gate.' On the western side of the Dzhungar Mountains, the territory is known in Kazakh as 'Zhetisu,'[1] referring to the seven rivers that flow from the glacial peaks of these mountains to Lake Balkhash (Figure 6.1). Throughout history, these river valley 'gates' connected China and the Far East, through the mountains, with western Central Asia.

The environment of the Eastern Steppe Zone varies between sandy deserts, semi-arid grasslands, open steppe grasslands, and mountainous regions. The ecological variation between these grass zones is associated with extreme differences in precipitation, annual temperature change, soil quality, and elevation, all which affect the potential strategies for human occupation in each zone. In the Dzhungar region, for example, the annual cycle of the continental climate traditionally played a considerable role in the patterns of movement of both animals and nomadic populations, especially in the mountain and desert regions where the difference between summer and winter pasture resources is pronounced.

In fact, it is the generally consistent (over the long term) seasonal variation in pasture-resources in the Zhetisu region that enables us to model some of the environmental restrictions to pastoral land-use in the mountains and deserts. Specifically, in the summer the desert regions cannot support large herds of domestic cattle and horses, while the high mountain pastures offer rich green meadows. In the winter, the opposite is the case, when mountain pastures are covered in deep snow, while at lower elevations a more temperate climate allows for winter pasturing. This current environmental trend provides the basic framework for simulating the movement patterns of prehistoric pastoralists in the region.

One of the main questions for archaeologists working in the Eurasian Steppe region concerns the origins and development of pastoral nomadism. When mobile pastoralism emerged as an economic and social strategy, what the scale and extent of mobility and contact was between populations across the steppes in prehistory, remain vital questions for scholars of this region.

During the mid-second millennium BC, 'Bronze Age' societies are known to have inhabited most of the steppe region, as well as the mountain ranges between present-day Kazakhstan, China, and southern Siberia. The most characteristic elements of the Bronze Age archaeology, such as copper and arsenical bronze jewelry and decorated hand-made ceramic vessels, reflect the shared metallurgical tradition and domestic styles of these societies (Chernykh 1992; Sorokin 1966). Although a primary focus of Soviet archaeologists, the details of the domestic economy of these groups is only roughly understood, with a general consensus that 'agro-pastoralism' typified the subsistence strategies of the region (Shilov 1975). This reconstruction is rooted in the findings of domestic fauna in burial and settlement contexts, interpreted by association with ethnographic data concerning steppe populations. However, the past decade of new archaeology in the region has revealed that there is a wider variation in both settlement and subsistence strategies across the steppes than previously thought (Chang and Grigoriev 1999). Oddly, to date there have been few reconstructions of economies in light of localized ecological constraints *and* potential social practices. Thus it is difficult to compare patterns of land-use, mobility, and interaction between various regions and populations across the steppe, which may be better indicators of economic activity than simple faunal reconstructions.

In addition to questions of subsistence, the material culture of the Bronze Age in this region sparks questions concerning trade and regional interaction. As mentioned, the Bronze Age 'culture-groups' of the Eastern Eurasian Steppes are primarily known from their characteristic ceramic vessels, metal artifacts, and cist burials, which are surprisingly widely distributed across a vast territory from the Ural Mountains to southeastern Kazakhstan and Kyrgyzstan (Kuz'mina 1986). The broad similarities in material culture styles led Soviet archaeologists to develop a complex Bronze Age culture history of 'Andronovo tribes' across the steppe, and to delineate a number of regional variants along stylistic, and typological lines of argumentation (e.g. Margulan *et al.* 1966).

Though this typology is today an issue of debate for regional specialists, the expanse of roughly similar archaeological material across the Eurasian Steppes does raise significant questions concerning the nature of interaction and cultural diffusion through Central Asia during the second millennium (Potemkina *et al.* 1995; Kuz'mina 1994).

Therefore, the modeling of mobility patterns, land-use, and the development of social landscapes of Bronze Age steppe societies is a crucial step in understanding the dynamics of economy and interaction among populations across Eurasia. The potential for interaction, trade, and warfare are tied to the ways these societies occupied space and how they defined that space over spatial and temporal scales. If populations of the second millennium were highly mobile, perhaps the potential for interaction across large distances would also have been high; if their social landscapes were more confined, then other mechanisms must be proposed to explain the extent of material similarities across the region.

Modeling Bronze Age pastoralism in the Koksu River Valley

Given the difficulties of reconstructing prehistoric nomadic patterns from traditional archaeological techniques (Cribb 1991), digital methods offer an opportunity to contextualize the archaeology of mobile pastoralists using data that are otherwise analytically difficult to manipulate. To illustrate a digital approach using the scalar paradigm outlined above, I have selected a few data sources collected from recent archaeological studies in Koksu River Valley of eastern Kazakhstan.[2] These archaeological and ecological data represent different scales of analytical and actual information relevant to our questions of nomadic landscape construction. These data sources include: 1 Paleo-climatic reconstruction (large-scale) and qualified land-cover (large and medium scale); 2 Potential mobility pathways (large and medium scale); 3 distribution of settlements and burials (medium scale); and 4 rock-art (small-scale). The methodological approach entails combining and delimiting these various data sets so that they produce a geographic depiction of the patterns of movement and the areas of high potential of interaction across the pastoral landscape. The primary function explored below is that of 'flow accumulation' over the landscape, which is essentially the degree of travel over a range of pathways that are optimized according to criteria of different scales. The following sections describe the data sources, how they were manipulated in GIS, and the implications of the calculations for prehistoric pastoralism.

Study zone

The Koksu River Valley is located in the southern range of the Dzhungar Mountains, forms an east–west grassland corridor between sub-alpine pastures and lowland, arid semi-deserts. The detailed study zone is approximately 2,500 sq. km, and extends from the point where the Koksu River emerges from steep-walled upland canyons to the territory where it flows out of the Dzhungar Mountains (Figure 6.2). The study zone includes highland zones with elevations over 3,000 meters above sea level, as well as lowland depressions of less than 600 meters above sea level. The region is rich in archaeology primarily attributed to the Bronze Age (second millennium BC), Iron Age (first millennium BC), and Medieval periods, and ethnographically is host to semi-nomadic Kazakh herders.

Modeling pastures and land-cover

For the purpose of landscape modeling here, we will assume that the vegetation and climate of the study region during the mid-second millennium was broadly comparable with contemporary conditions.[3] When more detailed reconstructions are processed, the land-cover theme can be adjusted to reflect more comprehensive conditions of the second millennium. For pastoralists,

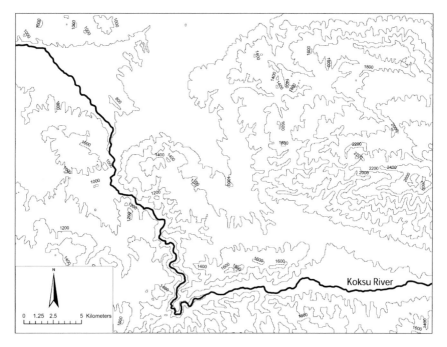

Figure 6.2 Detailed view of study zone.

perhaps the most important resource for their subsistence economy is green pasture. In the Dzhungar Mountains, the size and productivity of pastures are directly correlated with seasonality and altitude. As a general rule, high altitude pastures (> 1,400 m.a.s.l.) are more than three times as productive as pastures below 800 m a.s.l.[4] (Bykov 1974). Therefore, modeling the large-scale geography of pasture resources in upland zones entails rectifying the vegetational land-cover according to known botanical horizons at different altitudes (Sobolev 1960). Altitude horizons that significantly affect the grass-land botany of the Dzhungar region exist at 800 m, 1,000 m, 1,400 m, 2,300 m and 2,800 meters above sea level (Figure 6.2) (Goloskokov 1984).

To accurately render the pasture resources in the study zone, an NDVI[5] image was calculated in Arc-View Image analyst using Landsat TM 7 base data. An NDVI image assigns values ranging from − 1 to 1 for land-cover, according to the intensity of reflected chlorophyll in the vegetation (i.e. 'greenness'). Using ArcGIS 8.2, the NDVI image was reclassified, assigning qualitatively ranked 'productivity values' to vegetation indices greater than 0. Vegetation indices less than 0 represent poor vegetation coverage, i.e. areas of inadequate pasture potential. This revalued NDVI image was then resolved into four classes of grassland types according to known botanical composition of pastures at various altitude horizons (Goloskokov 1984; Sobolev 1960). These include: 1 Alpine meadows; 2 Sub-alpine meadows; 3 Mountain steppes; and 4 semi-arid steppes (Figure 6.3). This data theme

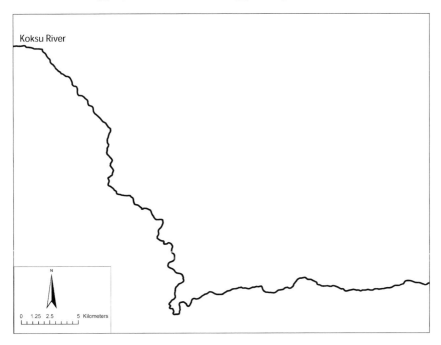

Figure 6.3 Course of Koksu River.

acts as one of the large-scale factors that determine spatial and temporal cycles of pastoral movement.

Pasture accessibility and potential pathways

With a proposed map of the summer pasture resources we can then begin to model the potential movements of pastoral groups across the landscape. The first element of landscape-use explored is herd movement, delimited by the availability of optimal grass resources. The assumption here is that herders would be more likely to move their animals over pathways where the animals can feed, whether *en route* to longer term pasture locations, or to designated social arenas (e.g. settlements). This type of optimization only partly reflects reality, in that the ethnographic record certainly shows instances of nomadic migrations over areas without adequate pasture resources. However, there are few instances when pastoralists explicitly avoid rich pastures in their movement to summer camps, for example. Thus, to link herding pathways to corridors of rich grass should be taken as a best case scenario, while other criteria will enable us to propose reasons why particular pathways might be selected, or avoided, in spite of their ecological potential (e.g. socio-political factors).

To produce a map of likely pathways, I first calculated a theme that shows the cost benefit of traveling from settlement camps to pastures, ranked according to the quality of pasture. In this map, distance to settlements is set against productivity of the pasture, so that in some case, even more distant pastures are qualified as more easily traveled, given their high yield (Figure 6.4). This qualified layer is then set as a cost layer, and using the Flow Accumulation function in Spatial Analyst, a network of potential pathways between settlements and the richest pastures is produced (Figure 6.5). This pathway map reflects the widest scale possibility for traveling across the landscape, provided good grass resources, and as pathways flow into one another (i.e. share a common track), the pathway is ranked as more likely (i.e. given a higher value). This enables a route to each pasture cell (set at 30 m^2) to be compared, and gives preference to those routes that offer accessibility to the best pastures.

The selection of potential pathways based solely on the availability of grass may best reflect the movement of pastoralists if the only consideration was providing good pastures for their herds. However, social and personal factors play a role in the decision-making logic of herders, such as where they can meet with their kinsmen, avoid hostile or inhospitable neighbors, or take advantage of secondary geographic resources, such as good hunting areas, water sources, etc. Therefore, the pathway model should also reflect preferences for some destinations over others. For the model presented here, I selected some medium-scale data, settlements, and categorized a 2 km zone around them to represent 'proximal zones of interaction.' This distance

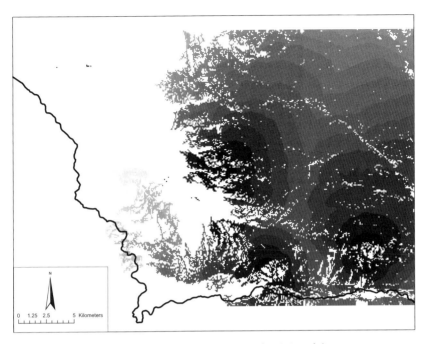

Figure 6.4 Distance to settlements set against productivity of the pasture.

was gauged according to the average distance between settlement groups (approx. 1.5 km). Then, using the pasture resources again as the restrictive factor, least cost/greatest benefit pathways were calculated between these zones (Figure 6.5). The resulting pathways reflect the 'best' way to simultaneously provide for herds, and move between settlements. The pathways also suggest likely orbits for localized herding around settlements. Yet, since we are interested in not only establishing zones of interaction around known archaeological locales, additional data must be considered along with settlements to illustrate the variety of potential movements of groups, and flush out the less obvious locales of interaction across the landscape.

Ritual landscapes

The technique illustrated above shows how large-scale data, such as landcover and pasture resources, may have contributed to the selection of discrete pathways for movement in relation to medium-scale contexts such as settlements. However, along these pathways, mobile groups would experience socially constructed contexts of a variety of scales within the landscape at different times. Therefore, in order to test the relationship between pasturing movements, and other pathways that define the social spheres of

141

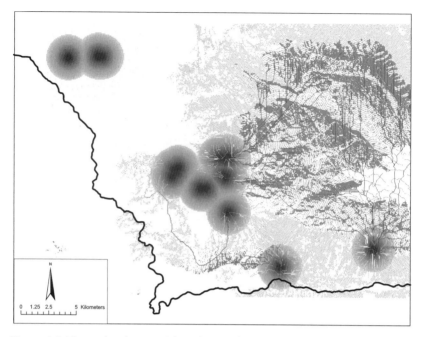

Figure 6.5 Network of potential pathways between settlements and the richest pastures.

groups, the routes between pastures and settlements are compared with routes between rock-art, burials and other destinations.

Since the movement between various locales in the landscape does not always entail feeding herds, other delimiting factors to traveling over the landscape must be considered. There are many potential factors that play into route selection, such as the location of lakes, streams, walls, field boundaries, and sacred areas; one considered here is topography. The basic assumption is that pathways over flatter terrain are preferable to those up and down cliffs. Using percent slope as a source for calculating cost of travel, I produced a map that preferences routes over flatter topography. Assessing travel between pasture areas and rock-art, as well as rock art and settlements using slope as the delimiting factor, I produced a flow accumulation map similar to the one seen for travel to rich pasture resources, yet with additional pathways over some lowland areas where green pasture is not available (Figure 6.6). By comparing the pathways to rock-art (based on ease of terrain) with the location of other socially constructed contexts, the types of constructed contexts that fall along these pathways can be assessed. When compared with the pathways for herding (based on rich pasture locations), the pathways that trace routes between pastures and rock-art, and between settlements and rock-art, illustrate a pattern of pathways, which

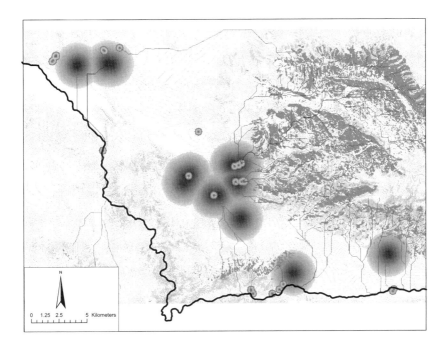

Figure 6.6 Flow accumulation map for travel to rich pasture resources noting additional pathways over lowland areas.

pass over a number of burials (Figure 6.7). This may suggest that ritual sites were not visited as frequently on herding migrations (i.e. were unrelated to locations of rich pasture), and instead implies that movements independent of herding needs were employed for ritual purposes.

As greater numbers of decision impacting factors are incorporated, it is important to depict how they affect social interaction and landscape use over temporal scales as well as across space. Temporal information is more difficult to model directly; however, some of the modeled results inherently educate us about the potential seasonality or usage patterns of particular areas of the landscape.

If we return to the pathways modeled between settlements and pastures (Figure 6.5), there are a few conspicuous sites that have no pathways to them. These settlements are located in a lowland area, where summer pasture resources are extremely poor. Even when travel tolerance is set extremely high, productive herding pathways do not reach these features given the availability of rich summer pastures. Thus, from an annual perspective, these features might best be interpreted as 'winter' settlements – or at least 'not summer' settlements. By association, I infer that since the population would be upland during the summer, the sphere of social and

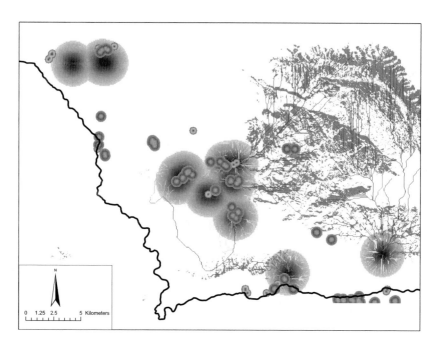

Figure 6.7a Pathways tracing routes between pastures and rock-art.

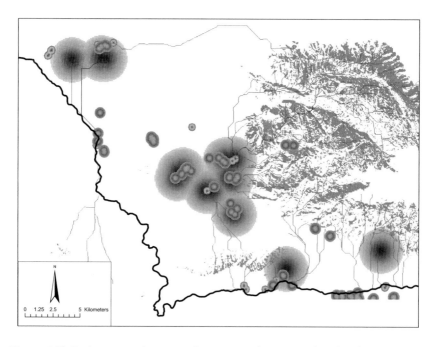

Figure 6.7b Pathways tracing routes between settlements and rock-art.

ritual interaction would also migrate. From this reconstruction seasonality can be assigned to the rock-art and burials in the lowland region.

In addition to constructed contexts, the usage of pastures can be assessed according to the degree of resource degradation due to pasturing animals. Since there are clear pathways that illustrate the frequency of animal 'traffic' over certain areas, it can be suggested that the host pastures to the 'most likely traveled' pathway would be devoured first, and would force the use of secondary pasture tracks in a knowable time frame. Of course this type of calculation would depend on the productivity of pasture resources, the number of animals and their nutritional needs (cf. Larin 1962; Chekeres 1973).

Discussion

In the cases tested above, some basic assumptions about pastoralists have been made: 1 that they desire good pasture for their animals; and 2 they will choose easier travel routes when not feeding their herds. These assumptions are admittedly circumstantial, but seem to produce an output that is consistent with data from other scales (e.g. locations of burials). To produce a comprehensive model, there are many data that may change the current picture. For example, population dynamics could be modeled to show the degree of stress on the landscape, or herd size could be assigned to different regions to revalue the way resources would likely be valued. All of these potential adjustments, however, bring us back to the goal of this chapter – to theoretically and analytically relate various scales of data to simultaneously impact the outcome of archaeological reconstructions and interpretations.

Combining data such as land-cover with settlements and mobility patterns to rock-art locations shows how an array of factors can produce rather different landscape views, depending on how scale was qualitatively assigned to the data. Settlements were selected to have a wider landscape impact than rock-art (reflected in the distance buffers around them). This scalar assignment has an effect on the 'communication' between data sources in the digital environment. Digital archaeological modeling thrives on the ability to test countless iterations of data of different scales to more accurately reconstruct some of the potential ways humans experience their landscape. In the case study here, combining large-scale, medium-scale and small-scale data to preference various patterns of mobility, illustrated that a variety of pathways may accurately define the pastoral landscape. These patterns are not random, but in fact represent the compression of a number of ecological and social factors that are weighted in a particular way. To produce different results, one need simply reclassify the scale and impact of their data. The most 'real' model is only distinguished according to the kinds of questions that are being tested. This kind of simulation is not anti-positivist, but rather balances qualitative attributes of certain data classes, with the quantitative reality of that data's scalar impact. Independent correlation is achieved when models align seemingly unrelated scales of data over common spatial or temporal contexts.

In closing, digital archaeological tools such as GIS and remote sensing offer useful methods for comparing actual three and four-dimensional data in an analytical space that processes multi-scalar data, and produces synthetic output that helps archaeologists interpret social and environmental relationships in the past. In order to begin to reconstruct the way human societies, like mobile pastoralists of Eurasia, experienced their landscape in prehistory, we must continue to explore the correlations between social and ecological data of various scales.

Acknowledgements

The archaeological research underpinning these reconstructions was funded by the National Science Foundation and George F. Dales Foundation. The archaeology and paleo-climatic studies were conducted in collaboration with Dr. Alexei Mar'yashev (Institute of Archaeology) and Dr. Bulat Aubekerov (Institute of Geology), Almaty, Kazakhstan. In addition, conversations with Dr. Dana Tomlin (University of Pennsylvania) were instrumental to the GIS modeling.

Notes

1 Also known in Russian as 'Semirech'ye.'
2 The Dzhungar Mountains Archaeology Project (1999–2003) which I co-direct with Dr. Alexei Maryashev (Inst. of Archaeology, KZ).
3 For summary of the stability of steppe vegetation during the late Holocene, see Khotinskiy (1984: 196–7), also more generally (Kremenetski 2002). For complete discussion of paleoclimate and paleovegetation of the case study region, see Ph.D. thesis by author (2004).
4 During the summer growing season (June–August).
5 Normalized Difference Vegetation Index.

References

Anshuetz, K. F., Williams, R. H. and Scheick, C. L. (2001) 'An archaeology of land-scapes: Perspectives and directions'. *Journal of Archaeological Research* 9: 157–211.

Barfield, T. (1989) *The Perilous Frontier: Nomadic Empires and China*. Cambridge, MA: Basil Blackwell.

Barth, F. (1964) *Nomads of South Persia*. New York: Humanities Press.

Bykov, V. A. (1974) *Bilogicheskaya Produktivnost' Rastitel'nosti Kazakhstana (Biological Productivity of the Vegetation of Kazakhstan)*. Alma-Ata: Nauka.

Chang, C. and Grigoriev, F. P. (1999) 'A preliminary report of the 1994–1996 field seasons at Tuzusai, an Iron Age site (*c.* 400 BC–100 AD) in Southeastern Kazakhstan'. *Eurasia Antiqua* 5: 1–20.

Chekeres, A. I. (1973) *Pogoda, klimat, I otgonno-pastbishchnoe zhivotnovodstvo (Weather, Climate and Distant Pasture Stock Breeding).* Leningrad: Gidrometeoizdat.

Chernykh, E. N. (1992) *Ancient Metallurgy in the USSR: The Early Metal Age.* Cambridge: Cambridge University Press.

Cribb, R. (1991) *Nomads in Archaeology.* Cambridge: Cambridge University Press.

Frachetti, M. and Chippindale, C. (2002) 'Alpine imagery, alpine space, alpine time; and prehistoric human experience', in Nash, G. and Chippindale, C. (eds) *European Landscapes of Rock-Art*, pp. 116–43. London: Routledge.

Giddens, A. (1984) *The Constitution of Society: Outline of a Theory of Structuration.* Cambridge: Polity Press.

Goloskokov, V. P. (1984) *Flora Dzhungarskogo Alatau (Flora of the Dzhungar Mountains).* Almaty: Nauka Kazakhskoi SSR.

Ingold, T. (1993) 'The temporality of the landscape'. *World Archaeology* 25: 152–74.

Kuz'mina, E. E. (1986) *Drevneishie skotovody ot Urala do Tian'-Shania.* Frunze: Ilim.

Kuz'mina, E. E. (1994) *Otkuda prishli indoarii? material'naia kul'tura plemen andronovskoi obshchnosti i proiskhozhdenie indoirantsev.* Moskva: MGP 'Kalina'.

Larin, I. V. (1962) *Pasture Rotation; System for the Care and Utilization of Pastures.* Jerusalem: Israel Program for Scientific Translations.

Mar'yashev, A. N. (1994) *Petroglyphs of South Kazakhstan and Semirechye.* Almaty: Akademiia Nauk.

Margulan, A. X., Akishev, K. A., Kadirbaev, M. K. and Orazbaev, A. M. (1966) *Drevnaya Kul'tura Tsentral'nogo Kazakhstana (Ancient Cultures of Central Kazakhstan).* Almaty: Nauka Kazakhskoi SSR.

McGlade, J. (1995) 'Archaeology and the ecodynamics of human modified landscapes'. *Antiquity* 69: 113–32.

Potemkina, T. M., Stefanov, V. I. and Korochkova, O. N. (1995) *Lesnoe Tobolo-Irtysh e v kontse epokhi bronzy.* Moskva: Institut Arkheologii.

Salzman, P. C. (1972) 'Multi-resource nomadism in Iranian Baluchistan', in Irons, W. and Dyson-Hudson, N. (eds) *Perspectives on Nomadism*, pp. 60–8. Leiden: E. J. Brill.

Shilov, V. P. (1975) 'Modeli skotovodcheskikh khoziaistv stpenikh oblatei Evrazii v epokhu eneolita i rannego bronzogo veka (Models of pastoral economies in the steppe regions of Eurasia in the Eneolithic and early Bronze Ages)'. *Sovetskaya Arkeologiya* 5–16.

Sobolev, L. N. (1960) *Kormovye Resursy Kazakhstana (Fodder Resources of Kazakhstan).* Moscow: Nauka.

Sorokin, V. S. (1966) *Andronovskaya Kultura.* Moscow: Nauka.

Spooner, B. (1973) *The Cultural Ecology of Pastoral Nomads.* Addison-Wesley Module in Anthropology No. 45. Reading, MA: Addison-Wesley.

7

WHAT YOU SEE IS WHAT YOU GET?

Visualscapes, visual genesis and hierarchy

Marcos Llobera

Introduction

The intention of this chapter is to introduce the reader to a few ideas and methods on how to explore visual patterns of past landscapes using standard GIS tools. It also attempts, very timidly, to extend the limited toolkit currently available to landscape archaeologists by introducing some very basic GIS techniques.

Our understanding of the relevance of visual patterns in the past has been dominated by very few topics which to a certain extent evoke remnants of old approaches to the study of space (although they are not thought of that way). So far most of the studies have been concerned almost exclusively with the topic of intervisibility (Wheatley 1995; Lake *et al.* 1998) i.e. to what degree sites maintain visual contact with each other (Tilley 1994). Most of the discussion concentrates on the monuments themselves, i.e. locations, rather than exploring, for instance, what kind of visual structure sites or monuments generated and/or the relationship that these may have had with the visual areas they define. Within GIS and archaeology, concern with the visual area itself was very briefly noted by Lock and Harris (1996) while discussing the Neolithic landscape surrounding the hillfort of Danebury, in particular, with reference to the non-overlapping nature of the viewsheds associated with the long-barrows in that landscape.

The retrieval and study of visual patterns associated with past cultural landscapes is a huge topic which is yet to be fully explored mainly because of the lack of proper methodologies. Current technical limitations, together with a heavy criticism of the study of visual aspects and the increasing promotion of multi-sensorial and/or other senses, have not necessarily aided the development of new techniques and ways of thinking (e.g. Gillings and Goodrick 1996). Most of these criticisms are valid ones, though unfortunately they have not always been terribly constructive. In this respect, works such as the one conducted by Watson and Keating on sound (Watson and Keating 1999) represent a welcome and innovative development. In spite of all these limitations, visual information remains of vital importance for understanding past landscapes, for vision is the sense that in most cases is responsible for structuring space. Of course, this does not deny the fact that other senses play an important role in forming our understanding of the landscape, as pointed out by several authors (e.g. Gillings and Goodrick 1996).

Independent of how significant visibility is in playing a role at a social, political or symbolic level, the existence of a visual structure associated with a cultural landscape is undeniable. Such a structuring may or may not have had a specific purpose, and may or may not have been part of a conscious effort. Clues about the importance of the visual, and the role that it might have had, can be found in the structure itself (its 'robustness') and/or its combination with other archaeological information.

In this chapter the notion of *visualscape* is introduced as a generic term within a GIS context to talk about the visual structure in a landscape. Questions about how soon this structure or pattern arose and how it changed as it was emerging are examined. These issues are important from a practical perspective, as a way to incorporate the uncertainty into our dataset, and at a theoretical level, as a way to obtain new insights into their significance. The possibility of determining the contribution that the viewshed of each site or monument may have had on this structure is also explored as well as the notion of a visual hierarchy.

Visualscapes

The concept of visualscape was introduced elsewhere as: 'The *spatial representation* of any *visual property* generated by, or associated with, a *spatial configuration*' (Llobera 2003).

It is an operational concept, that within a GIS context, attempts to unify, organize and extend both the scope and methodology, of works focusing on the study of visual space as found in disciplines such as geography, archaeology, architecture and urbanism.

High among the different reasons for defining this concept is the idea that every cultural landscape generates, or can be associated with, a visual structure. While not identical (no mention is made here about light), this idea resonates with Gibson's *optic array* notion (Gibson 1986) in that both stress the presence of a structure or patterning. Recovering this structure and understanding its properties requires that we go beyond concentrating exclusively on specific locations and that we examine the patterns as a whole, e.g. where do changes in visibility occur? With what intensity? How does the visual prominence of a location change from different viewpoints? Emphasis shifts from being solely interested in what happens at the sites to understanding the visual structure at large; its relationship with the sites that generated it, and so forth.

Another important aspect associated with a *visualscape* is the notion that by focusing on different elements of the cultural landscape we can vary the scope, scale, nature and intent of the visual analysis. This possibility allows us to incorporate another of Gibson's contributions: that of *perception as the education of attention*. The visual structure generated by different elements in the landscape may delineate areas with different significance and activity patterns. So for instance, if we were to take a group of monuments clustered together, we would want to distinguish the areas from where the entirety of the monuments is visible from those where only the façade and/or entrance is visible. Each of these areas, particularly the latter cases, may define places where different activities, and indeed, social expectations occur.

Cumulative and total viewsheds

Cumulative viewsheds can be thought of as a type of *visualscape* describing the visual structure generated by a set of monuments or sites. This description is rather crude as it employs simple spatial representations, usually points (or some other GIS spatial primitives) to represent the monuments or sites, and only records the number of uninterrupted lines-of-sight that connect each location with the monuments.[1]

An initial step, when considering the visual pattern generated by the *cumulative viewsheds* is to determine how likely the pattern is to have emerged by pure chance; this can be answered in various ways. One way is by conducting some sort of *Monte Carlo* simulation by which we generate the *cumulative viewshed* from *n* random locations (*n* usually being the same number as that of monuments or sites) *r* number of times, comparing (statistically) the results with the original *cumulative viewshed*. Another may be achieved by using a *total viewshed*,[2] another type of *visualscape* similar to the *cumulative viewshed*, where the viewshed for each location[3] in the DEM is calculated and added together. Once calculated, it is relatively trivial to check statistically how much the visual pattern of any *cumulative viewshed* reflects the pattern inherent in the topography of the landscape. The main limitation of the *total viewshed* is the intensity of computation it requires, as opposed to the *Monte Carlo* approach. A few years ago this intensity would have been prohibitive (Lake *et al.* 1998); however, as technology advances, the possibilities of computing *total viewshed*s for sizeable DEMs are increasing rapidly. Not only are commodity computers becoming faster but it is also possible to employ software (e.g. CONDOR, a generic scheduling package) that allows distributing computational loads across a non-dedicated network of machines. This system has already been successfully used to compute the *total viewshed* for several archaeological landscapes across a network of computers (Llobera *et al.* forthcoming) quite rapidly. As Llobera (2003) has shown, a *total viewshed* should not only be considered as an (intensive) alternative to the *Monte Carlo* approach (just

150

because we can compute them!) but as a construct that is worth studying in its own right, and from where other information can derive (e.g. visual prominence).

Being a natural extension of *cumulative viewsheds, total viewsheds* suffer from the same limitations as the former (see Fisher *et al.* 1997; Lake *et al.* 1998; Gillings and Wheatley 2000). Among these, those of a 'practical' nature, such as the lack of atmospheric attenuation or the effect of vegetation, are harder to resolve. Other ones, of a more methodological nature, like the edge effect, are resolved, or properly handled, by following simple principles (Lake *et al.* 1998; Llobera *et al.* forthcoming).

Visual genesis

If we accept *cumulative viewsheds* as an expression of the structure generated by a set of monuments or sites, it would be highly beneficial if we could understand the process of their construction. We need to avoid, at least initially, the temptation of accepting the visual structure described by the *cumulative viewshed*[4] as a *de facto* pattern (an aspect very much implicit in most studies), as a pattern that was actually present or recognizable at any point in time.

There are several reasons why drawing conclusions from the *cumulative viewshed* alone (i.e. in its final stage) may be unwise; from a practical point of view, the data that we are using may have derived from an aerial photography survey (as in this case) that without further ground-proving resulted in the inclusion of many 'sites' that did not exist or were misclassified. Another, common problem is the limitation that arises from our own 'periodization' of the data (a common practice in landscape projects), i.e. assigning sites to particular periods. Some of these periods may encompass a long spell of time (several generations) in which case the order in which sites were constructed would have played a crucial role in the emergence of the visual structure. From a theoretical perspective, understanding how this visual pattern was constructed can shed some light on how territories were generated (if visibility was an active element) and perceived, as well as providing us with some idea of the intentionality of the builders (independently of whether it is part of a conscious effort or not). All of these aspects may be investigated through a series of concrete questions such as: how 'stable' is the visual pattern we observe (i.e. how many sites need to be absent before the pattern changes?) How 'early' is the pattern determined? How many sites are required? Which locations maintained the same 'level of visibility'? How much does this level fluctuate?

Data from the Yorkshire Wolds (see Figure 7.1) will be used to illustrate how some of these questions may be explored. Only the faintest of archaeological implications will be sought here given space constraints and the intention to focus on methodology. For a more detailed description of the

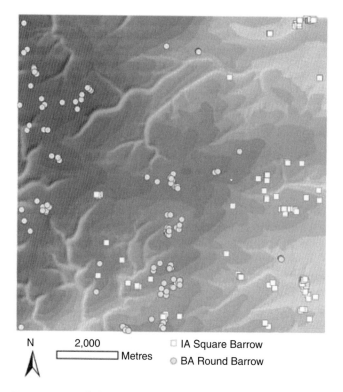

N   2,000
              Metres   □ IA Square Barrow
                        ○ BA Round Barrow

Figure 7.1 Yorkshire Wolds archaeology.

archaeology of the area the reader is referred to (Stoertz 1997; Bevan 1997; Giles 2000). The *cumulative viewshed* for both Bronze Age (BA) round barrows and Iron Age (IA) square barrows are presented in Figures 7.2 and 7.3 respectively.

In order to explore some of the questions mentioned above, the following experiment was constructed (see Figure 7.3):

1   The final *cumulative viewshed* (*fcv*) for all of our sites was calculated and normalized (*nfcv*), so that the number of lines-of-sight are expressed from 0 to 100.

2   A percentage *p* of the total number of viewsheds forming the original *cumulative viewshed* was selected (without replacement). The initial percentage should amount to a sensible number of sites, i.e. it is dependent on the total number of sites we have.

3   Given this percentage, a sample *cumulative viewshed* (scv_i) was generated and normalized, same as our original *cumulative viewshed* ($nscv_i$).

4   The (absolute) difference between the normalized *cumulative viewsheds* ($dif = nfcv - scv_i$) was obtained.

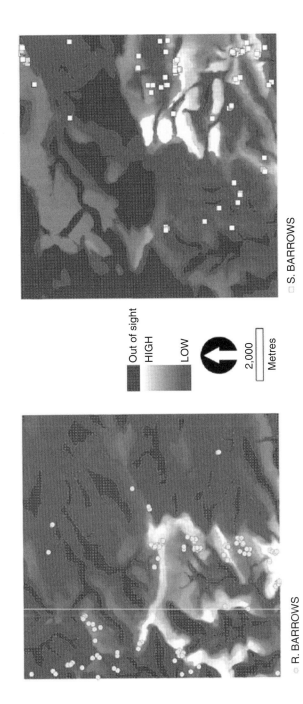

Out of sight

HIGH

LOW

2,000
Metres

□ S. BARROWS

○ R. BARROWS

Figure 7.2 Cumulative viewshed for the BA round and IA square barrows respectively.

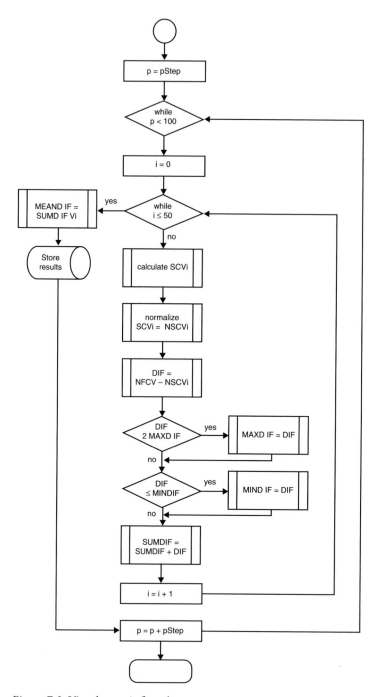

Figure 7.3 Visual genesis flowchart.

5   The average, maximum and minimum difference was noted.
6   This process was repeated *n* times (here *n* = 25, so *i* goes from 1 to 25 inclusive).
7   The *p* % is increased until say, *p* = 95%.

Results

The results of the simulations are presented in Figures 7.4 and 7.5, for the round and square barrows respectively.

The horizontal axis indicates the number of sites that participate in each sample *cumulative viewshed*. The vertical axis describes the percentage of error with respect to the final *cumulative viewshed*. A figure of 100 per cent would mean that when the final (normalized) viewshed was compared against a sample (also normalized) *cumulative viewshed*, the maximum difference, in this case 100, was registered at each location. As it stands, this can never be the case, for obvious reasons. For the BA round barrows, we observe that with only five barrows the maximum (high) error recorded was of 16.8 per cent; this value represents the average error found for the entire study area (i.e. image) out of 25 iterations. It is possible that at some locations this error could have been much greater (or smaller). The average difference between the *cumulative viewshed* using this amount of barrows and the final *cumulative viewshed* was about 10.1 per cent; the smallest

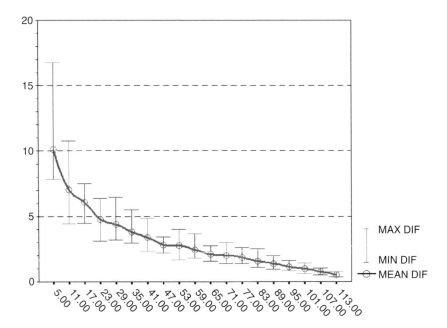

Figure 7.4 Visual genesis for BA round barrows.

155

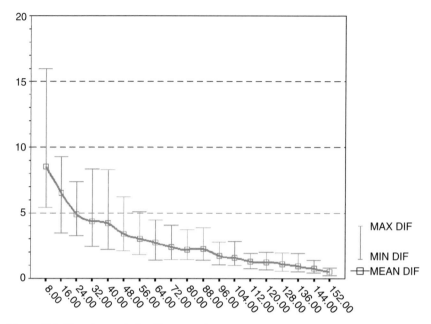

Figure 7.5 Visual genesis for IA square barrows.

difference was 7.8 per cent. Close examination of these graphs provides us with numerous insights about the nature of the *cumulative viewsheds*.

By examining the trendline uniting the average difference obtained for each percentage, we can tell how quickly the emerging visual pattern converges to its final configuration.

Given the high level of clustering present among the monuments (see Figures 7.3 and 7.4) it is not surprising that both sets of monuments present a very similar pattern. Indeed, one can say that this high level of clustering will pervade most of the results. Care must be exercised if these types of graphs are to be compared side by side given the unequal number of monuments. We can distinguish various stages of convergence by considering the slope that an imaginary straight line would have along different sections of the trendline. A first rapid decline, particularly in the case of the round barrows, occurs after 24 monuments are in place, at which point the overall average difference becomes 5.0 per cent. This is followed by a second phase up to 47–53 round barrows for the BA and 72–80 square barrows for the IA, and a final phase when all monuments are considered. The steadiness of the decline observed (after 24+ barrows) is likely to be caused, in part, by the averaging effect when calculating the overall error for the entire study area.

It is interesting to note the overall variability surrounding the sample *cumulative viewsheds* (Figure 7.7). In both cases, this variability reduces with increasing number (as would be expected) but the magnitude of the

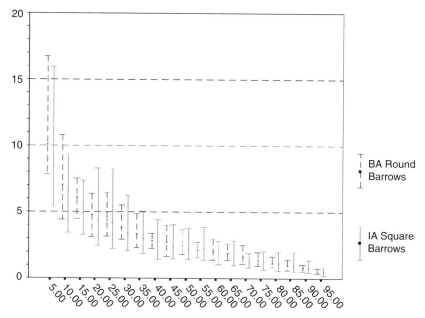

Figure 7.6 A comparison of the visual variability for round and square barrows.

variation is larger for square barrows than for round barrows. This is particularly true until at least 48 square barrows are in place, up to that point the average difference is about 6.0 per cent. This suggests that visual experience associated with square barrows was far richer and not as well 'defined' as the one associated with the round barrows (see discussion below on visual hierarchy). We can actually find out at which locations the incorporation of more barrows would have brought substantial changes in visual intensity.

Figure 7.8 shows the visual variability at each location in the study area for the round and square barrows. To obtain these images, all sample *cumulative viewsheds* were combined into a single image representing the standard deviation of the visual intensity at each location. The idea is simple, we want to know how the visual intensity at each location varied as the number of monuments used to generate the *cumulative viewshed* increased. Areas with large variability (large standard deviation) would have been less defined, more visually unstable, than those whose standard deviation was smaller. One way of interpreting this measure (certainly not the only one) would be to associate areas with large visual variability with areas that were not well defined visually, were not very stable. These were locations whose visual intensity changed through time as opposed to others that remained the same, and may have represented boundary locations or areas of symbolic importance. Perhaps the best way of utilizing this information is by employing it in connection with the final (normalized) *cumulative viewshed*.

157

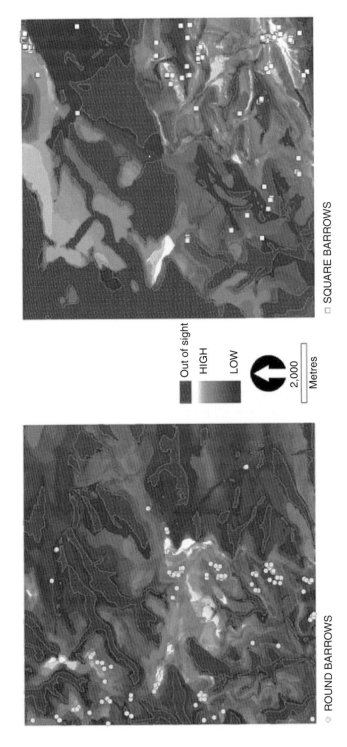

Out of sight

HIGH

LOW

2,000
Metres

□ SQUARE BARROWS

○ ROUND BARROWS

Figure 7.7 Visual variability at each location for round and square barrows.

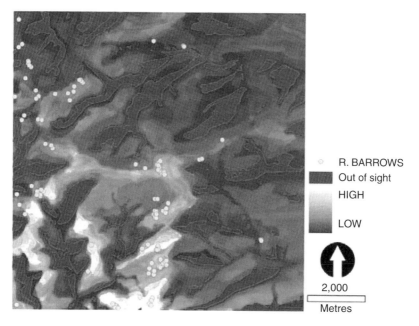

R. BARROWS
Out of sight
HIGH
LOW

2,000
Metres

Figure 7.8 Visual structure generated by round barrows after their visual variability
has been accounted for.

If we divide the latter by its visual variability, we will be able to determine
which locations remained visually intensive as the number of monuments
increased (Figure 7.8). This is probably one of the best (single) descriptions
we can generate to describe the visual structure generated by a set of sites or
monuments using conventional GIS methods.

Visual change

If *cumulative viewsheds* describe the visual structure related to a set of locations or monuments, the question about where and how did these changes
occur is something we are interested in examining. One way of exploring
this aspect using traditional GIS techniques, is combining the (final) *cumulative viewsheds* of each set of monuments (in this case corresponding to
two different periods, see Figure 7.9). In this particular case, this was
achieved by subtracting the normalized *cumulative viewsheds* from each
other. Negative values are associated with higher visual intensity during one
specific period (in this case BA), positive values with higher visual intensity
during the other period (IA) and zero values with locations where the visual
intensity remain the same. Another way of obtaining similar results is by
reclassifying the *cumulative viewsheds* into several categories (at most four
for best results) and cross-tabulating the categories associated with each set

159

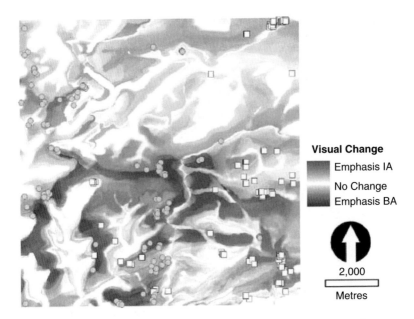

Visual Change

Emphasis IA
No Change
Emphasis BA

2,000

Metres

Figure 7.9 Visual change.

of monuments (Llobera 1999). The image obtained contains an enormous amount of information (it is recommended that the reader spends some time examining it and drawing his/her own interpretations).

It is quite likely that these changes, as they appear in the image, would not have been noticeable by the individuals moving and dwelling in the landscape. However, they are useful for the researcher to understand what changes took place over a long period of time. In this particular case, visual structure is quite homogeneous during each period (i.e. one does not find many 'islands' of different visual emphasis). The areas in the landscape where visual emphasis changed are clearly marked partly because of the overwhelming clustering mentioned earlier. There is a distinct change from east to west on the southern side of the study area while the northern side offers a much more ambiguous picture. A simple visual inspection shows that there are more square barrows found in BA visually intense/no change areas than round barrows in IA visually intense areas (with the exception of asset of barrows in the middle of the image). This could point to the fact that visual contact with round barrows during the IA was not pursued or may have been avoided.

Areas with no visual change may represent boundary areas, marking the separation between the visual range attributed to one set of monuments from that attributed to another set. This interpretation can in some cases be misleading for, as they appear here, these areas can also represent locations that would have been out of sight from both sets of monuments (as is the case inside dry streams or slacks). What is remarkable is the fact that highly visually intensive areas, as those appearing in the lower middle part of the image, lie very near to each other, separated by a very thin area of no visual change.

These are only a few of the many interpretations, presented here as provisional, that this type of image can provide. Many of these interpretations may be aided and/or improved through the creation of additional tables and univariate graphs (e.g. Figure 7.10), as well as by reclassifying the image using different criteria.

Visual hierarchy

In this section, the possibility of finding out how much the viewshed of each monument contributed to the final *cumulative viewshed* is explored. Can a 'visual weight' be assigned to each monument? This 'weight' could be used to rank monuments which could then be checked against other archaeological information, throwing some insight into the significance of the monuments and their social, political or symbolic role in the landscape.

The question about how this weight may be calculated is ultimately a matter of choice; however, it is beneficial when deciding upon this criterion to consider the nature of the viewshed itself. It has already been mentioned that viewsheds are relatively crude, for at best, they identify locations connected by at least one uninterrupted line-of-sight with the viewpoint/s (see Llobera 2003). At the moment, the possibility of deriving other (more revealing) sorts of information such as how much to/from the viewpoint

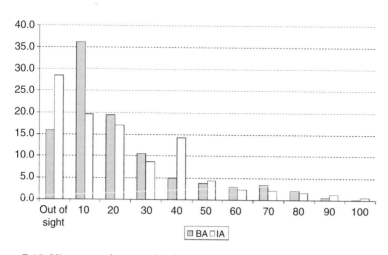

Figure 7.10 Histogram showing the distribution of locations according to the visual intensity generated by round and square barrows.

can be seen, is restricted. Hence all we have is positional information provided by the viewshed, i.e. what locations are in sight or not.

One possible way of defining the visual weight of a monument would be by simply counting the number of locations (grid cells) that are visible to/ from the viewpoint. In a raster GIS, this may be used as an estimate of the total area in view. While this is a perfectly valid measure, particularly if we want to rank monuments by the size of their viewshed, it may generate results that have little relation with the final *cumulative viewshed*. One could envisage a monument having a large viewshed that hardly coincides with that of other monuments. It would be a different matter if the viewshed closely coincided with those of other monuments. In fact, the more the viewshed of a single monument coincides with those of the rest of the monuments the better (the higher its weight). Essentially, this is the same as saying that the more a viewshed coincides with areas of high visual intensity, as given by *cumulative viewshed*, the more weight it should have. One way of calculating this information is by adding up the visual intensity at each location in a viewshed. Monuments for which this sum is large will have higher visual weights. As it stands, the measure is perfectly adequate, however, a further refinement may be included. If the value of this sum is divided by the actual number of 'visible' locations (or 'visible' area), we should, in principle, be able to distinguish monuments with a large viewshed (i.e. by default covering areas of any visual intensity, high and low) from those whose viewshed is not perhaps as large but much more concentrated on locations with higher visual intensity.

The following formula describes these operations in a compact way:

$$w_1 \frac{\sum_{r=0}^{n} NCV(r) \cdot r, (r)}{\sum_{r=0}^{n} V_i(r)}$$

where,

w: 'visual weight' for each monument i
r: location (i.e. each grid cell)
n: number of grid cells in the raster
$NCV(r)$ visual intensity at location r in the normalized cumulative viewshed (0–1.0)
$V_i(r)$ in sight index at location r [0, 1]

Figures 7.11 and 7.12 show round and square barrows, arranged in decreasing order according to their visual weight (calculated using the previous formula). Presenting visual weights in this fashion helps us to identify

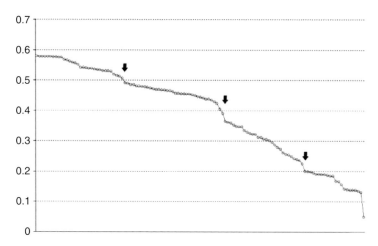

Figure 7.11 Visual weight for round barrows in decreasing order.

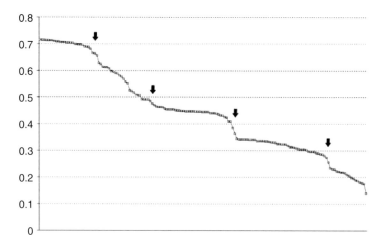

Figure 7.12 Visual weight for square barrows in decreasing order.

visually clusters of monuments that share similar values. This can be achieved by checking for noticeable jumps along the trendline. We can use any clustering technique to group monuments according to their visual weight. Figures 7.13 and 7.14, show these clusters for both round and square barrows, after *Jenk's Optimization method* has been employed. This clustering technique seeks to minimize the variance *within* a class by minimizing the sum of squared deviations from the class mean while at the same time maximizing the variance *between* class means.

The colour scheme used in both images can be interpreted on the one hand, as identifying the different clusters, and on the other showing where

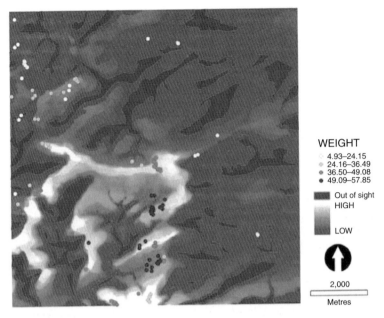

WEIGHT

  4.93–24.15
  24.16–36.49
  36.50–49.08
  49.09–57.85

Out of sight
HIGH

LOW

2,000

Metres

Figure 7.13 Visual clustering of round barrows.

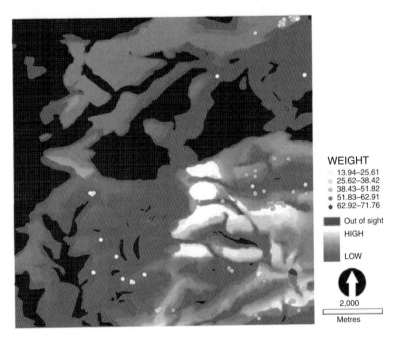

WEIGHT

  13.94–25.61
  25.62–38.42
  38.43–51.82
  51.83–62.91
  62.92–71.76

Out of sight
HIGH

LOW

2,000

Metres

Figure 7.14 Visual clustering of square barrows.

the most 'influential' barrows are located. On the basis of their location, the interpretation of these clusters suggests different roles or functions. These become apparent when we separate the clusters and generate the *cumulative viewshed* associated with each of them. This process of disaggregating the visual structure for the round barrows is shown in Figure 7.15. One should keep in mind, while looking at this sequence, that these patterns are created *from* the monuments in each cluster. Shown in this manner the sense attached to each cluster becomes very revealing. Cluster one is responsible for defining the visual core, where the highest visual intensity is found (reader must note the spatial definition and intensity). Cluster two extends

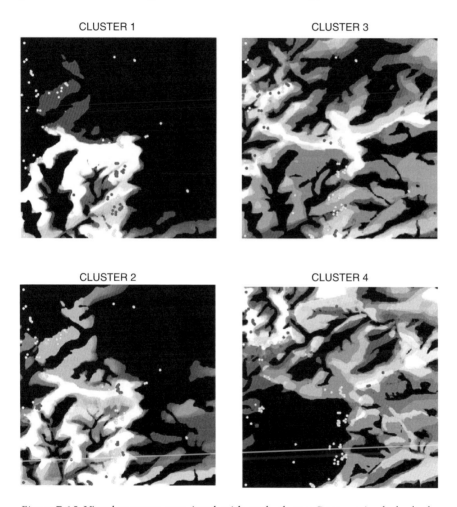

Figure 7.15 Visual patterns associated with each cluster. Barrows in dark shades represent those barrows belonging to the cluster and responsible for the pattern. The lighter, the higher the visual intensity.

this core to the immediate surroundings in a south to north direction (intensity in the core has dropped). Cluster three is the most extensive cluster; barrows can be seen throughout the entire region, and they are also responsible for visually marking the middle ridge across the study area. Finally, cluster four is absolutely divorced from the core, it kind of resembles the set of residuals in a regression, although it is responsible for high visual intensity areas in the northwest. In the case of the round barrows, the main cluster is concentrated on the central southern region, as opposed to the second cluster that seems to be on the fringes of the area of greatest visual intensity though in a disaggregated manner (i.e. separated into several subclusters). For the square barrows (not shown here), the overall pattern is similar to that of the round barrows, inner and more concentrated barrows to outer and more dispersed ones. This is not surprising given the existing spatial clustering of the monuments, as mentioned earlier.

Final comments

The aim of this chapter was predominantly methodological, to introduce the reader to some new ways of thinking and analysing visibility in an archaeological landscape. The techniques proposed here utilize standard GIS methods, hence they should be easily reproduced by a wider community.

Given their novelty and the fact that they can still be considered as being work in progress, it is hard to provide at this point a comprehensive description of the array of implications and interpretations that may derive from them. It is also likely that some functionality may undergo slight changes and refinements. Still they are illustrative of the enormous possibilities available through the use of GIS, possibilities that can incorporate many of the practical limitations that archaeologists face (e.g. classification limitations, 'periodization') and at the same time precipitate new insights, and new ways of thinking about old topics.

Notes

1 No reference to the asymmetry caused by the use of offsets at the target and observer's position will be discussed here (see Fisher *et al.* 1997).
2 This is the terminology used by Llobera (2003): previously *total viewshed* was introduced by Lee and Stucky (1998) as *viewgrid* and *dominance viewgrid*.
3 Location here usually refers to the point at the centre of each grid cell.
4 Putting aside the role that vegetation and other factors may have had on it.

References

Bevan, B. (1997) 'Bounding the landscape: place and identity during the Yorkshire Wolds Iron Age', in *Reconstructing Iron Age Societies* (ed. Gwilt, A. and Haselgrove, C.). Oxford: Oxbow Monograph 71, pp. 181–91.

Fisher, P., Farrelly, C., Maddocks, A. and Ruggles, C. (1997) 'Spatial analysis of visible areas from the Bronze Age cairns of Mull.' *Journal of Archaeological Science* 25: 581–92.

Gibson, J. J. (1986) *The Ecological Approach to Visual Perception.* New Jersey: Lawrence Erlbaum.

Giles, M. (2000) 'Open-weave, close-knit: archaeologies of identity in later prehistoric landscapes of East Yorkshire.' Vols 1–2. Unpublished PhD, University of Sheffield.

Gillings, M. and Goodrick, G. T. (1996) 'Sensuous and reflexive GIS: exploring visualisation and VRML', *Internet Archaeology* 1 (http://intarch.ac.uk/journal/issue1/gillings_toc.html).

Gillings, M. and Wheatley, D. (2000) 'Vision, perception and GIS: developing enriched approaches to the study of archaeological visibility', in *Beyond the Map* (ed. G. Lock). Amsterdam: IOS Press, pp. 1–28.

Lake, M. W., Woodman, P. E. and Mithen, S. J. (1998) 'Tailoring GIS software for archaeological applications: an example concerning viewshed analysis'. *Journal of Archaeological Science* 25: 27–38.

Lee, J. and Stucky, D. (1998) 'On applying viewshed analysis for determining least-cost-paths on digital elevation models'. *International Journal of Geographic Information Systems* 12: 891–905.

Llobera, M. (1999) 'Landscapes of experiences in stone: notes on a humanistic use of a GIS to study ancient landscapes'. Unpublished DPhil thesis, Oxford University.

Llobera, M. (2003) 'Extending GIS based analysis: the concept of visualscape'. *International Journal of Geographic Information Science* 1(17): 25–48.

Llobera, M., Wheatley, D. and Cox, S. (forthcoming) 'Calculating the inherent structure of a landscape (total viewsheds): high-throughput computing in archaeology'. *CAA 2004.*

Lock, G. R. and Harris, T. M. (1996) 'Danebury revisited: an Iron Age hillfort in a digital landscape', in *Anthropology, Space and Geographic Information Systems* (ed. Aldendefer, M. and Maschner, H.). Oxford: Oxford University Press, pp. 214–40.

Stoertz, C. (1997) *Ancient Landscapes of the Yorkshire Wolds: Aerial Photographic Transcription Analysis.* Swindon: Royal Commission on the Historical Monuments of England.

Tilley, C. (1994) *The Phenomenology of a Landscape.* Oxford: Berg.

Watson, A. and Keating, D. (1999) 'Architecture and sound: an acoustic analysis of megalithic monuments in prehistoric Britain'. *Antiquity* 73: 325–36.

Wheatley, D. (1995) 'Cumulative viewshed analysis: a GIS-based method for investigating intervisibility, and its archaeological application', in *Archaeology and Geographic Information Systems: A European Perspective* (ed. Lock, G. and Stančič, Z.). London: Taylor and Francis, pp. 171–86.

Part V

VIRTUAL WORLDS

8

'DIGITAL GARDENING'

An approach to simulating elements of
palaeovegetation and some implications
for the interpretation of prehistoric sites
and landscapes

Benjamin R. Gearey and Henry P. Chapman

Introduction

The study of prehistoric sites and landscapes is approached from a number
of often divergent perspectives, which tend to polarise between the essentially 'processual' (e.g. Edwards 1998) through to the 'sensual/experiential'
(e.g. Tilley 1994). This broad span of approaches to the study of the past
generates a wide range of information that although diverse, may not
always be mutually exclusive. However, attempts to integrate the different
paradigms remain few and far between and as such the potential synergy
that might result from closer integration often remains largely unrealised
(Chapman and Gearey 2000).

In this chapter, a new method is presented for the simulation and investigation of prehistoric landscapes that attempts to combine approaches from
the multi-disciplinary arena that constitutes 'landscape archaeology'. A case
study of an Iron Age lowland landscape is presented that explores the
potential for integrating 'scientific' methods and data with 'experiential'
approaches to the understanding of an archaeological site. Archaeological,
palaeoecological, topographical and hydrological data are manipulated
within a Geographical Information System (GIS) environment to explore
the palaeoenvironment of the site during its period of usage. The GIS is then
used to investigate the impacts of this reconstruction on the interpretation
of the site, compared with one which does not consider this additional data.
A 'digital narrative' approach is used to explore the two resulting landscapes in which the potential contrasts in sensual experience are examined.
It demonstrates that failure to include issues of the palaeoenvironment (cf.
Bender *et al.* 1997) may lead to incomplete interpretations of past landscapes. It is shown that, whilst palaeoecological data can never be precise
with respect to the exact location and structure of vegetation at specific

times, it is possible to explore the possible alternative explanations that such data might present. It is argued that closer communication between palaeo-ecologists and archaeologists at all stages of research might lead to a clearer understanding of the issues that might in future be fruitfully examined.

Current approaches to 'sensual' interpretations of landscape and the use of GIS

Recent archaeological approaches to the interpretation of prehistoric land-scapes have focused particularly on the understanding of 'space' and 'place', and have thus become increasingly concerned with theoretical issues. It has become recognised that the subtleties of embodied space, essentially the experience of 'being in the world', is important in the interpretation of the spatial relationships between monuments, spaces between monuments and the route ways that connect them (cf. Tilley 1994). Thus the positioning of petroglyphs might be explained through their intervisibility and viewsheds (Bradley 1993), or the interpretations of monuments might be made on the basis of the impact that natural and anthropogenic landscape features might have (cf. Thomas 1993; Tilley 1994), or the way a monument might be viewed from afar (Devereux 1991). Domestic space has similarly been examined from the perspective of exploring the views from the doorways of individual houses within a Bronze Age settlement (Bender *et al.* 1997).

The resulting approach is complex, based upon the subjective interpret-ation of observed landscape relationships, visual, spatial or otherwise. Con-clusions are drawn using perspectives based largely upon personal experience – this is the principal reason for this approach in favour of quantitative approaches. The concepts of space and place (cf. Tuan 1977) are corrobor-ated with issues of movement – 'Movement through space constructs "spatial stories", forms of narrative understanding' (Tilley 1994: 28).

There have been a number of critiques of this 'phenomenological approach' to landscape interpretation. For example, it might be argued that such approaches rely upon a particular reading of the landscape that might be contradicted in a number of pragmatic ways (Fleming 1999 contra Bender *et al.* 1997). However, this does not alter the usefulness of such humanistic and experientially based approaches to interpreting landscapes. Consequently, this should not be seen as a criticism of method, but a critique of a particular interpretation.

Computer modelling enables a visualisation of past landscapes: assessing visibility for a particular period, for example, requires the removal of modern, physical landscape components. The usefulness of being able to quantify and statistically assess visual patterns has led to developments in the spheres of computer archaeology, and particularly in the use of GIS. The potential to perform complex analyses utilising GIS has in turn led to a positive feedback into archaeological theory. Absence of any overlap in the viewsheds from various long barrows, for example, has been argued to illustrate the existence of separate territories during the Neolithic (Wheatley 1995; Lock and Harris 1996). Another study statistically examined the importance of the sea within viewsheds (Fisher *et al.* 1997), whilst Lake *et al.* (1998) tested hypotheses regarding the positioning of hunter-gatherer sites. Conversely, the use of such 'cumulative viewshed analysis' (*sensu* Wheatley 1995) has been used to identify significant 'places' as those that may be seen from a range of different monuments (cf. Llobera 1996).

Problems and potential of palaeoenvironmental reconstruction of past landscapes

Although the role of environmental archaeology in reconstructing past landscapes is well established, it remains the case that assimilating such data into broader theories of landscape such as those discussed in the previous section has been occasionally acknowledged but rarely attempted. A range of factors dictates the accuracy and precision of palaeoenvironmental inter-pretation using any given technique (e.g. Birks and Birks 1980) and it is beyond the scope of this chapter to discuss these at length. Attempts have been made in recent years to provide more robust interpretation of palyno-logical data, probably the most commonly employed technique for the reconstruction of past environments, notably through the study of pollen taphonomy and the creation of theoretical and empirical models to calcu-late vegetation source areas for pollen deposition. Many of these models exploring the relationship between pollen rain and vegetation structure have concentrated on pollen deposition in lake and forest hollow sampling sites in fully forested environments (Tauber 1967; Andersen 1970; Webb *et al.* 1981; Jackson 1990; Sugita 1993, 1994; Calcote 1995).

Although quantitative reconstructions of palaeovegetation have been attempted using these models (e.g. Bradshaw and Holmqvist 1999), the issue of directly 'reconstructing' vegetation both temporally and spatially is fraught with difficulties, not least involving scale and resolution. As Edwards (1982: 6) has observed: '. . . the various stages of palaeoecological inference represent levels of increasing abstraction and perhaps decreasing credibility.' 'Placing' vegetation in the landscape using palaeoecological data may be seen as moving towards the upper limits of this credibility. However, this does not alter the fact that such data are significant with respect to a number of issues, such as the likely effect of trees, shrubs or grassland on the human experience of 'being' in different habitats (Evans *et al.* 1999).

Working on a macroscopic scale, Bennett (1989) produced a map of the dominant woodland in the United Kingdom up to *c.* 5000 BP based on palynological data. A recent GIS-based study by Spikins (2000) adopted a different approach and considered vegetation pre-5000 BP by including a range of factors including elevation and soil type in order to predict vegetation patterns. Whilst a positive and welcome start, the value of this study for landscape interpretation was reduced by the low-resolution approach and by the lack of verification of results through primary data or through reference back to the archive of palynological studies. As such, the model remains untested. The advent of large-scale woodland clearance post-*c.* 5000 BP and the subsequent opening up of the landscape in the United Kingdom substantially increased the diversity of the landscape and vegetation mosaic. Many different habitats are reflected in the available palaeoenvironmental data, including woodland, grazed woodland pasture, arable land, wasteland, heathland and so on. Once this diversity is encountered the interpretation of the pollen record becomes even more problematic (cf. Edwards 1982) and the question becomes, for many areas, not only 'where were the trees', but also 'where was the cultivation?', 'where was the scrubland?' etc. Some recent work has begun to address this issue taphonomically (Sugita *et al.* 1999).

With respect to archaeological considerations, without a substantial network of palaeoenvironmental sampling sites it becomes very difficult to locate this vegetation 'patchiness' temporally and spatially. In some situations, the analysis of the plant macrofossil or coleopteran record from a given site alongside the pollen record can provide more specific evidence of local and extra-local vegetation (e.g. Dinnin and Brayshay 1999). Likewise, the use of 'three-dimensional' pollen diagrams has enabled a certain degree of spatial discrimination to be introduced into palaeoenvironmental reconstruction (e.g. Smith and Cloutman 1988). Even when specific vegetation units can be accurately mapped spatially and temporally, the precise physical character of this environment cannot be easily established.

Towards an integrated approach

Despite the problems outlined above, it is our contention that approaches to landscape interpretation based upon embodied space might be enhanced through a more rigorous consideration of the palaeoenvironment (Chapman and Gearey 2000; Exon *et al.* 2000). As the preceding sections have alluded, the location and character of vegetation will clearly have the potential for influencing a number of factors in the interpretation of archaeological sites and landscapes, with visibility and movement being two of the more obvious.

The general absence of effectively integrated palaeoenvironmental data is a result of the factors regarding not only the nature of palaeoenvironmental data as briefly discussed in the previous section, but also of conceptions relating to its perceived applicability and utility. 'Locating' vegetation in the palaeolandscape, for example, has rarely been attempted, with recent attempts to 'place' trees in the landscape meeting with hostility (Gaffney pers. comm.). This is due in part to the issue of credibility referred to above. Some elements of the palaeolandscape may be reconstructed with more certainty and clarity than others and certain studies have made good progress in assessing the role of landscape scale processes in prehistoric site location and human activity (Tipping *et al.* in press).

However, the general lack of integration between palaeoecology and landscape theory means that such issues are rarely addressed or debated. Moreover, this problem is seemingly exacerbated by the attitude of many archaeologists to the utility and applicability of palaeoecological data alongside the tendency of environmental archaeologists and palaeoecologists to shun the integration of 'theory' into their reconstruction of palaeolandscapes, although there are some notable exceptions to this condition (e.g. Brown 1997; McGlade 1995; Tipping *et al.* in press). This results in what may be termed the 'paradox' of environmental archaeology – the production of data essential to the understanding of past landscapes, versus its apparent insufficient accuracy for consistent and meaningful integration. Although we acknowledge the inherent difficulties with specific uses of palaeoenvironmental data, such as extrapolating from sub-fossil pollen grains preserved in sediment sequences the position and character of the vegetation from which it was derived, this should not dissuade attempts to explore both the means by which this might be attempted as well as the resulting implications for sites, landscapes and people.

The initial problem may therefore be identified as one of synthesis; identifying the best approach to combining the aims, methods and approaches of the different paradigms – the scientific versus the humanistic. This is a large and complex issue. Although the interpretation of palaeoecological data is an imperfect art and in the current state of knowledge it is not possible to be certain about the precise position of trees or the composition of vegetation communities and their changes through time, it is possible to utilise sufficiently robust data sets to provide outlines of various 'alternative' scenarios. The remainder of the chapter thus presents a case study that attempts to integrate a range of archaeological, topographical and palaeoecological data in this manner. The GIS is employed to explore these possibilities and their potential implications for 'sensual' responses to the site within its landscape context.

Sutton Common: a case study

This case study uses the site of Sutton Common, a double Iron Age enclosure situated to the north of Doncaster, UK (see Whiting 1936; Parker Pearson and Sydes 1997). This site was chosen due to the existence of a range of palaeoecological (see below), topographical (Chapman and Van de Noort 2001) and hydrological data (Van de Noort *et al.* 2001; Chapman and Cheetham 2002) and the previous identification of a 'route' through the site based upon impact and visual awareness (Parker Pearson and Sydes 1997).

The postulated Iron Age route across the site suggests that it was approached from the west through the smaller enclosure, over a causeway lying across a palaeochannel, now infilled with biogenic and minerogenic deposits, and into the larger enclosure as the final destination (Parker Pearson and Sydes 1997; Figure 8.1). The reasoning behind this lay first in the

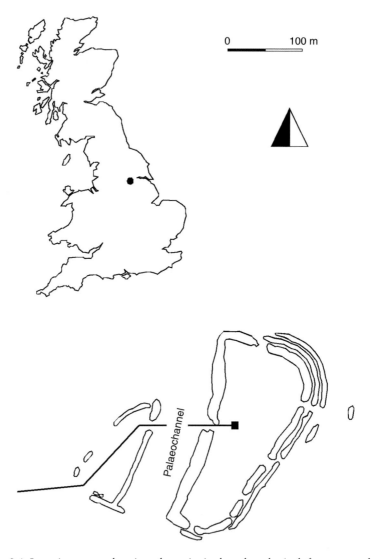

Figure 8.1 Location map showing the principal archaeological features and the route through the site as postulated by Parker Pearson and Sydes (1997).

176

arrangement of earthworks of the smaller enclosure such that a western approach would have been met by a series of 'ditch followed by bank' arrangements, typical of 'defensive' structures. Second, the various excavations at the site had identified a limestone-revetted bank on the western edge of the larger enclosure, built using stone obtained from a distance in excess of a kilometre to the west. It was argued that such a building medium within a wetland landscape reflected an attempt to provide a powerful visual component on approach to the structure. This interpretation is compelling, but hypothetical. It is not the purpose of this chapter to challenge this route, but rather to use it as a basis for the exploration of the effects of simulated vegetation.

Data and methods

The digital landscape surface

The digital landscape model was based upon a surface created from a high-resolution differential GPS survey of the earthworks and the surrounding area. A total in excess of 5,000 survey points were recorded three-dimensionally across the site at a range of resolutions in accordance with the density of archaeological features (cf. Fletcher and Spicer 1988). These data were consequently modelled within a GIS environment (ArcGIS version 8.3) to produce an interpolated digital surface of the site.[1] In addition, the Iron Age earthworks were digitally reconstructed on the basis of a previous survey (Whiting 1936) to a height of one metre above the current surface – almost certainly lower than their height during the Iron Age.[2] No account was taken of the possibility of timber constructions or other structures on top of the earthworks. The results from this process provided a digital elevation model (DEM) constructed of 'cells' each representing an area measuring 1 × 1 m, and each with an attribute relating to absolute height.

Hydrology

The recreation/regression of elements of the palaeoenvironment was based upon a series of deterministic parameters. Data relating to the highest recorded water table were already available, having been collected at 50 monitoring points (piezometers) covering an irregularly shaped study area. These data were modelled using GIS to create a second DEM at the same 1 × 1 m resolution, correct to absolute heights (see Van de Noort et al. 2001; Chapman and Cheetham 2002). In order to reconstruct areas of past wetland an increase of 0.3 m height was made to the resulting surface, providing the likely shape of the water table at a level that broadly corresponded to the vertical position of deposits containing preserved organic remains identified during excavation. No allowance was made for seasonal fluctuations. By subtracting the topographic DEM from the water table DEM, a third model was generated representing hypothetical areas and depths of standing water in the period following monument construction (Figure 8.2).

Palaeovegetation

The palaeoecological data from the site consists of pollen sequences obtained from three different contexts. The first is a radiocarbon-dated pollen diagram from nearby Shirley Pool that provides a pollen record that can be regarded as having an extra-local (*sensu* Jacobson and Bradshaw 1981) record of vegetation change (Schofield 2001). Palynological sequences through the fills of the Iron Age ditches (Bunting 1998) provide information on vegetation during the period following site construction. The pollen record from such contexts probably reflects vegetation changes in a likely radius of *c.* 50 m of the sampling site (Andersen 1970; Sugita 1994; Calcote 1995). The third context consists of the organic horizons within the palaeochannel which provide evidence of the local, wetland vegetation between the two enclosures (Lillie 1997). Further information was also available

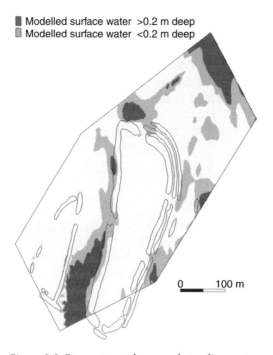

■ Modelled surface water >0.2 m deep
▫ Modelled surface water <0.2 m deep

0   100 m

Figure 8.2 Reconstructed areas of standing water on the site in relation to the two enclosures.

from work undertaken by Brayshay and Hale (in Parker Pearson and Sydes 1997) who also carried out palynological investigations at the site.

Together these data suggest that the original dryland vegetation cover of lime-oak-elm woodland had been largely cleared before or at the time the enclosures were constructed in the Iron Age. Some hazel and perhaps a little oak remained as wood/scrubland nearby, but open habitats with grass and other herbaceous communities had replaced much of the woodland cover on drier land. The pollen spectra from all three sampling contexts, however, indicate that *Alnus* (alder) remained a significant part of the local vegetation. *Alnus* dominates the pollen spectra from Shirley Pool indicating that this site was carr woodland for most of the Holocene, although there is evidence that the alder cover may have been cleared at some point during the Iron Age (Schofield 2001). All the samples from contexts closely associated with the enclosures such as ditch fills contain *Alnus* as a significant component of the vegetation on the site (up to 60 per cent total land pollen).

Certain limitations exist when inferring vegetation structure from these data, many of which are common to palynological analyses in general. The data are too imprecise to permit a reconstruction of the vegetation at a specific point in time. What can be created, however, is an abstract model of the palaeoenvironment of Sutton Common, bounded by broad, but finite, parameters. The pollen record shows that the Iron Age vegetation was not the closed woodland of the earlier Holocene – little elm, lime or oak remained locally by this time – nor was the area around the enclosures an intensively farmed landscape, such as is found in the present day. Open areas of herbaceous communities and pastureland were established on and around the site. Alder and hazel woodland were the most significant arboreal components in the vicinity, with alder the dominant taxa.

Alnus glutinosa has reasonably specific ecological preferences (McVean 1955, 1956). It will tolerate sporadic but not prolonged waterlogging, and is often found on the banks of streams and rivers, as well as in damp woodland (Orme and Coles 1985; Rackham 1995). On swampy ground alder trees grow closely together, forming an alder carr. These ecological parameters may be used to identify likely locations of alder tree stands during the Iron Age at Sutton Common, with the damper areas of soils the most probable locations of alder growth as identified as the shallow wetlands, and supported by the evidence from both the micro- and macro-fossil records. The potential areas of alder can thus be predicted from the GIS model of standing water and water depth. The heights of the DEM cells representing the topographic surface within these predicted areas of the model can then be increased randomly within the likely height parameters for alder trees (Figure 8.3), simulating the physical presence of trees within the landscape model. Other locations can be excluded, such as the interior of the enclosures, the causeway and the ditches around the site where contemporary clearance for construction had taken place (Figure 8.4).

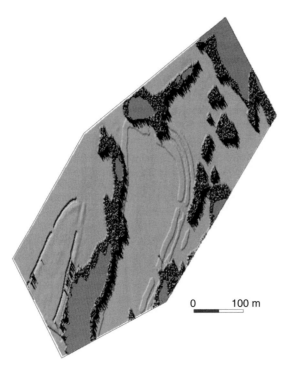

Figure 8.3 Areas of modelled alder vegetation and areas of deep water added to the reconstructed archaeological landscape.

Integration

Specific features of the archaeo-environmental record can therefore be used to regress the Sutton Common landscape towards an approximation of one possible reality of that during the Iron Age. Certain possibilities can be investigated within the bounds of what may be referred to as a 'probability envelope' for the palaeoenvironment. Whilst exact details cannot be known, it is possible to move towards an approximation of this envelope within the GIS model by defining its boundaries. In other words a 'minimum' surface (in the model) will represent the landscape with no attempted reconstruction/regression, whilst the 'maximum' surface will represent the same area including certain variables (i.e. in this case wetland extent and alder cover) established within semi-quantitative parameters. As such the following models do not purport to be strict 'reconstructions' of the landscape, but rather are produced to provide a heuristic tool that enables the exploration of the 'probability envelope'. It is likely that the 'actual' Iron Age landscape (in terms of alder vegetation and hydrology) lay somewhere between the 'minimum' and 'maximum' models. The two models may as

180

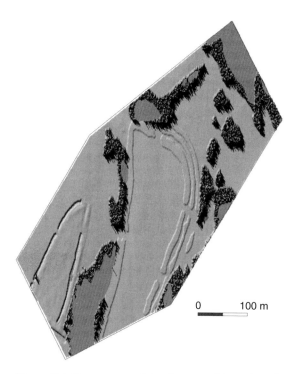

Figure 8.4 Reconstructed landscape with archaeological features cleared of alder vegetation.

such be considered as relativist tools for engaging with alternative versions of past realities.

Interpretation

To examine the effect of this 'reconstructed' vegetation on visibility patterns whilst moving through landscape, the two models can be compared and contrasted. First, the visual changes can be examined following a route through the 'minimum model': the topographic surface excluding any environmental factors (cf. Chapman 2000). Second, the same route using the same observer positions is followed but with the 'reconstructed' vegetation and surface water: the 'maximum model'. From each position, visibility was analysed from a location 1.7 m above the ground to simulate eye position. A 'digital narrative' was thus constructed for each route on the basis of changes in visibility patterns.

Narrative 1 – the 'minimum model'

Position 1 (Figure 8.5a–d): The route through the site begins inside of the smaller enclosure, within the boundary of the area of hydrological monitoring. From this location the immediate locality (the interior of the smaller enclosure), the route behind and the route in front, including most of the

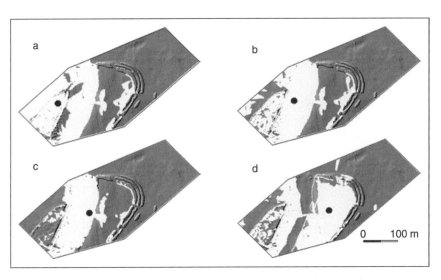

Figure 8.5a–d Changes in visibility patterns when moving through the 'minimum' landscape.

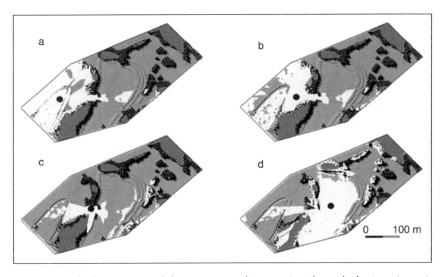

Figure 8.6a–d Changes in visibility patterns when moving through the 'maximum' landscape.

182

palaeochannel, are all visible. The western edge of the larger enclosure is clearly visible, including the white limestone revetment. The distant rows of banks marking the eastern edge of the larger enclosure are also visible on the horizon, although the view of the interior of the enclosure is restricted.

Position 2 (Figure 8.5b): Upon exiting the smaller enclosure the view to the west becomes increasingly restricted, although the view of the palaeo-channel area remains nearly complete. The limestone revetted western bank of the larger enclosure remains clearly in view and there is some visibility of the tops of the distant banks marking its eastern boundary. Its interior remains mostly out of sight except for those areas that can be seen through the entrance.

Position 3 (Figure 8.5c): Following the causeway, across the infilled palaeo-channel to approach the entrance to the larger enclosure, the viewshed becomes more restricted locally. The palaeochannel remains in view, but the view behind (to the west) decreases and the view ahead into the larger enclosure remains limited. Overall, upon approaching the larger enclosure the viewshed becomes increasingly locally focused.

Position 4 (Figure 8.5d): Once the larger enclosure is entered the viewshed becomes internally focused. Almost the whole of the interior of the enclosure is visible, although the exterior has become mostly out of sight, other than through the breaks in the enclosure banks and the western edge of the palaeochannel.

Narrative 2 – the 'maximum model'

Position 1 (Figure 8.6a): From the first position almost the entire interior of the smaller enclosure is visible, along with the area outside to the west. Part of the palaeochannel is visible, but the trees lining the edge of the deeper water restrict a complete view. The trees do not just create a barrier to the archaeology and landscape here, but also provide small pockets of invisibility concealed by them. The limestone revetment is not visible, although it is possible that an indication of this feature may have been seen through small gaps between the trees. The interior of the larger enclosure is limited to that area directly through the entrance, although the tops of the trees to the east of it are visible.

Position 2 (Figure 8.6b): Dropping down into the palaeochannel area the view behind (west) is increasingly obscured. The view along the channel to the north increases but, despite being positioned within it, the view to the north is only increased slightly compared to Position 1. There is no increased visibility of the limestone revetment and pockets between the trees remain out of sight. There is no significant change to the view of the interior of the larger enclosure destination.

Position 3 (Figure 8.6c): Just before the entrance to the larger enclosure the visible area becomes much smaller and more restricted so that only the area immediately behind and a small proportion of that in front remain within sight. More of the interior of the eastern banks of the larger enclosure is visible, although this remains limited, with a localised focus to the viewshed.

Position 4 (Figure 8.6d): Upon arriving inside the interior of the larger enclosure the visual area is restricted to a greater extent by the perimeter earthworks. This marks the 'arrival' part of the route such that none of the outside landscape may be seen other than through the entrance. This inward-looking focus is emphasised by the view to the tops of the trees on the outside.

Discussion

The narratives constructed from the changing visibility from the two scenarios present alternative understandings of the landscape. While it is perhaps stretching inference too far to suggest emotional response to changing viewsheds, a number of themes may be drawn from comparison of the two. Using the 'minimum model', the viewshed changes from clear view of the immediate area and middle distance, but with limited visibility of the destination, to an increased localisation of the areas visible as the causeway was crossed. Upon arrival within the larger enclosure the view was inward looking, with a focus on the interior. The 'maximum model' presented a similar sequence of visual 'events' with a reduction in visibility as the approach was made, resulting in an inward-looking 'arrival'. However, here the themes identified from the analysis of the 'minimum model' were exaggerated. This is particularly emphasised by the localisation of the viewshed upon the approach to the larger enclosure, where the inclusion of vegetation provides a visual barrier to much of the palaeochannel area. Similarly, upon arrival in the larger enclosure, the inward-looking view is further emphasised by visibility of the surrounding treetops – perhaps highlighting the difference between outside and inside.

The analysis of the two models raises a number of questions about the site, including the role of the white limestone revetment of the western bank of the larger enclosure. Whilst the 'minimum model' retains visibility of this feature throughout the approach to the larger enclosure, the reconstructed vegetation on the 'maximum model' substantially restricts the view. Assuming a view of this feature was important, two hypotheses may be developed: either this revetment was intended to be seen in fragmented form through the vegetation, or the trees in this area were removed.

Reconstructed vegetation appears therefore to emphasise visibility themes encountered by topography alone, but also highlights inconsistencies and raises questions through the difference observed between the two. Effectively, a 'probability envelope' has been defined between the 'maximum' and 'minimum' models of palaeoenvironmental reconstruction within the parameters of hydrology and alder coverage. Iron Age 'reality' probably lies within the 'probability envelope' somewhere between the two and, whilst this reality remains unknowable, these models provide the heuristic basis for further exploration and explanation and the erection of hypotheses.

Discussion of the method

The approach used in this study has aimed to examine the potential effect of simulated palaeovegetation on the interpretation of the archaeological remains on Sutton Common, using a postulated route through the site as a constant to provide a basis for comparison. There are a number of potential issues and limitations with such an approach. These may be classified in relation to the two principal phases of research – palaeoenvironmental reconstruction/simulation and landscape interpretation.

The simulation of the palaeolandscape is fraught with potential error and uncertainty. In terms of the archaeology, the reconstruction of the earthworks has been arbitrary, with no firm data relating to the heights of banks. Furthermore, the surrounding topography has been considered 'real' without consideration of processes including sedimentation, accretion, desiccation and compaction which will each have an influence on the morphology of the landscape.

In terms of the palaeovegetation, hydrology formed the only variable used for the predictive modelling of alder locations, and this was not considered in relation to seasonal fluctuations. Other factors that might influence the positions of vegetation include slope and aspect, and anthropogenic influences. More specifically, whilst alder appears to have been the dominant contemporary tree species, it is the only taxon that was modelled and thus the results may be considered to be limited, since other trees and shrubs, including hazel, are known from the palynological record. Whilst alder accounts for up to 60 per cent of the total land pollen (TLP), this is not directly proportional to the distribution of alder in the local vegetation. More research needs to be undertaken in order to understand exactly what pollen diagrams represent in terms of the floral distribution. Furthermore, the model simulating the vegetation was run only once.

The interpretation of the simulated landscape also has its own limitations. First, the example outlined shows the application of the method along a pre-determined pathway through the site. This has been constructed on the basis of earlier research, and upon current understanding of the site's relationship with the surrounding wetland and elements of its architecture. It is not however unequivocal and, consequently, this is just one of many possible pathways through the site. Indeed, a route postulated from an assessment of the architecture of the site is not the best starting point for beginning to interpret the architecture, as this leads to a degree of circularity. However, for the present purposes, this route served as a vehicle for exploring the application of a new approach. Other applications of GIS might suggest different routes through the landscape, such as those based on cost-surface analyses and prominence (cf. Bell and Lock 2000; Llobera 2001).

Perhaps more fundamentally, the present study has focused upon visibility to the exclusion of the role of the other senses, which limits the process of 'embodying' space as a method of interpreting archaeological landscapes. The primacy of visibility in many studies has been criticised as an imposition of inappropriate modern, western ideals (Rodaway 1994). Furthermore the role of visibility within sensual perception has been shown to be more complex than commonly thought (Wheatley and Gillings 2000).

There are clearly many uncertainties with any method aimed at integrating diverse data and approaches from contrasting paradigms. However, this should not preclude attempts to do so. Indeed, it is perhaps time to engage more with the available data rather than being overly concerned about error tolerances and the inadequacies of different data types. Where uncertainty arises it is more important to explore the available data in order to narrow down options, and this can be achieved through the development of hypothetical landscape simulation and heuristics. Within a heuristic framework these limitations are acceptable. Whilst a level of accuracy sufficient for unambiguous reconstruction cannot be achieved, the 'probability envelope' approach provides a benchmark that might be refined.

In the present study the method has been developed in order assess the potential for changes to the pattern of interpretation rather than to achieve absolute answers. GIS provide the possibility of combining various layers of data of varying accuracy that might be explored and engaged as a whole. Through such an approach it is possible to address current questions, to refine them, and to develop new ones.

Conclusions

This chapter has demonstrated the application of a method that has sought to combine data from various sources with the approaches to the study of past landscapes from disciplines that are often largely separate in terms of aims and methods. It has demonstrated some implications of including the possible distribution of vegetation, based on palaeoecological analyses. Whilst precise reconstruction of archaeological sites and their landscapes will never be possible, it is nevertheless possible to model and simulate certain components within broadly definable parameters. This approach has allowed the construction of alternative narratives and also permitted the creation of hypotheses regarding specific archaeological interpretations of the site of Sutton Common. The method illustrated here is not advocated as either the best or only approach and it is important that future work should continue to debate and investigate the possibilities that palaeolandscape simulation and digital embodiment can provide.

Notes

1 See Chapman and Van de Noort 2001 for full details of the GIS-based approach to modelling the topography of Sutton Common.
2 See Chapman 2001 for a consideration of the potential errors involved in this process.

References

Andersen, S. (1970) 'The relative pollen productivity and pollen representation of north European trees and correction factors for tree pollen spectra'. *Danmarks Geologiske Undersogelse* II 96: 1–96.

Bell, T. and Lock, G. (2000) 'Topographic and cultural influences on walking the Ridgeway in later prehistoric times' in G. Lock (ed.) *Beyond the Map: Archaeology and Spatial Technologies*. Amsterdam: IOS Press.

Bender, B., Hamilton, S. and Tilley, C. (1997) 'Leskernick: stone worlds; alternative narratives; nested landscapes'. *Proceedings of the Prehistoric Society* 63: 147–78.

Bennett, K. D. (1989) 'A provisional map of forest types for the British Isles 5,000 years ago'. *Journal of Quaternary Science* 4: 141–4.

Birks, H. J. B. and Birks H. H. (1980) *Quaternary Palaeoecology*. London: Edward Arnold.

Bradley, R. (1993) *Altering the Earth*. Edinburgh: Society of Antiquaries of Scotland Monograph Series Number 8.

Bradshaw, R. and Holmqvist, B. H. (1999) 'Danish forest development during the last 3000 years as reconstructed from regional pollen data'. *Ecography* 22: 53–62.

Brown, A. G. (1997) 'Clearance and clearings: deforestation in Neolithic Britain'. *Oxford Journal of Archaeology* 16: 133–46.

Bunting, M. J. (1998) 'Sutton Common 1998: a palynological investigation of palaeoenvironmental data preservation and potential'. Unpublished report, Department of Geography, University of Hull.

Calcote, R. (1995) 'Pollen source area and pollen productivity: evidence from forest hollows'. *Journal of Ecology* 83: 591–602.

Chapman, H. P (2000) 'Understanding wetland archaeological landscapes: GIS, environmental analysis and landscape reconstruction; pathways and narratives', in G. Lock (ed.) *Beyond the Map: Archaeology and Spatial Technologies*. Amsterdam: IOS Press.

Chapman, H. P. (2001) 'Understanding and using archaeological surveys – the "error conspiracy" ', in Z. Stančič and T. Veljanovski (eds) *Computing Archaeology for Understanding the Past – CAA2000. Computer Applications and Quantitative Methods in Archaeology*, 19–23. Oxford: BAR International Series 931: Archaeopress.

Chapman, H. P. and Cheetham J. L. (2002) 'Monitoring and modelling saturation as a proxy indicator for *in situ* preservation in wetlands: a GIS-based approach'. *Journal of Archaeological Science* 29: 277–89.

Chapman, H. P. and Gearey B. R. (2000) 'Palaeoecology and the perception of prehistoric landscapes: some comments on visual approaches to phenomenology'. *Antiquity* 74: 316–19.

Chapman, H. P. and Van de Noort. R. (2001) 'High-resolution wetland prospection, using GPS and GIS: landscape studies at Sutton Common (South Yorkshire), and Meare Village East (Somerset)'. *Journal of Archaeological Science* 28: 365–75.

Devereux, P. (1991) 'Three-dimensional aspects of apparent relationships between selected natural and artificial features within the topography of the Avebury complex'. *Antiquity* 65: 894–8.

Dinnin, M. H. and Brayshay, B. (1999) 'The contribution of a multiproxy approach in reconstructing floodplain development', in S. B. Marriott and J. Alexander (eds) *Floodplains: Interdisciplinary Approaches*. Bath: Geological Society of London Special Publication 163.

Edwards, K. J. (1982) 'Man, space and the woodland edge: speculations on the detection and interpretation of human impact in pollen profiles' in M. Bell and S. Limbrey (eds) *Archaeological Aspects of Woodland Ecology*, pp. 5–22. British Archaeological Reports International Series 146.

Edwards, K. J. (1998) 'Detection of human impact on the natural environment: palynological views', in J. Bayley (ed.) *Science in Archaeology*. London: English Heritage.

Evans, C., Pollard, J. and Knight, M (1999) 'Life in woods, tree-throws, "settlement" and forest cognition'. *Oxford Journal of Archaeology* 18: 241–54.

Exon, S., Gaffney V., Yorston R. and Woodward A. (2000) 'Stonehenge landscapes: Journeys through real-and-imagined worlds'. Oxford: Archaeopress.

Fisher, P., Farrelly C., Maddocks, A. and Ruggles, C. (1997) 'Spatial analysis of visible areas from the Bronze Age cairns of Mull'. *Journal of Archaeological Science* 24: 581–92.

Fleming, A. (1999) 'Phenomenology and the megaliths of Wales: a dreaming too far'. *Oxford Journal of Archaeology* 18: 119–25.

Fletcher, M. and Spicer, D. (1988) 'Clonehenge: an experiment with gridded and non-gridded survey data' in S. P. Q. Rahtz (ed.) *Computer and Quantitative Methods in Archaeology*, pp. 309–24. Oxford: British Archaeology Reports International Series 446(ii).

Jackson, S. T. (1990) 'Pollen source area and representation in small lakes of the north-eastern United States'. *Review of Palaeobotany and Palynology* 63: 53–76.

Jacobson, G. L. and Bradshaw, R. H. W. (1981) 'The selection of sites for palaeovegetational research'. *Quaternary Research* 16: 80–96.

Lake, M. W., Woodman, P. E. and Mithen S. J. (1998) 'Tailoring GIS software for archaeological applications: an example concerning viewshed analysis'. *Journal of Archaeological Science* 25: 27–38.

Lillie, M. (1997) 'The palaeoenvironmental survey of the Rivers Aire, Went, former Turnbridge Dike (Don north branch), and the Hampole Beck', in R. Van de Noort and S. Ellis (eds) *Wetland Heritage of the Humberhead Levels, an Archaeological Survey*, pp. 47–80. Hull: Humber Wetlands Project, University of Hull.

Llobera, M. (1996) 'Exploring the topography of mind: GIS, social space and archaeology'. *Antiquity* 70: 612–22.

Llobera, M. (2001) 'Building past landscape perception with GIS: understanding topographic prominence'. *Journal of Archaeological Science* 28: 1005–14.

Lock, G. R. and Harris T. M. (1996) 'Danebury revisited: an English Iron Age hillfort in a digital landscape', in M. Aldenderfer and H. D. G. Maschner (eds) *Anthropology, Space, and Geographic Information Systems*, pp. 214–40. Oxford: Oxford University Press.

McGlade, J. (1995) 'Archaeology and the ecodynamics of human-modified landscapes'. *Antiquity* 69: 113–32.

McVean, D. N. (1955) 'Ecology of Alnus glutinosa (L.) Gaertn. II: seed distribution and germination'. *Journal of Ecology* 43: 61–71.

McVean, D. N. (1956) 'Alnus glutinosa (L.) Gaertn.V: notes on some British alder populations'. *Journal of Ecology* 44: 321–30.

Orme, B. J. and Coles, J. M. (1985) 'Prehistoric Woodworking from the Somerset Levels: 2. Species Selection and Prehistoric Woodlands'. *Somerset Levels Papers* 11: 7–24.

Parker Pearson, M. and Sydes, R. E. (1997) 'The Iron Age enclosures and prehistoric landscape of Sutton Common, S. Yorkshire'. *Proceedings of the Prehistoric Society* 63: 221–59

Rackham, O. (1995) *Trees and Woodland in the British Landscape*. London: Weidenfeld & Nicolson.

Rodaway, P. (1994) *Sensuous Geographies*. London: Routledge.

Schofield, J. E. (2001) 'Vegetation succession in the Humber wetlands'. Unpublished PhD thesis, University of Hull.

Smith, A. G. and Cloutman, E. W. (1988) 'Reconstruction of Holocene vegetation and history in three dimensions at Waun-Fignen-Felen, an upland site in South Wales'. *Philosophical Transactions of the Royal Society of London* B322: 159–219.

Spikins, P. (2000) 'GIS models of past vegetation: an example from northern England, 10,000–5000 BP'. *Journal of Archaeological Science* 27: 219–34.

Sugita, S. (1993) 'A model of pollen source area for an entire lake surface. *Quaternary Research* 39: 239–44.

Sugita, S. (1994) 'Pollen representation of vegetation in Quaternary sediments: theory and method in patchy vegetation'. *Journal of Ecology* 82: 881–97.

Suigita, S., Gaillard, M.-J. and Bostrom, A. (1999) 'Landscape openness and pollen records: a simulation approach'. *The Holocene* 9: 409–21.

Tauber, H. (1967) 'Investigations of the mode of pollen transfer in forested areas'. *Review of Palaeobotany and Palynology* 3: 277–86.

Thomas, J. (1993) 'The politics of vision and the archaeologies of landscape', in B. Bender (ed.) *Landscape: Politics and Perspectives*. Oxford: Berg.

Tilley, C. (1994) *A Phenomenology of Landscape. Places, Paths and Monuments*. Oxford: Berg.

Tuan, Y.-F. (1977) *Space and Place: The Perspective of Experience*. London: Edward Arnold.

Van de Noort, R., Chapman, H. P. and Cheetham, J. L. (2001) '*In situ* preservation as a dynamic process: the example of Sutton Common, UK'. *Antiquity* 75: 94–100.

Webb, T. III, Howe S. E., Bradshaw, R. H. W. and Heide, K. M. (1981) 'Estimating plant abundances from pollen percentages: the use of regression analysis'. *Review of Palaeobotany and Palynology* 34: 269–300.

Wheatley, D. (1995) 'Cumulative viewshed analysis: a GIS-based method for investigating intervisibility, and its archaeological application', in G. Lock and Z. Stančič (eds) *Archaeology and Geographical Information Systems: A European Perspective*, pp. 171–85. London: Taylor & Francis.

Wheatley, D. and Gillings, M. (2000) 'Vision, perception and GIS: developing enriched approaches to the study of archaeological visibility', in G. Lock (ed.) *Beyond the Map: Archaeology and Spatial Technologies*. Amsterdam: IOS Press.

Whiting, C. E. (1936) 'Excavations at Sutton Common 1933, 1934 and 1935'. *Yorkshire Archaeological Journal* 33: 57–80.

9

AT THE EDGES OF THE LENS

Photography, graphical constructions and cinematography

Graeme P. Earl

Archaeological sites, whether real or virtual, are not passive places. To work on an excavation or survey is to become physically and emotionally involved with landscapes, themselves sedimented in contextual practice. This chapter has been based largely on fieldwork in southern Spain and at the site of Quseir al-Qadim[1] in Egypt, and is as such a product of these places and experiences. It is now commonplace to associate archaeological practice with such experience and with the unfolding and development of narratives (see, for example, Joyce 2002; Schrire 1995). As the surveyor stands at the total station or wanders with the staff, so the landscape is defined by looking up and down and striding a fixed distance; as the geophysicist walks line after line so the landscape is partitioned into grids and transects, positive and negative, black and white; as the excavator cuts through a feature, the feature is created anew and named; as the computer specialist pins trench plans to AutoCAD like butterflies so the place planned becomes one of Cartesian spaces. Finally, the graphical reconstructors of the past draw on these experiences, where accessible, and present a solidified, modelled world to be consumed or explored, itself constrained by the structures and metaphors of computational technology.

The archaeological computer graphics literature has wrestled with the process of reconstruction and its relationship to these archaeological activities for many years, with the process given a definition in 'virtual archaeology' by Reilly in 1990 (1991). A key debate has been the power of the computer image to deceive and the requirement to authenticate. I wish to argue that while authentication is important in terms of data-linked-to-model, so too are critiques of the visual deceits used in reconstruction work, the environment in which they are consumed, and the complex processes, beyond the data, implicated in their construction.

Over the last decade computer graphics technologies have blossomed in the media. Films such as *Terminator 2* showed the potential beauty of computerised models and within ever shorter spaces of time the methods showcased on our screens (Bizony 2001) have become available on our desktops. More recent films provide a visual spectacle in which the computerised elements are for the most part indistinguishable from elements produced by other techniques. Considerable attempts are made to conceal the constructed nature of Computer Graphic Imagery by association with more traditional, less precise techniques (Brooker 2003: 298–9). It is this assimilation of graphical techniques within a familiar context – the framed, intercut cinematic experience – that empowers the technology. Similarly, in the use of photographic stills, attempts to match contrast and grain to matte imagery (seen extensively in architectural modelling), aim to incorporate reconstructed elements seamlessly within a photograph. This ostensibly calls for a reading of the model as captured reality and consumption as a photographic image. Such techniques are powerful but problematic for those attempting to critique representations of the past that incorporate them (see Zubrow this volume).

Archaeology's use of such methods began in collaborative projects with consultants and/or computer scientists, with graphics techniques being applied to archaeological data, in order to extend and embellish internal visions of the archaeological past. Later, a growing corpus of computerised archaeological visual reconstructions of sites appeared over the flourishing Internet while television documentaries began to use graphics as a matter of course to convey the frequently complex spatial arrangements previously left to the conventional reconstruction painting: the medium in many cases setting up a dichotomy between computed visualisations of fact, and painted or drawn interpretations of the data with a basis in style and emotion. Archaeological computer graphics, seen in some cases to present a virtually real past, often existed without critique or explanation, conflated periods, data and interpretations, and were directed by aesthetic choices (exemplified in a criticism levelled by Frischer *et al.* (2001) at Forte and Siliotti's *Virtual Archaeology* (1997); see also Huggett and Guo-Yuan 2000; Miller and Richards 1995).

The world of archaeological computer graphics has changed and developed. The dichotomies between theoretical and presentational graphics that previously appeared so clear-cut now spread across a broad spectrum. Much attention has been paid to reflexive and transparent methodologies for presenting the past (Pollard and Gillings 1998; Earl and Wheatley 2001; Eiteljorg 2000), how construction of pasts demonstrates and impacts the interpretative process as it unfolds (Barceló 2000), and indeed what it is to construct graphical pasts (Gillings 2000). The broader questions have moved more closely to parallel those raised in wider contexts. How can we explore space and movement amongst and between our archaeological worlds? How can the ways in which we represent spaces define our understanding and that of those less constrained by archaeological rhetoric? What if anything is the real value of three-dimensional computer modelling to archaeology? If there is value, what are the problems which must be addressed? Finally, can a set of computational methodologies overcome these problems and offer value to the archaeologist?

It seems that computation does not hold all of the answers. Moser has considered in great detail the construction of specific archaeological knowledge through visual media, demonstrating how complex the issues are. In the introduction to *Ancestral Images* she states that:

> [e]ssentially these images have been taken for granted. They have been seen as unproblematic and self explanatory rather than as complex documents which drew on a range of pictorial devices in order to create meaning. The major reason why reconstructions have been neglected as a subject worthy of study is that they have been perceived as divorced from the serious practice of science.
>
> (Moser 1998: 1–2)

Such imagery is pervasive and we might all identify the considerable range of representational devices through which our envisioning of the past has been shaped. In the case of the Roman reconstructions on which my work concentrates, the list of visual stimuli goes ever onward, drawing from children's books, visits to sites, film, television, plays, and time spent surrounded by and working with classical architecture. Although the technology used to build computer graphic models from such experience moves on, it does so seeking focus from its history and from the environment within which technological processes are exacted. Our literature has discussed the dangers of computing dictating archaeological process – as the epithet goes, tools in desperate search for applications – and this remains a valid criticism in many cases. However, broader issues providing the context for the production and use of archaeological images have been considered to a lesser degree in the computational literature. Use of graphics is certainly problematic but equally offers considerable potential in terms both of representing archaeological thought and impacting it. Different questions may need to be asked, beginning perhaps with whether one might ever consider illustration to be *dangerous* (distorting an empirical, extant, objective reality measured in lines and correlates) and whether *aesthetic* choices are in themselves inferior to objectified, authentic visualisations. Perhaps we have buckled ourselves into straitjackets, based on empirical affirmation of process, which no computer artist would recognise. As Wheatley noted in a paper at CAA in 1996:

> The disparaging of such techniques as animated walk-through and photorealistic rendering is misguided, and based on an irrational avoidance of aesthetic and personal experience.
>
> (2000: 126)

The perceived transition from artist to technician in the early stages of graphics technologies' adoption seems to have produced a mutual distrust and avoidance that survives even now. The continuing reality of this distinction is most clearly defined in the introduction to the largest collection of academic papers on computer reconstruction in archaeology to date. The authors divide representations between artistic *illustration* which is:

> not an explanation of the past, but a personal and subjective way of seeing it' and a virtual model which is 'a representation of some ... features of a concrete or abstract entity'. Visualisation is thus the 'mapping of abstract quantities into graphical representations ... We should not create wonderful imaginative illustrations of the past, but should use geometry to explain some properties of the data set.
>
> (Barceló *et al.* 2000: 9–10)

The term 'visualisation' carries with it the sense of a graphical externalising of data held within a computer – a duplicate able to utilise visual response to convey facts. However, virtual archaeology does not attempt to imitate reality (or to be based on translating real data into real images) but instead defines the *simulation* of aspects of reality as a sensual form of communication. We are well versed in the interpretation of sensual information and it is this precisely that virtual reality and other forms of graphical representation may stimulate (Brody 1991; Carr and England 1995; Heim 1993; but also Edgar and Bex 1995: 94–6; Wann *et al.* 1995). However, much of our literature implies that virtual reconstructions create living worlds from otherwise dead data, monolithic worlds in which the newly recovered past becomes open to interpretation, summarised and clarified – in essence a visual time machine (Sanders 1999). This is at its most extreme in relationships between text and virtual archaeologies published on the Internet. Reconstruction then is to be the impressive end-product of a scientifically rigorous process of archaeological data mining, resulting in visualisation of a past recovered from that information. This association between computation and objectified science is pervasive and in computer graphics tends towards a readiness to accept computer reconstructions from a less critical stance than artist's impressions. In truth, a great many of the reconstructions discussed to date involve a considerably less interpretatively dedicated approach than that of, for example, Sorrell (1981) or James (1993) – exemplars of the potential to combine uncertainty, the nature of archaeological evidence, emotion and professional obligation.

Graphics and the photographic metaphor

If we accept that the creation of archaeological reconstructions has as one ultimate aim the definition of specific views then as modellers we have much to learn both from existing visual art forms and from work in human computer interfaces. In photography we have an interesting correlate to archaeological computer graphics, particularly if we accept the inherent difficulties of our rigorous discipline and start to look upon ourselves as artists as much as scientists. Clarke describes Niépce's first photograph, characterised by its 'ambiguity . . . crude format and poor quality' as 'not so much an image as an archaeological fragment' (1997: 12). Such questions of ambiguity and interpretative potential are fundamental to our reconstruction project, with the photographic literature having already dealt in depth with key issues relevant to archaeological modellers: approaches such as sequentially documenting the process of reconstruction through a series of images have been represented in the photographic canon for decades, particularly in photographic art installations.

The importance of such techniques lies in their demonstration of the authorship of the image: its personality. The photograph provides a snapshot – an unchanging point in time defined by the specific, if contingent, choices of the photographer – and various attempts are made to approach this subjectivity. In turn this personal significance is seen to be of increasing value to archaeology (Bateman 2000; Shanks 1997). At Quseir al-Qadim photographs record/define the excavation but the medium also serves to document the daily life of those photographed and, by association, those whose photographs are collected. Through photographic critique (Hamilton 1997: 99) it becomes clear that our archaeological record shots, our snaps and our portraits are imbued by the feelings and knowledge of their photographers, and that this must be considered as the background to the conscious colouring, framing, orientation and other decisions which define them: for example, the varied saturation and contrast in lighting and focus used to define the complexity and subtlety of a scene (Brooker's 'positive and negative space' – 2003: 293). In addition, by understanding a body of photographic work in the light of a perceived pervading cultural influence the interrelationship between photograph and culture might also be explored.

A photograph, then, does not portray the life in a person, rather it portrays the life as desired or as understood by the photographer, and mediated through the performance of photography. To Barthes the photograph is disturbing, being the 'advent of myself as other: a cunning disassociation of consciousness from identity' (1993: 12). Any photograph, not merely portraiture, is as framed as a portrait and as Shanks notes, 'photography and drawing are constituted by interest' (1997: 76). In learning practical photography we are taught that emotion can be defined in this disassociative process simply through lighting and angle: arrogance and diffidence may be defined in turn by lowered lighting and a low angled lens, and by bright ambient light. In part this is seen in professional CGI[2] in the application of photographic norms: the rule of thirds used in photography, painting and cinematography is now seen extensively in professional graphics. What is seen far less is the deliberate subversion of normalising styles, such as the definite symmetry seen in some urban photography.

Archaeologists adopt photographic techniques in a number of ways. First, in the direct creation or critique of archaeological photographs. Second, in the incorporation of photographic images in CGI composites, whether as mattes or textures. Third, the virtual camera uses photographic and cinematographic metaphors and is constrained by them. Finally, photographs are created and distorted to create photomontage or panoramas. The last of these, the ever-increasing range of interactive photographs (Cummings 2000; Edmonds and McElearney 1999; Gidlow 2001; Goodrick 1999), demonstrates the pervasiveness of established photographic techniques. A digital panorama remains framed and constrained by choice and methodology – but the framing is obscured by the novelty of the approach. Thus, a representation of a given *scene* viewed in a bubble has all the restrictions present in the stitched originals (or in the mirror and lens technology if a one-shot approach is used). The viewer remains at a fixed point and the landscape as viewed is a construct of the complex optical and decision-making process barring the viewer, through the viewed, from the implied reality. Those with rapid web access will be familiar with the spin panorama style, and its spatial metaphors. However, it is noticeable that those who have not come into contact with such images are surprised as the photograph seamlessly translates into rotating view. Indeed we see this technique employed deliberately in presentations – the unexpected visual – but the depth of this impression, although powerful, will be short-lived. It is seldom that archaeological graphics attempt to introduce visual variety in this way, or in a different meaning defined perhaps as Barthes' photographic 'surprise' (1993) or by Eco (1982). When successful such elements *force* an appreciation of the constructed nature of the image, although this does not seem to be the stimulus to the proliferation of archaeological bubbles.

Once learned, the style of a representative system such as the bubble world is exploited more broadly, as the rules defining its reality become clear. The black and white photograph reveals the complexity of this process. Clarke believes that this represents 'the way in which the "realism" of photography is part of a structure of illusion to which we accede' (1997: 23). In making my combined photographic and CGI views of Quseir I have made black and white the dominant format for what I considered as a simple aesthetic choice and in order to situate reconstruction within modes of critique understood in terms of the photograph. However, one might argue that in producing images in the professional genre, excepted by those using colour specifically to challenge modes of representation and consumption (for example Cornell – see Jeffrey 1981: 228), I failed in my interest in making the subjectivity of my work more apparent. Photography and photorealist CGI is thus a realm of contradictions – the image presents varying levels of interpretation including a view of the point of focus as recorded and at the same time the solidification of this pattern of light as the result of technology, choice, and power (Wolff 1993).

> [T]he photograph, for all its capacity to reproduce the literal, retains the values and hierarchies so much associated with what might be viewed as its opposite: academic painting . . . Any photograph is dependent on a series of historical, cultural, social and technical contexts, which establish its meanings as an image and as an object.
>
> (Clarke 1997: 18–19)

The context of consumption is key to the photograph: the distinction, to use Clarke's example, between a photograph withdrawn from a wallet, magazine prints on varying 'qualities' of paper or as a part of a contact print (1997: 19). The context here is one of reproduction, modes and environments defining the object reproduced (Benjamin 1936, discussed in Bateman 2000), with representations incorporating previous ways of seeing – previous representations and expressions of accepted fact. For these reasons Molyneaux (1997) calls for study and documentation of the context of image production (see Hall 1997: 25). In archaeological reconstruction terms the context of production and consumption references the choice of representative forms such as hypermedia, the variety of museum display, accompaniments to documentaries or texts, and archaeological graphics presented as art. In each of these it is possible to identify trends in the visual styles, without suggesting that such context should constrain the range of attempts made to convey the variety of archaeological practice through CGI.[3] The familiar cut-away model or the variously faded architectural images are ways traditionally associated with presenting the spatial form alongside, for example, a description of a given excavation. However, this convention should not prohibit a photorealistic rendering or composite piece. One may recognise here a static imposition of style in technological representation that is far less apparent in the diversity of painted or drawn images used to illustrate our discipline. In general our digital paint box is far more diverse than that currently employed, and far less open to diversity than the real canvas of our counterparts.

The artist Alan Sorrell believed firmly in the power of the image and the importance of attractive imagery – not stripped bare but rather imbued, blossoming, hazy and at the same time real (Sorrell 1981). Following Sorrell then, I suggest that an *engaging* scene must be provided before we can make room for imagination – there is some undefined level of detail/visual excitement from which our extrapolation grows to a degree *in accordance* with that prescribed by the artist. In the most part current virtual worlds, by comparison, are closer to the architectural sketch or schematic; they encourage a different form of consumption, perhaps less clearly defined, tied in only to the vocabulary of line and shade. But in leaving this imaginative latitude should we stop short of photography? In other words, should photorealistic reconstruction be tempered?

Unfolding through a number of articles the photorealism debate considers the power of the image to deceive and the dangers inherent in a technology that can make appear real what is in fact based on supposition, one rationale being that enhanced data might logically provide for enhanced visual fidelity. The debate considers a variety of means to represent uncertainty and thus to limit the deception, making for a *transparent* construction methodology (Forte 2000). Compositional (at times confrontational) modes of representation might be useful tools in the *authenticated* construction of archaeological pasts.[4] These employ realistic techniques but incorporate, for example, other images to demonstrate some of the underlying stimuli to the reconstruction. In making such deviations from traditional photorealistic imagery, powerful as they can be, the aim is to expose the modes of representation to critique rather than as specific indications of the relationship between fact and model (Eiteljorg 2000; Pletinckx *et al.* 2001). This is not a semantic distinction: the latter attempts to distinguish model elements on grounds of process certainty – a visual map of how authentic a reconstruction is – whilst the former highlights the constructed nature of the image itself. It defies the idea that an authenticated archaeological reconstruction can exist, except with the symbolic terms read from a particular image. These terms, clearly situated in cultural context, act very differently depending on their mode and locus of consumption.

Methodologically based authenticating strategies are open to debate. Taken to its extreme, one might argue that to authenticate a painted reconstruction one must buy paint and canvas, carry out research, learn to paint, and then paint it. Conversely, if the choice was rather not to authenticate visually, or to use visual means to emphasise the contingent processes rather than the perceived truth, then the artist's skill and knowledge are allowed to wash over us whilst the consumer considers the information available to him or her. We accept that much of the image will be based on subjective decision-making but we welcome this, and move on. Again at the extreme we see that to produce a variety of images in order to convey uncertainty behind the components of an illustration suggests that by so doing the process is made transparent: to produce a variety of images to convey uncertainty in the use of the same components suggests that the process can never be transparent. This is worrying to those of us who consider reconstruction modelling to be both interpretatively useful and a powerful means for presenting the specifics of archaeological practice. Essentially we are required to accept the contingent nature of the production of our models: that to show all of the conflicting information available is an impossible project, and that by attempting it the modeller will produce an image restricting the engagement with itself at the heart of the visual reconstruction project.

The argument remains an important one in the light of the various attempts to show links between data and images. It allows the multiple conventional reconstructions of James (1997) and related CGI attempts (Junyent and Lores 2000; Roberts and Ryan 1997; Ryan 1996) to be considered in tandem, crucially providing for the incorporation of the most realistic graphical techniques, whilst emphasising that models do not authenticate, in the sense of providing a reversible route between data and views. Of course, successful authentication strategies are of profound benefit to the modelling endeavour and represent the contingency of models on archaeological assumption and choice (Frischer *et al.* 2000; Kantner 2000; Ryan 2001).

> There is nothing wrong in going from o to Constantinopolis, or in presenting, within the same model, alternative views of how the site might have originally looked. To the contrary. The important part is that when we add information beyond what is archaeologically attested we need to flag our supplements or alternatives interpretation of the data by means of signs.
>
> (Frischer *et al.* 2001: 8)

I do not suggest that this be ignored. Rather that, in the way authentication has been represented and critiqued in the painted and drawn reconstruction literature (for example Adkins and Adkins 1989), the means to indicate the origin of our reconstructions need not always detract from the visual impact of the images themselves. It is after all a problem wrestled with in art, photography and cinematography: each frequently producing a divergent set of responses. Photorealist artists such as Estes take many photographs of their subject from different angles and distances, using them to define the scene as appropriate, perhaps even projecting one of the images onto the canvas. A three-dimensional understanding of the space is constructed via the many angles represented in the photographs, with this space redefined in two-dimensional form in the finished product. In photorealist works then the photographs are used to capture a moment (Barthes' *death* – 1993), in terms of otherwise changing shadows and colour, motion of objects and people, and a concentration on extreme detail viewable in any sequence and over an extended period of time. In a similar way, archaeological reconstructions use images of objects and scenes in the world around the modeller to create a three-dimensional space. This is then transformed via collage of archaeological data, through practice. Photorealism attempts to confront the distinction between photographic production as process and painting as interpretation and semiology. In their frequent depiction of conventionally mundane subjects photorealists present images to be consumed and not analysed. Alternative approaches incorporate different effects emphasising the construction of realities, introducing aberrations into otherwise realistic portrayals. Similarly, photography attempts to deconstruct these standard modes of presentation: the manipulative landscape photography of Uelsmann or abstract, extreme urban photography using high contrast and unusual compositions or views.

Cinematography and animation

A belief that the contingent nature of graphical reconstructions makes them irreducible to component motivations and data does not preclude their critique. Moving to look at cinematography I would suggest that reconstruction animations may benefit from its principles and informed by its theory.

> Cinematography is the process of taking ideas, words, actions, emotional subtext, tone and all other forms of non-verbal communication and *rendering them in visual terms*.
>
> (Brown 2002: ix; original emphasis)

Cinematography provides a diversity of experience in the definition of artificial imagery, movement through landscape and also in the critique of those views. The film style is one that is understood in context, hence the considerable efforts seen specifically to subvert audience perception through variation from the cinematic norms. What we must consider is whether archaeology should fear the incorporation of cinematic devices (and their attendant influence) in the presentation of pasts, and indeed whether the cinematographer should be encouraged in it. Bateman has argued that the presentation of archaeological pasts adopting the metaphors and styles of film 'enables the objectification of the archaeological material through the technologically mediated separation from its production' (2000: 4). However, the consumption of the image may be such that the significance of this separation is illusory: the production of film being better understood than perhaps any other contemporary artform, with *behind the scenes* (and Barthes' *off camera*) key to the creation of film-going culture. In effect we need to consider the iconography of the film image in the same depth as the content and the genre as a whole (see, for example, Carnes *et al.* 1995; Wyke 1997).

The cinematography of the archaeological reconstruction image is *generally* the cinematography of spinning buildings on flat landscapes, of steady camera trucks or dollies, rapid zooms into and through unoccupied, clinical buildings. The over-use of diverse camera movement, coupled with non-cinematic approaches, detract from the power and interest of otherwise engaging archaeological visuals. The common oblique aerial shots (the 'reading perspective' – Ihde 1993 quoted in Gillings 2000) seem more to demonstrate the full detail of the models produced (at best, their form and context) than to serve a useful archaeological purpose. A sense of being in the landscape does not proceed from such detached views, unless one is interested for example in alternative modes of representation such as the shamanic or of some folkloric descriptions.[5]

This detachment of animated view from past space underpins much of the interest in interactive methodologies such as VRML[6] or its high-end virtual reality counterparts. A distinction is established between the definition of animated or static views (often staid and un-engaging) and virtual reality, but there is a place for both techniques (Goodrick and Earl 2003). In this consideration of the uses of film metaphors I would go further and suggest that the distinction between the two is in many cases very small. An unconstrained virtual reality world does not create a situated GIS or a mode of landscape experience – it is a three-dimensional mapping, defining a Cartesian landscape (Cosgrove and Daniels 1988; Gillings and Goodrick 1996; Hearnshaw and Unwin 1994). The VR we come across in archaeological contexts is usually limited to a particular human observer – height, field of view, depth of field if the technology allows, and further depth cues. Navigation without constraint, far from defining infinite free perception of the environment, leads to confusion and an inhibited sense of space. This does not restrict the creativity of virtual reality projects (see examples in Heim 1998) but rather determines one aspect of their perception.

Perception in virtual reality is a complex web of theoretical and practical issues (Gillings 1999; Heim 1993). Practically the virtual camera metaphor, seen in the virtual realities I have found available to the archaeologist, offers the multimedia director limited options. To gain the benefits of VR one must feel present in the scene and, where the technology does not provide a sufficient equivalence to perception in reality, an equivalence to the aberrations of the lens may act as a suitable alternative. This is able to draw upon existing techniques and also avoids in part Heim's notion of 'data idealism' – the 'idealism that equates reality with bytes and equates being with being digital' (1998: 139–40; Ellis 1995: 17–18). The world explored here is a construction and is perceived through some form of lens and indeed many archaeological virtual environments incorporate a considerable number of predefined viewpoints and sequences between these – an attempt to ensure that particular views and movements defined as important by the modeller are appreciated by the observer. Such predefined viewpoints *can* be exploited to considerable effect, offering a pre-constructed (not essentially linear) narrative sequence with the option to intercut or spatially link each successive orientation. Still, given a limited sample of the archaeological virtual reality models available online, the motivation seems frequently to be a means of limiting the very real problems of virtual navigation.

Construction of models in any system and for any output format involves constant, active engagement with the spaces modelled and the information drawn upon. Having produced a complex model the modeller is intimately familiar with the spatial relationships of the scene modelled. VR provides an interface through which others may approach a similar experience, but as I have suggested above, in order truly to experience the modelling processor one should be able to model. Ideally one might present, for example, visitors to a museum with an easy to use interface[7] for building a model and let them use it. Providing a VRML or other scene derived from this reconstruction process does not make it any more transparent – particularly if the VR system is indeed as constrained in many respects as its predefined, animated counterparts. The most fluid means of achieving a virtual experience would seem to be to create the model oneself, and even then one remains constrained to the technology. In this sense, the greatest trick the virtual camera pulls is to convince us that it does not exist – that it is in some way a neutral interface between a physically modelled world and an eye.

Cubitt (1998) argues that the computer, whether in VR or animation, offers the chance to produce a seamless narrative (a succession of vistas, interactions and modifications requiring no inter-cutting). This is the continuous pan, so revolutionary to the audience of Hitchcock, replicated with ease on a computer workstation and stripped of its carefully orchestrated impact. Such a linear stream of information is one to which we remain unused, both in our perception of the living world and as constructed via photography and cinema. Cinematography is there to project the personal onto a sheet of canvas or phosphorescent glass, via a format using preceding and following images as keys to the definition of the tone of those they surround. The director is reliant on the cinematographer for the translation of an imagined scene into a filmed *sequence* and the audience is familiar with the format. To follow the film camera through a real or virtual landscape (seen as a 'hideout', rather than a 'frame' for life – Barthes 1993), to employ rack focus to associate and disassociate subject and background, to rest just the *right* number of seconds on a passer-by; all this is to define places in which the characters and places we interact with live on, and lived before. The history of the scenes and their futures are in a sense made accessible through the motion of the camera. The virtual camera pretending to be the film lens of the camera deserves similar thought but it is far harder to breathe life into a faceted, simply shaded and lit world than a beautifully rendered and animated model. I suggest that when the virtual camera tries to be our eye (problematic given much perceptual theory) it confronts us with the truth of what we are doing – as the film implies a life outside (that actors walk on from somewhere and off to somewhere else; that places are occupied and used in different ways when the film crew leave) so the virtual world proves that there is no life at all, other than that constructed for us.

Conclusions

The very metaphor of the still or movie camera influences the subsequent views created. This influence is more pervasive than in reality since the camera is not a mediator with some abstracted, real world but is in fact the creator of a wholly digital landscape. Architectural theorists and practitioners (for example Ching 1996) have long recognised this stylistic/ technical impact. Lefebvre suggests that it is the medium and the style (incorporating linear perspective) which define the internalised spaces from which, in turn, the architect's designs emerge and are committed to paper:

> Within the spatial practice of modern society, the architect ensconces himself in his own space. He has a *representation of this space*, one which is bound to graphic elements – to sheets of paper, plans, elevations, sections, perspective views of facades, modules and so on. This conceived space is thought by those who make use of it to be true, despite the fact – or perhaps because of the fact – that it is geometrical: because it is a medium of objects, an object itself, and a locus for the objectification of plans.
>
> (Leach 1997: 144; original emphasis)

The computers upon which graphical pasts are constructed are masters of linear perspective – creating space in the terms of Lefebvre's architect: defining and at the same time defined by the medium.[8] By using linear perspective we are further complicating the archaeological aesthetic. Not only is the practice of producing reconstruction models cultural, but it is compounded by visual critique of subjects constructed in depth via Western principles 500 years old, through Western eyes attuned to the artistic, cinematic and photographic aesthetics of the last 200 years.

The perspective of the computer then is at variance from that of the painter. Perspective is generated via the computer modelling process whilst the painted image is defined by its *variance* from the rules. We have decided to use linear perspective. It is neither correct nor incorrect. It is, in Wartofsky's terms, defined by 'the theory of pictorial representation that we came to adopt' (1979: 274; Gillings 2000: 60) and when followed blindly fails in its project to represent reality. Whilst Da Vinci trained painters by abstracting depth as seen in the terms of linear perspective via a marked glass plate, the plate was not itself used in the production of the painting. The monitor and the software are inescapable plate and canvas combined, but other aspects of the modelling process are open to manipulation. Visual art is defined by varied adherence to rules, upon which the representative iconography (Moser 2001) builds. Those who understand the rules can break them effectively and with impact, but this requires the existence of the rules, their general application and their consumption by others versed if not in the rules themselves then in the subconscious appreciation of them. This alone is justification enough for archaeological modellers considering the photography, illustration and cinematography which together define much of the environment in which their work will be consumed, and the rules of which, when broken successfully, serve directly to impact the viewer or to enhance their awareness of the complex representative processes at work.

Archaeological graphics have drawn extensively upon the literature of computation but comparatively little on the extensive representation theories and upon cinematography and photography. I have suggested that these disciplines have much to offer both in terms of new ways for constructing our reconstruction graphics and for critiquing their style and representational impact. I have argued that, certainly in its earliest incarnations, archaeological reconstruction offered a succession of spinning views and rapid pans which served to objectify scenes and to distance the observer within an unnatural and unfamiliar visual environment. It seems to me only rarely that the modeller considers the specific emotional impact of the views generated of their models. Still, this chapter should not be read as a criticism of archaeological reconstruction practice. Considerable practical restrictions are faced by the archaeological modeller and ours is a relatively young discipline (Frischer *et al.* 2001), with the availability of technology having seen a sudden and rapid increase only in the last few years. Animation software now falls within the budgetary constraints of many archaeological institutions and consultancies, and its hardware requirements are becoming more realistic; but visually stunning graphics takes work. A scene might contain 50 lights and atmospheric effects, render times of many hours, and diverse post-production filters. The question is whether the output better satisfies the archaeologist's own impression of the place they are defining, and as such is a justified endeavour.

Adopting cinematic or photographic principles, and employing the wide range of CGI techniques necessary to stimulate us visually may be beyond the archaeologist, and we should not perhaps be surprised or disheartened by this. I look forward to the archaeologies that may result from development at the interfaces and from collaboration, including an opening out of our archaeological computing milieu. One might envisage greater variation in the imagery we produce and engage with, including perhaps collaged museum displays with composited images, animations, architectural renderings and the reconstruction data matched and focused in the reconstruction images – an insight into the contextualised production of a past view, framed in the languages of photography and cinema, to be read as a created object rather than as a computed reality. Still, I wonder whether, despite our knowledge of representation and of archaeological process, of perspective and the surprise, of changing light and absorbing, cultured ways of seeing, we must accept that the final consumption, distortion and appropriation of the images we produce are beyond our influence, and are all the better for it.

Notes

1 The Quseir al-Qadim project had its first season in 1999. It is based around excavation of Quseir al-Qadim (literally old Quseir), a site nine kilometres from modern Quseir on Egypt's Red Sea coast. In addition to the extensive remains of the late Ayyubid/Mamluk occupation of the site in the medieval period, recent excavation has identified the Roman port on the site as Myos Hormos, a key axis for the Roman Eastern trade (see http://www.arch.soton.ac.uk/Research/Quseir). Since then a further four seasons have been completed, in addition to extensive additional work by members of the Quseir Community Archaeology Project (Moser *et al.* 2002), and further work is planned. The majority of the digital work was carried out by myself, and as a result Quseir presented the ideal site for me to develop and implement a variety of visualisation techniques. I became interested in the creation of archaeological fictions surrounding Qusier, with graphical (re)construction requiring imagination and extrapolation, the creation of simulacra, contingent on personal and academic experience.

2 Computer Graphic Imagery.

3 The cinematographic and photographic principles discussed here are drawn from a largely First World context and in what is to come in three-dimensional modelling this significant impact must be addressed. In ongoing work in Egypt the question of how a reconstruction is understood has become a key element. Given the emphasis of the CGI aesthetic on a particular, narrow subset of visual symbology (in particular the metaphors of linear perspective, camera motion and architectural sketch), attempting to express personal spatial perceptions to an audience unfamiliar with such styles and unused to decoding their representational structures is complex and requires critique, but again we might ask how the drawings by our illustrators operate in Egypt. We have only begun to consider the representational traditions at work in the local community at Quseir from which many of my images derive, and also the diverse impact of the eventual (web or museum) consumption of them. The appropriate methodology would seem to be an inclusive one in which those consumers of modelled pasts play an active role in their externalisation, or indeed one in which the representation is fundamentally mediated by those defining ownership of the past. In turn this requires the provision of some approaches not tied to an exclusive technical vocabulary (Bateman 2000; Goodrick and Earl 2003) and to elite hardware.

4 They are clearly not new: examples of constructivism and related approaches to the photographic subject extending back through the last century (Clarke 1997: 188ff).

5 As we have begun to be at Quseir; see Glazier 2003.

6 Virtual Reality Modelling Language (see, for example, Ames *et al.* 1997; McCarthy and Descartes 1998).

7 An 'easy to use' interface presents problems in its own right. There are reasons for the complexity of modelling packages such as 3ds Max and provision of cutdown versions limits the creativity of the modeller – the diversity of approaches is

required for a vibrant reconstruction canon. Experimentation with the various interfaces and tools has certainly had a profound impact on much of my own work. In a cut-down version I could provide only component options; not the option to break apart what had been done and construct it in a new form.

8 This parallels Bateman's consideration and concerns regarding the perceived primacy of particular areas of visual representation for study, and questions of how to conceptualise the ' "self-explanatory" pole of our visual sphere' (2000: 1).

References

Adkins, L. and Adkins, R. (1989) *Archaeological Illustration*. Cambridge: Cambridge University Press.

Ames, A. L., Nadeau, D. R. and Moreland, J. L. (1997) *VRML Sourcebook*, New York: John Wiley.

Barceló, J. (2000) 'Visualizing what might be: an introduction to virtual reality techniques in archaeology', in J. Barceló, M. Forte and D. Sanders (eds) *Virtual Reality in Archaeology*. Oxford: BAR International Series.

Barceló, J., Forte, M. and Sanders, D. (eds) (2000) *Virtual Reality in Archaeology*. Oxford: BAR International Series.

Barthes, R. (1993) *Camera Lucida*. London: Random House.

Bateman, J. (2000) 'Immediate realities: an anthropology of computer visualisation in archaeology', *Internet Archaeology* 8 (accessed 10 August 2003).

Bizony, P. (2001) *Digital Domain*. London: Aurum Press.

Brody, F. (1991) 'How virtual is reality?', in T. Feldman (ed.) *Proceedings of the First Annual Conference on Virtual Reality 91*. London: Meckler.

Brooker, D. (2003) *Essential CG Lighting Techniques*. Oxford: Focal Press.

Brown, B. (2002) *Cinematography*. Oxford: Focal Press.

Carnes, M. C., Mico, T., Miller-Monzon, J. and Rubel, D. (eds) (1995) *Past Imperfect: History According to the Movies*. New York: Henry Holt.

Carr, K. and England, R. (eds) (1995) *Simulated and Virtual Realities: Elements of Perception*. London: Taylor & Francis.

Ching, F. D. K. (1996) *Architecture: Form, Space and Order* (2nd edn). London: John Wiley.

Clarke, C. (1997) *The Photograph*. Oxford: Oxford University Press.

Cosgrove, D. and Daniels, S. (eds) (1988) *The Iconography of Landscape*. Cambridge: Cambridge University Press.

Cubitt, S. (1998) *Digital Aesthetics*. London: Sage.

Cummings, V. (2000) 'The world in a spin: representing the Neolithic landscapes of South Uist', *Internet Archaeology* 8 (accessed 10 August 2003).

Earl, G. P. and Wheatley, D. W. (2001) 'Virtual reconstruction and the interpretative process: a case-study from Avebury', in D. W. Wheatley, G. P. Earl and S. J. Poppy (eds) *Contemporary Themes in Archaeological Computing*. Oxford: Oxbow.

Eco, U. (1982) 'Critique of the image', in V. Burgin (ed.) *Thinking Photography*. London: Thames & Hudson.

Edgar, G. K. and Bex, P. J. (1995) 'Vision and displays', in K. Carr and R. England (eds) *Simulated and Virtual Realities: Elements of Perception*. London: Taylor & Francis.

Edmonds, M. and McElearney, G. (1999) 'Inhabitation and access: landscape and the internet at Gardom's Edge', *Internet Archaeology* 6 (accessed 10 August 2003).

Eiteljorg II, H. (2000) 'The compelling computer image – a double-edged sword', *Internet Archaeology* 8 (accessed 10 August 2003).

Ellis, S. R. (1995) Virtual environment and environmental instruments, in *Simulated and Virtual Realities: Elements of Perception*. K. Carr and R. England (eds). London: Taylor & Francis, pp. 11–51.

Forte, M. (2000) 'About virtual archaeology: disorder, cognitive interactions and virtuality', in J. Barceló, M. Forte and D. Sanders (eds) *Virtual Reality in Archaeology*. Oxford: BAR International Series.

Forte, M. and Siliotti, A. (1997) *Virtual Archaeology: Great Discoveries Brought to Life Through Virtual Reality*. London: Thames & Hudson.

Frischer, B. Niccolucci, F., Ryan, N. and Barceló, J. (2001) *From CVR to CVRO: The Past, Present, and Future of Cultural Virtual Reality*. Available HTTP: <http://www.cvro.org> (accessed 10 August 2003).

Frischer, B., Favro, D., Liverani, P., De Blaauw, S. and Abernathy, D. (2000) *Virtual Reality and Ancient Rome: The UCLA Cultural VR Lab's Santa Maria Maggiore Project*. Available HTTP: <http://www.cvrlab.org/humnet/smm.html> (accessed 10 August 2003).

Gidlow, J. (2001) 'Rock art and bubble worlds', in D. W. Wheatley, G. P. Earl and S. J. Poppy (eds) *Contemporary Themes in Archaeological Computing*. Oxford: Oxbow.

Gillings, M. (1999) 'Engaging place: a framework for the integration and realisation of virtual-reality approaches in archaeology', in L. Dingwall, S. Exon, V. Gaffney, S. Laflin and M. van Leusen (eds) *Computer Applications and Quantitative Methods in Archaeology* 97, Oxford: Archaeopress.

Gillings, M. (2000) 'Plans, elevations and virtual worlds: the development of techniques for the routine construction of hyperreal simulations', in J. Barceló, M. Forte and D. Sanders (eds) *Virtual Reality in Archaeology*. Oxford: BAR International Series.

Gillings, M. and Goodrick, G. T. (1996) 'Sensous and reflexive GIS: Exploring Visualisation and VRML', *Internet Archaeology* 1 (accessed 10 August 2003).

Glazier, D. (2003) ' "We make the diamond shine". Archaeological communities of Quseir, Egypt'. Unpublished thesis, University of Southampton.

Goodrick, G. (1999) 'Virtual reality at Avebury', in L. Dingwall, S. Exon, V. Gaffney, S. Laflin and M. van Leusen (eds) *Computer Applications and Quantitative Methods in Archaeology* 97, Oxford: Archaeopress.

Goodrick, G. and Earl, G. P. (2003) 'A manufactured past: virtual reality in archaeology'. Forthcoming in *Internet Archaeology*.

Hall, S. (ed.) (1997) *Representation: Cultural Representations and Signifying Practices*. London: Sage.

Hamilton, P. (1997) 'Representing the social: France and frenchness in post-war humanist photography', in S. Hall (ed.) *Representation: Cultural Representations and Signifying Practices*. London: Sage.

Hearnshaw, H. M. and Unwin, D. J. (eds) (1994) *Visualization in Geographic Information Systems*. Chichester: John Wiley.

Heim, M. (1993) *The Metaphysics of Virtual Reality*. Oxford: Oxford University Press.

Heim, M. (1998) *Virtual Realism.* Oxford: Oxford University Press.

Huggett, J. and Guo-Yuan, C. (2000) '3D interpretative modelling of archaeological sites – a computer reconstruction of a medieval timber and earthwork castle', *Internet Archaeology* 8 (accessed 10 August 2003).

James, S. (1993) 'How was it for you?', *Archaeological Review from Cambridge* 12(2): 85–100.

James, S. (1997) 'Drawing inferences', in B. L. Molyneaux (ed.) *The Cultural Life of Images.* London: Routledge.

Jeffrey, I. (1981) *Photography: A Concise History.* London: Thames & Hudson.

Joyce, R. (2002) *The Languages of Archaeology: Dialogues, Narratives and Writing.* Oxford: Blackwell.

Junyent, E. and Lores, J. (2000) 'Virtual reality as an extension of the archaeological record: reconstruction of the Iron Age fortress of Els Vilars (Arbeca, Catalonia, Spain)', in J. Barcelo, M. Forte and D. Sanders (eds) *Virtual Reality in Archaeology.* Oxford: BAR International Series.

Kantner, J. (2000) 'Realism vs. reality: creating virtual reconstructions of prehistoric architecture', in J. Barcelo, M. Forte and D. Sanders (eds) *Virtual Reality in Archaeology.* Oxford: BAR International Series.

Leach, N. (ed.) (1997) *Rethinking Architecture.* London: Routledge.

McCarthy, M. and Descartes, A. (1998) *Reality Architecture.* Hemel Hempstead: Prentice Hall.

Miller, P. and Richards, J. (1995) 'The good, the bad, and the downright misleading: archaeological adoption of computer visualisation', in J. Huggett and N. Ryan (eds) *Computer Applications and Quantitative Methods in Archaeology 94.* Oxford: BAR International Series.

Molyneaux, B. L. (ed.) (1997) *The Cultural Life of Images.* London: Routledge.

Moser, S. (1998) *Ancestral Images.* Stroud: Sutton.

Moser, S. (2001) 'Archaeological representation: the visual conventions for constructing knowledge about the past', in I. Hodder (ed.) *Archaeological Theory Today.* Cambridge: Polity Press.

Moser, S., Glazier, D., Phillips, J., El Nemer, L. N., Mousa, M. S., Richardson, S., Conner, A. and Seymour, M. (2002) 'Transforming archaeology through practice: strategies for collaborative practice and the Community Archaeology project at Quseir, Egypt', *World Archaeology* 34(2): 220–48.

Pletinckx, D., Silberman, N. and Callebaut, D. (2001) *How to Tell a Scientifically Validated Story.* Available HTTP: <http://www.cs.ukc.ac.uk/people/staff/nsr/cvro/pletinckx.pdf> (accessed 10 August 2003).

Pollard, J. and Gillings, M (1998) 'Romancing the stones: towards a virtual and elemental Avebury', *Archaeological Dialogues* 5(2): 143–64.

Reilly, P. (1991) 'Towards a virtual archaeology', in K. Lockyear, S. Rahtz (eds) *Computer Applications and Quantitative Methods in Archaeology 90.* Oxford: BAR International Series.

Roberts, J. C. and Ryan, N. (1997) *Alternative Archaeological Representations within Virtual Worlds.* Available HTTP: <http://www.cs.ukc.ac.uk/people/staff/nsr/arch/vrsig97/vrsig.html> (accessed 10 August 2003).

Ryan, R. (1996) 'Computer based visualisation of the past: technical "realism" and historical credibility', in T. Higgins, P. Main, and J. Lang (eds) *Imaging the Past.* London: British Museum Press.

Ryan, N. (2001) *Documenting and Validating Virtual Archaeology.* Available HTTP: <http://www.cvro.org> (accessed 10 August 2003).

Sanders, D. (1999) 'VR for archaeological research and education', in L. Dingwall, S. Exon, V. Gaffney, S. Laflin and M. van Leusen (eds) *Computer Applications and Quantitative Methods in Archaeology 97.* Oxford: Archaeopress.

Schrire, C. (1995) *Digging Through Darkness: Chronicles of an Archaeologist.* Charlottesville: University Press of Virginia.

Shanks, M. (1997) 'Photography and archaeology', in B. L. Molyneaux (ed.) *The Cultural Life of Images.* London: Routledge.

Sorrell, M. (ed) (1981) *Reconstructing the Past.* London: Batsford.

Wann, J. P., Rushton, S. and Monwilliams, M. (1995) 'Natural problems for stereo-scopic depth-perception in virtual environments', *Vision Research* 35(19): 2731–6.

Wartofsky, M. W. (1979) 'Picturing and representing', in C. F. Nodine and D. F. Fisher (eds) *Perception and Pictorial Representation.* New York: Praeger.

Wheatley, D. W. (2000) 'Spatial technology and archaeological theory revisited', in K. Lockyear, T. Sly and V. Mihailescu-Birlitsa (eds) *Computer Applications and Quantitative Methods in Archaeology 96.* Oxford: BAR International Series.

Wolff, J. (1993) *The Social Production of Art* (2nd edn). London: Macmillan.

Wyke, M. (1997) *Projecting the Past.* London: Routledge.

Part VI

DISSEMINATING THE DATA

10

ELECTRONIC PUBLICATION IN ARCHAEOLOGY

Julian D. Richards

. . . the theme of my paper is this use of computers, to do *useful* things, not *clever* things.

Rahtz (1986: 3)

Introduction

For the last 30 years the role of computers in archaeology has tended to focus upon pioneering activities in data recording and analysis (see Richards and Ryan 1985; Lock 2003; Zubrow this volume). Computers have seemed largely peripheral to publication. Now, with the development of multimedia applications and the growth of the Internet as a global means of communication, computers are able to play an increasing role in dissemination and publication. For the next 30 years this role will place information technology at the centre of mainstream archaeological endeavour. However, the application of Information Technology is not unproblematic. Technology, innovation and systems of knowledge have always interacted (Huggett 2003). The medieval library, the printed book, and library classifications have each transformed and reordered knowledge. Internet and digital technologies will have a profound effect on archaeological theory and practice. This chapter places current developments in electronic publication within an international and cross-sectoral context. It outlines the development of electronic publication in archaeology and examines current trends, discussing the potential and constraints of existing technologies and applications.

Technological change is likely to have a significant effect upon all aspects of communication and publication. Although the printed book is still the primary means of dissemination for popular fiction, reference books have been usurped by the Internet as the first stop for many researchers. Google rather than the *Encyclopedia Britannica* is now the primary source of information. Radio and television continue to be important communication media but TV companies make increasing use of web sites for supporting and follow-up material. As technologies converge the alliance between television and the Internet will grow (Gates 1996). This chapter is primarily concerned with scholarly communication, but it is worth noting that changes in the academic sector also have a broader impact on popular education, communication and entertainment (Hills and Richards 2004).

Changes in publication practices

The trend towards electronic publication has partly been driven by problems with traditional media, but partly it is led by the anticipated advantages of new technologies.

Research in many fields is held back by the relatively slow process of peer-reviewed journal publication, which is in conflict with the rapid rate of discovery and the pressure to claim intellectual ownership for new ideas and discoveries ahead of rivals. Those within the particle physics research community solved this problem by establishing a networked library of pre-prints of papers submitted for publication (Ginsparg 1998). HTML (Hyper Text Markup Language) was created by Tim Berners-Lee at CERN in the late 1980s to provide online typesetting features for the exchange and dissemination of pre-prints. A major feature of HTML was the ability to link text and images to another document through the use of hypertext links. When this standard way of rendering electronic documents was combined with the development of international networks of computers, the Internet was born.

Allied to the problem of delays in traditional publication was the problem of its cost. Although felt most keenly in the sciences, spiralling journal inflation has put library budgets under pressure across all disciplines, reflected in periodic exercises in cutting the number of subscriptions. Publishers have responded by competing to produce yet more titles, fuelled by the pressure to publish which has been forced on academics by research assessment exercises and competition for tenure. In both the United States and Europe libraries and academics have formed consortia, such as SPARC (the Scholarly Publishing and Academic Resources Coalition) (http://www.arl.org/sparc/), to try to encourage lower cost publishers. Some have sought to take publishers out of the equation altogether. Steven Harnad (2001) and others have argued that it is absurd that the results of public-funded research should only be made available by commercial publishers who charge the scholarly community to read the fruits of their own labours. They have developed the pre-print model and proposed the development of institutional e-print archives of grey literature where each university should mount papers by its researchers in its own computer servers, catalogued according to emerging metadata standards, cross-searchable within both subject-specific and institutional gateways and portals, and made freely available over the Internet (Pinfield *et al.* 2002).

Despite anxieties about the longevity and academic status of e-prints, the model has found favour with many university librarians. They are aware not only of the cost of subscribing to paper journals, but also of the cost of housing them. With shelf space taking up valuable real estate and institutions developing policies for information access rather than library holdings, many universities see electronic publication as the way forward. With new generations of students, and even older generations of lecturers, increasingly expecting to do their research at a computer screen, most Higher Education institutions have developed integrated campus information and library networks, incorporating the networking of study bedrooms. The larger commercial publishers have responded by creating electronic versions of their paper titles, often providing 'free' electronic access, thrown in with the paper subscription. However, as journal runs on paper begin to be relegated to the stacks, it is already clear that the electronic version is seen as providing the primary means of access for most readers. Publishers have also sought to maintain their market share by bundling multiple titles with subscription packages, encouraging libraries to take on more titles than local demand would strictly require. Smaller scholarly publishers, such as period and county archaeological societies, will need to form consortia or face being 'squeezed-out' by these commercial pressures.

Electronic publication in archaeology

The potential of electronic publication in archaeology has been rehearsed on several occasions (for example, Rahtz *et al.* 1992; Wolle and Shennan 1996; Heyworth *et al.* 1996). It combines an option to publish much more material than is economic on paper with the ability to publish a greater variety of material, including unlimited colour images and new media such as sound, video, and virtual reality models. It is also argued that electronic publication allows authors to make their actual data available in spreadsheets, databases, and GIS, providing the reader with a level of access to data which will allow them to test interpretations and to develop rival theories, thereby contributing to a process of democratisation of archaeological knowledge (Gaffney and Exon 1999). It is further suggested that electronic hypertext encourages new forms of writing, breaking away from traditional linear narrative, and permitting multi-vocal statements and interpretations (Hodder 1999a, 1999b; Holtorf 2003). Such initiatives also require new approaches to post-excavation and writing (Beck 2000). Denning (2003) and Holtorf (2003) have suggested that new approaches to hypertext may be required if it is to be used effectively.

On the other hand, it can be argued that electronic publication allows the author to present the dumping of raw undigested field data as a virtue, rather than as an opt out from the professional responsibility of adequate post-excavation analysis. Many readers also claim that they find non-linear publications confusing and disorientating. There is considerable cultural resistance towards electronic publication. It can be seen as transient and ephemeral, lacking in academic respectability and, because of the ease of copying electronic files, more open to plagiarism and copyright infringement.

Experiments in electronic publication in archaeology go back to the pre-history of hypertext, although at the time their possible future impact was largely unappreciated outside specialist circles. The advantages of hypertext for the structuring of archaeological reports and archives were often repeated but there were few applications outside the academic sector (Rahtz *et al.* 1989, 1992). A pioneering electronic publication and archive was developed for the site at Wadi Ziqlab using an Apple product, Hypercard (Banning 1993), and an experimental hypermedia programme, Microcosm, developed in Southampton University, was tested for the site at St Veit Klinglberg (Wolle and Shennan 1996). Rahtz *et al.* (1992) illustrated an attempt to produce a version of Oxford Archaeological Unit's report on Rough Ground Farm marked up in SGML.

Many multimedia publishing ventures began life as new ways of present-ing contextual information as part of museum or heritage exhibitions, such as the World of the Vikings project (Maytom and Torevell 1993), or a pro-ject to record Tibetan Thangka painting (Makkuni 1992). Others were funded as teaching support projects, such as the Archaeology Disc of images of British stone circles (Martlew 1991). In the United States, a team at the University of North Carolina developed 'Excavating Occaneechi', a CD-ROM that was both an excavation report and a teaching resource (Davis Jr *et al.* 1998). However, such initiatives required special project funding, and it is only when the use of CD offers cost-savings, perhaps by cutting down on the high costs of publishing large paper reports that it has been taken up within the routine publication of archaeological fieldwork.

CD-ROM publication will undoubtedly remain popular in this role for several years, particularly as a replacement for microfiche, and in conjunc-tion with a traditional print volume (see Dibble and MacPherron 1995; Thomas 1995; Powlesland 1997). A CD-ROM can hold 650–700 Megabytes (Mb) of digital information and can be read on the majority of personal computers. One particularly interesting approach is what has been chris-tened the WEB-CD. Files are prepared in HTML within a web format application, but then distributed off-line on CD. This overcomes problems with access to broadband Internet whilst not requiring any specific soft-ware, beyond a web browser. It has been used effectively for the distribution of archive reports and data to a distributed network of specialists (Powlesland *et al.* 1998) but in many ways can be seen as an interim solution pending comprehensive Internet access. In the meantime publication on CD offers a similar model to print publication in that purchase requires a tangible object to change hands. CD-ROMs can be packaged and sold in bookstores and unless they are mounted on a network it is necessary for each reader to have access to a disc, so the potential for avoiding paying for a publication is limited. Similarly, once acquired, the user has ownership, and can rely on the data being available, unlike the Internet where content is made available at the discretion of the 'publishing body'.

CD-ROMs are unpopular with libraries, however, as they are easily lost or damaged and difficult to access across a network without special efforts. Moreover they are dependent upon the existence of specific hardware devices and certain to go the way of 12-inch vinyl records, cassette tapes, and 5¼ inch floppy discs in a few years. Publication on CD-ROM raises specific anxieties for the long-term survival of the content, unless steps are taken to preserve it using other media.

Web-based publication

Online publication using the Internet is widely seen as a longer-term and more sustainable option for electronic publication. The 2003 Oxford Internet Survey reported that only 4 per cent of the British population lacks ready access to a place where they could sign on to the Internet. Whereas only 64 per cent of adults in Britain had used the Internet, 98 per cent of those still at school are Internet users. According to the Office for National Statistics, by 2003, 48 per cent of UK households had home Internet access, compared to 9 per cent in 1998. Initial anxieties about limiting access and disenfranchising the developing world have been largely overcome by the rapid growth in worldwide Internet access. For archaeologists in large parts of Asia, Africa and the Middle East it has become easier to access documents on the Internet than to gain access to an academic library. Despite localised problems with bandwidth, publication on the Internet now provides instant international access to archaeological publications, from across all age groups and class groupings (Vince *et al.* 1997). Speed of publication can also be greatly increased, providing immediate and uncensored access to news stories. Unlike a CD-ROM, an Internet publication can also be dynamic. Papers can be updated and revised, and discussion lists can provide commentaries and debate. By the same token, however, this transience can be a cause of concern. The ability to alter conclusions is seen as threatening and dangerous. The instability of web sites and addresses is a major barrier to the acceptance of web-based electronic publication. The fact that anyone can create a web publication may be liberating and egalitarian, but can also create problems for readers trying to decide which publications can be regarded as trusted sources.

In Britain, one of the first Internet archaeological journals was published by Southampton University. *Online Archaeology* was published for just one issue and no longer survives. In 1996, graduate students in Sheffield set up *Assemblage*, (http://www.shef.ac.uk/assem/) a journal which combined academic papers with news and ephemera, and still survives. The first fully-refereed online journal in archaeology was *Internet Archaeology* (http://

intarch.ac.uk/) founded in 1996. *Internet Archaeology* was initially funded through eLib, the UK universities electronic libraries programme. Its aim was to publish papers which exploited hypertext and made the most of new media, such as online searchable databases, clickable maps, and virtual reality models. A secondary aim was to provide access to underlying data and to allow readers to investigate the data upon which interpretations rested. In many ways journal was a misnomer as there was no restriction on length and several 'papers' were the equivalent of multi-volume print monographs. Despite being composed using HTML markup and available in web browsers it deliberately mirrored traditional print conventions, with volume and part numbers, and Harvard-style citation procedures. Most papers also follow a fairly traditional linear table of contents to aid navigation and reduce culture shock. The journal also chose not to alter anything after publication, making a virtue of stability in a dynamic field, in order to win the confidence of authors and readers. The journal was archived by the Archaeology Data Service so that long-term preservation was assured. All papers were peer-reviewed and there was a high rejection rate for unsuitable material. It was able to claim, with the support of successive panel chairs, that in UK research assessment exercises in Archaeology, refereed electronic publications would be judged according to the same criteria as print equivalents.

So long as access was free readership figures were extremely high, with some 25,000 registered users; *Internet Archaeology* became the Google 'Number One Hit' for searches on 'Archaeology'. Many authors came to the journal because they appreciated the instantaneous international readership that electronic online publication provided. Nonetheless, fieldworkers have been slow to take advantage of full electronic publication. The excavation report by Wickham-Jones and Dalland in Volume 5 (1998) represented its first experiment in site publication. Wickham-Jones described her experiences in a follow-up article (1999). Whilst the bells and whistles offered by electronic publication were appreciated by authors and readers they were not necessarily so popular with funding bodies providing publication subventions. It is undoubtedly true that an exact electronic equivalent of a paper publication is probably cheaper on a page-per-page basis, due to the removal of printing and distribution costs. This has been demonstrated in the *SAIR* project (see below) where PDF publication of large backlog reports was found to cost about a third of traditional print journals. Although server and preservation costs are additional charges these are generally lower than for print publications. Most authors, however, are not content with simple text and want to add more interactive features, which inevitably increases publication costs.

There is no doubt that *Internet Archaeology* was a great success of the eLib programme as the subject matter provided a wide variety of media types and presented a volume of material that would have been impossible to publish in conventional publication. Several have tried to emulate it, but it is still unusual as a full multimedia journal for which it would be impossible to have a print equivalent. Other traditional paper journals, such as *Antiquity*, have also begun to see the advantages of an electronic component to provide access to supplementary material (http://antiquity.ac.uk/), but still depend upon subscriptions to their printed version. However, it is clear that true e-publication comes at a cost. When *Internet Archaeology* came to the end of its *eLib* funding in 2001, and introduced subscriptions, this was greeted with mixed reactions. Despite the spectacular growth of e-commerce there is a strong reaction against charging on the Internet and many correspondents found it difficult to accept that even 'free' web sites had a real cost, even if they were not bearing it. By 2003 most UK universities teaching archaeology, and a significant number of North American ones, had taken out institutional subscriptions. There was also a small number of individual subscribers and some who had taken advantage of a new pay-per-article or pay-per-issue service. Nonetheless, this is uncharted territory and with no existing exemplars – in any subject – it is difficult to develop the business model for an archaeological e-journal.

Internet Archaeology has benefited from a partnership with the Archaeology Data Service (ADS), the UK archaeology digital data archive. The ADS makes archives available free of charge online, either as downloads of the data files, and sometimes with online searchable interfaces. Several writers have promoted the importance of making primary archaeological data available digitally (e.g. Gaffney and Exon 1999). Most recently the Council for British Archaeology Publication User Needs Survey (PUNS) advocated multiple forms of publication, as appropriate for different audiences, and recommended that all data archives should be made available on the Internet, free of charge (Jones *et al.* 2001). This begins to blur the traditional distinction between archive and publication and allows a seamless gradation between the two (Richards 2002). *Internet Archaeology* has published a number of examples, such as a discussion of landscape archaeology in Ave Valley, supported by the raw fieldwalking data from ADS (Millett *et al.* 2000) and the excavation report of the Anglian and Anglo-Scandinavian settlement at Cottam, with links to the archive reports and excavations data files held by ADS (Richards 2001).

In the United States a rather different situation has arisen. Although wider access meant that the Internet was embraced earlier, its exploitation for archaeological publication has hitherto been limited to a small number of individual experiments, which are generally project web sites rather than peer-reviewed publications. The *SAA Bulletin*, the Society for American Archaeology's newsletter, has been placed online, and the SAA has also experimented with electronic occasional papers, but there are no exclusively online archaeological e-journals. There has been an emphasis on the e-monograph, but a failure to develop exemplars (Aldenderfer 1999). At

UCLA a project to develop a digital e-print template was established under the auspices of the Digital Archaeology Lab, with funding from the Ahmanson Foundation. Its aim was to plug the gap between archaeologists and web designers by providing a multipurpose excavation report template into which authors could slot their own materials. The template itself was completed but there appears to have been no take-up, reflecting several problems. Potential authors were nervous about questions of status and identity of their reports and few projects actually had a full range of digital materials so that a full digital monograph would represent a cost saving. With the closure of ADAP, the USA also lacks a central archive for digital archaeological data; responsibility for preservation of electronic publications is falling upon libraries.

SGML and XML

Most web-based forms of electronic publication use HTML as the mark-up language. HTML is a dialect of SGML (Standard Generalised Mark-up Language) which uses tags to determine how a file is displayed, or rendered, in a web browser such as Internet Explorer. At Tufts University the Perseus Project (Smith 1992) made early use of SGML to formalise the structure of archaeological information, and also encoded several thousand early Greek and Latin documents using SGML, and latterly XML, markup. Similarly the National Museum Project of the Museum of Norway (Holmen and Uleberg 1996) has made extensive use of SGML for tagging digitised documentary archives relating to archaeological sites, and giving them structure. It too has begun to tag documents in XML. Whereas HTML tags indicate the format of a document, XML tags can indicate the content. As well as specific tags for obvious items such as title and author it is likely that if agreed standards are developed it will be possible to make use of subject-specific tags. In the case of an archaeological excavation report, for example, where there are widely followed conventions which indicate content, it would be possible to tag items such as <site location> or <pottery report>. This would allow intelligent web robots and harvesters to find specific items of data that a reader was interested in, treating an electronic text with XML tags as if it were an online database. In addition, future users would also be able to tailor or personalise their web browser to display specific content in a certain way. Although an XML document contains no information about how to display the data it describes, a style sheet can be used to apply formatting. Just as Internet Explorer renders an /HTML heading tagged as <H1> in a certain way, so web browsers of the future might be programmed to perform actions according to content. XML is already valuable in allowing the same text to be rendered differently according to display device. These ideas underlie what Tim Berners-Lee (2001) has outlined as his vision for *The Semantic Web*, in which all web content will be structured. There are few actual archaeological examples of the application of XML as yet. Gray and Walford (1999) recommended it as a means of structuring archaeological reports and enabling comparison. Mecksepper (2003) has discussed its application to the dissemination of grey literature reports. Sugimoto (2002) has described its use in structuring a database of archaeological aerial photographs. In England, the OASIS project (Hardman and Richards 2003) has developed an online form for the collection of information about fieldwork and archives which allows the uploading of electronic versions of grey-literature reports for access in an on-line virtual library. The form exports data with XML tags for ease of loading into local or national databases. The next stage needs to be the development of a standardised system of tagging of the grey literature reports themselves (see Falkingham 2004)

In the United States, John Hoopes (2000) has proposed that the Society for American Archaeology should develop a peer-reviewed web gateway for the dissemination of archaeological reports. A problem with self-publication is that it can be difficult to locate relevant papers if they may appear anywhere on the Internet, rather than in a specific journal. Under the Open Archives Initiative (OAI), XML is used to tag index records for papers with appropriate metadata keywords, so that they can then be harvested by automated search tools and indexed in online virtual library catalogues.

Portable Document Format

Another file format which has been widely used to distribute and exchange documents via the Internet is the Portable Document Format (or PDF), a *de facto* standard developed by Adobe. PDF files require the use of the Adobe Acrobat reader, a plug-in, or program that runs within the web browser, to view the documents on screen. The PDF reader is free to download, but unlike HTML files which can be created in any text editor, creating PDF files requires the purchase of the proprietary Adobe Acrobat PDF writer. Although they have limited hypertext functionality it is possible to search and index PDF files. They have become very widely used as they are often generated as part of the conventional printing process, or as a result of scanning an existing paper page. Thus they are a relatively convenient means of creating an electronic version of a paper publication, and are used by most journal publishers as a means of distributing a parallel electronic version. PDF files can be published and distributed anywhere, including in print, as email attachments, on the web, or on floppy disc or CD-ROM. Unlike HTML files they retain the formatting of the paper page and so page numbers in citations and references are stable. PDF documents retain the look and feel of a word-processed document and, when printed, they look the same as when displayed. However, though appropriate for documents that users are likely to print, rather than read online, their fixed formatting means that they never fit well on a computer screen. PDF documents can also be very big and there is often a significant download time, and difficulties in navigation. Users sometimes complain that opening PDF files causes their computer systems to crash. The main disadvantage of PDF is the uncertainty surrounding its long-term preservation. As a proprietary format it is dependent upon support from Adobe.

Nonetheless PDF has been used to make sets of back runs of publication series available by digitisation. At the time of writing out-of-print Council for British Archaeology Research Reports (http://ads.ahds.ac.uk/catalogue/library/cba/rrs.cfm) and the complete run of the Proceedings of the Society of Antiquaries of Scotland (http://ads.ahds.ac.uk/catalogue/library/psas/) going back to 1851, were available as PDF files. Whilst not strictly speaking electronic publication such initiatives greatly enhance access of existing paper publications. Web access statistics for the CBA Research Reports indicate very high levels of usage, which given the low initial print runs, probably represents a higher level of usage for the online versions than for the original printed volumes.

In Britain, Historic Scotland has experimented with a new publication series, entitled *Scottish Archaeological Internet Reports* (http://www.sair.-org.uk/) using PDF as the file format, and replacing conventionally printed reports in the *Proceedings of the Society of Antiquaries of Scotland*. However, this is not really electronic publication in the true sense, but rather electronic dissemination of a conventionally formatted report, and some users have been disappointed that the potential of electronic publication is not being exploited more, rather than it being used as a cost-saving exercise.

Conclusion

It is a salutary thought that it was at an early Computer Applications Conference in 1986 that Sebastian Rahtz reminded the audience that despite the fact that Unix was developed as a text-processing environment, most 'archaeological computer hackers' were still focused on trying to do clever things (1986: 3). Email was not yet in widespread usage; the Internet had not even been thought of, but Rahtz foretold that the most useful applications of computers would be (a) to disseminate data quickly, (b) to provide access to data separately from thoughts about it, and (c) to provide different views of the same data to different readers. Rahtz concluded by posing the question: 'If the database becomes available, how does the excavator bring out what he considers important?' (1986: 13). If we can publish everything, how do we still guide the reader through a coherent story? How do we avoid drowning in data, yet simultaneously embrace e-publication and widen access? Almost 20 years on these questions have still not been answered, but lie at the heart of issues in electronic publication in archaeology.

References

Aldenderfer, M. S. (1999) 'Data, digital ephemera, and dead media: digital publishing and archaeological practice'. *Internet Archaeology* 6. Online at http://intarch.ac.uk/journal/issue6/aldenderfer_index.html

Banning, E. B. (1993) 'Hypermedia and archaeological publication: The Wadi Ziqlab project', in J. Andresen, T. Madsen and I. Scollar (eds) *Computing the Past. CAA92: Computer Applications and Quantitative Methods in Archaeology.* Aarhus: Aarhus University Press, pp. 441–7.

Beck, A. (2000) 'Intellectual excavation and dynamic Information Management Systems', in G. Lock and K. Brown (eds) *On the Theory and Practice of Archaeological Computing.* Oxford: Oxford University Committee for Archaeology Monograph No. 51, pp. 73–88.

Berners-Lee, T. (2001) 'The Semantic Web' *Scientific American* 501, May 2001.

Davis, Jr R. P. S., Livingood, P. C., Ward, T. and Steponaitis, V. P. (1998) *Excavating Occaneechi Town: Archaeology of an Eighteenth-Century Indian Village in North Carolina.* Chapel Hill: University of North Carolina Press.

Denning, K. (2003) ' "The Storm of Progress" and archaeology for an online public' *Internet Archaeology* 15. Online at http://intarch.ac.uk/journal/issue15/denning_index.html

Dibble, H. and McPherron, S. (1995) *Combe-Capelle on CD-ROM.* Philadelphia: University Museum Press.

Falkingham, G. (2004) 'Exploring XML and markup: a case study into the multi-layered presentation of archaeological grey literature'. Unpublished MSc dissertation, University of York.

Gaffney, V. and Exon, S. (1999) 'From order to chaos: publication, synthesis and the dissemination of data in the Digital Age', *Internet Archaeology* 6. Online at http://intarch.ac.uk/journal/issue6/gaffney_index.html

Gates, B. (1996) *The Road Ahead.* London: Penguin Books.

Ginsparg, P. (1998) 'Electronic research archives for physics', in I. Butterworth (ed.) *The Impact of Electronic Publishing on the Academic Community.* London: Portland Press, pp. 32–43.

Gray, J. and Walford, K. (1999) 'One good site deserves another: electronic publishing in field archaeology', *Internet Archaeology* 7. Online at http://intarch.ac.uk/journal/issue7/gray_index.html

Hardman, C. and Richards, J. D. (2003) 'OASIS: dealing with the digital revolution', in M. Doerr and A. Sarris (eds) *CAA2002: The Digital Heritage of Archaeology. Computer Applications and Quantitative Methods in Archaeology 2002.* Archive of Monuments and Publications Hellenic Ministry of Culture, pp. 325–8.

Harnad, S. (2001) 'The self-archiving initiative. Freeing the refereed research literature online', *Nature* 410: 1024–5.

Heyworth, M., Ross, S. and Richards, J. D. (1996) 'Internet archaeology: an international electronic journal for archaeology', in H. Kamermans and K. Fennema (eds) *Interfacing the Past: Computer Applications and Quantitative Methods in Archaeology CAA95.* Leiden: University of Leiden, Analecta Praehistorica Leidensia 28, pp. 517–23.

Heyworth, M., Richards, J. D., Vince, A. and Garside-Neville, S. (1997) 'Internet Archaeology: a quality electronic journal' *Antiquity* 71(274): 1039–42.

Hills, C. and Richards, J. D. (2004) 'The dissemination of information', in J. Hunter and I. Ralston (eds) *Archaeological Resource Management in the UK* (2nd edition). London and New York: Routledge.

Hodder, I. (1999a) *The Archaeological Process: An Introduction*. Oxford: Blackwell Publishers.

Hodder, I. (1999b) 'Archaeology and global information systems'. *Internet Archaeology* 6. Online at http://intarch.ac.uk/journal/issue6/hodder_index.html

Holmen, J. and Uleberg, E. (1996) 'The national documentation project of Norway – the archaeological sub-project', in H. Kamermans and K. Fennema (eds) *Interfacing the Past: Computer Applications and Quantitative Methods in Archaeology CAA95*. Leiden: University of Leiden, Analecta Praehistorica Leidensia 28, pp. 43–6.

Holtorf, C. (2003) 'The future of electronic scholarship', *Internet Archaeology* 15. Online at http://intarch.ac.uk/journal/issue15/holtorf_index.html

Hoopes, J. W. (2000) 'Beyond the World Wide Web: present and future venues for scholarly online publication', *Society for American Archaeology Newsletter* 18(5): 20–2.

Huggett, J. (2003) 'The past in bits: towards an archaeology of information technology', *Internet Archaeology* 15. Online at http://intarch.ac.uk/journal/issue15/huggett_index.html

Jones, S., MacSween, A., Jeffrey, S., Morris, R. and Heyworth, M. (2001) *From the Ground Up. The Publication of Archaeological Projects: A User Needs Survey*. Council for British Archaeology. Online at http://www.britarch.ac.uk/pubs/puns/index.html

Lock, G. (2003) *Using Computers in Archaeology*. London and New York: Routledge.

Makkuni, R. (1992) 'The electronic capture and dissemination of the cultural practice of Tibetan Thangka painting', in P. Reilly and S. Rahtz (eds) *Archaeology in the Information Age: A Global Perspective*. London and New York: Routledge, pp. 323–51.

Martlew, R. (1991) 'Every picture tells a story: the Archaeology Disc and its implications', in K. Lockyear and S. P. Q. Rahtz (eds) *Computer Applications and Quantitative Methods in Archaeology 1990*. BAR International Series 565, Tempus Reparatum, Oxford, pp. 15–19.

Maytom, J. and Torevell, K. (1993) 'The world of the Vikings: an interactive video project', in J. Andresen, T. Madsen and I. Scollar (eds) *Computing the Past. CAA92: Computer Applications and Quantitative Methods in Archaeology*. Aarhus: Aarhus University Press, pp. 449–56.

Mecksepper, C. (2003) 'The publication of archaeological excavation reports using XML'. *Literary and Linguistic Computing* 18: 63–75.

Millett, M., Queiroga, F., Strutt, K., Taylor, J. and Willis, S. (2000) 'The Ave Valley, northern Portugal: an archaeological survey of Iron Age and Roman settlement', *Internet Archaeology* 9. Online at http://intarch.ac.uk/journal/issue9/millett_index.html

Pinfield, S., Gardner, M. and MacColl, J. (2002) 'Setting up an institutional e-print archive', *Ariadne* 31. Online at http://www.ariadne.ac.uk/issue31/eprint-archives/

Powlesland, D. (1997) 'Publishing in the round: a role for CD-ROM in the publication of archaeological field-work results', *Antiquity* 71(274): 1062–6.

Powlesland, D., Clemence, H. and Lyall, J. (1998) 'West Heslerton WEB-CD. The application of HTML and WEB tools for creating a distributed excavation archive in the form of a WBE-CD', *Internet Archaeology 5*. Online at http://intarch.ac.uk/journal/issue5/westhescd_index.html

Rahtz, S. P. Q. (1986) 'Possible directions in electronic publication in archaeology', in S. Laflin (ed.) *Computer Applications in Archaeology 1986*, Birmingham: University of Birmingham, pp. 3–13.

Rahtz, S. P. Q., Carr, L. and Hall, W. (1989) 'New designs for archaeological reports', *Science and Archaeology* 31: 20–34.

Rahtz, S. P. Q., Carr, L. and Allen, T. (1992) 'The development of dynamic archaeological publications', in P. Reilly and S. Rahtz (eds) *Archaeology and the Information Age: A Global Perspective*. London and New York: Routledge, pp. 360–83.

Richards, J. D. (2001) 'Anglian and Anglo-Scandinavian Cottam: linking digital publication and archive', *Internet Archaeology 10*. Online at http://intarch.ac.uk/journal/issue10/richards_index.html

Richards, J. D. (2002) 'Digital preservation and access', *European Journal of Archaeology* 5(3): 343–67.

Richards, J. D. and Ryan, N. S. (1985) *Data Processing in Archaeology*. Cambridge: Cambridge University Press.

Smith, N. (1992) 'An experiment in electronic exchange and publication of archaeological field data', in G. Lock and J. Moffett (eds) *Computer Applications and Quantitative Methods in Archaeology 1991*, BAR International Series 577, Tempus Reparatum, Oxford, pp. 49–57.

Sugimoto, G. (2002) 'eXtensible Archaeology: an XML application for an archaeological aerial photograph database', *Archaeological Computing Newsletter* 60: 9–16.

Thomas, R. (1995) 'Publishing archaeological excavation reports on CD-ROM', *The Field Archaeologist* 24: 15–16.

Vince, A., Richards, J. D., Ross, S. and Heyworth, M. (1997) 'Publishing archaeology on the Web: who reads this stuff anyway?' *Internet Archaeology 3*. Online at http://intarch.ac.uk/journal/issue3/vince_index.html

Wickham-Jones, C. (1999) 'Excavation publication and the Internet', *Internet Archaeology 7*. Online at http://intarch.ac.uk/journal/issue7/wickham_index.html

Wickham-Jones, C. and Dalland, M. (1998) 'A small mesolithic site at Fife Ness, Fife, Scotland' *Internet Archaeology 5*. Online at http://intarch.ac.uk/journal/issue5/wickham_index.html

Wolle, A.-C. and Shennan, S. J. (1996) 'A tool for multimedia excavation reports – a prototype', in H. Kamermans and K. Fennema (eds) *Interfacing the Past. Computer Applications and Quantitative Methods in Archaeology CAA95*. Leiden: University of Leiden, Analecta Praehistorica Leidensia 28, pp. 489–95.

11

COMPUTERS, LEARNING AND TEACHING IN ARCHAEOLOGY

Life past and present on the screen

Gary Lock

One of the delights of archaeology is that it is a very diverse interest, not just in its content and application but also in the areas of practice within which it takes place. Most, if not all, of those areas have been impacted by the growing use of computers in a web of different and inter-acting ways. At a purely pragmatic level computers are aiding and enabling the integration of large and complex datasets, and making them available to audiences in ways that could only be imagined just a few years ago. Because archaeology is a process based on interpretation, changing and contesting views and differing theoretical stances, however, the purely pragmatic is always embedded within a more thoughtful process of self-reflection and critique. This applies equally to the new world of Digital Archaeology and to the small country of University Teaching that some of us inhabit within that world. This chapter attempts to illustrate the reflexive relationship between the pragmatic and the conceptual and to assess the impact and potential of adopting a computer-based approach to teaching.

Over the last decade or so, computers have been central to many innovative developments in learning and teaching. Many of these have been focused on the concepts and applications of multimedia and, more recently, their delivery through the online technologies of the World Wide Web. Such applications are found within a diverse range of informal learning situations, reaching such proportions as to give rise to the 'edutainment' industry. In museums, for example, interactive displays are often effectively used to engage visitors in a dialogue with information so that the pace and direction of accessing a mix of text, images and sound is user-controlled and, perhaps most importantly, enjoyable (Lock 2003). The challenge for educators within more formal structures, such as universities as considered here, has been how to incorporate these new technologies into traditional learning and teaching frameworks that include controlled content, quality assurance and assessment.

These developments fit into the wider changing views of education, from the functionalist models of the 1950s and 1960s that saw education as a means of fitting individuals more effectively into society, to the more radical ideas of education as individual and group empowerment and autonomy developed in the 1970s and 1980s. This self-directedness within the learning experience recognises an individual's powers of critical awareness and responsibility for their own learning – two key issues which are central to this chapter.

Educationalists have attempted to isolate the characteristics of effective learning and teaching in Higher Education, which, although obviously related, are two very different things. Learning can be deep or surface, being defined by a series of opposing properties (Entwistled 1992) such as the intention to understand material rather than to simply reproduce it, relating ideas to previous experience rather than simply concentrating on the assessment requirements, relating evidence to conclusions rather than just memorising facts and procedures routinely, and interacting vigorously and critically with the content material rather than just accepting information and ideas passively. Equally, Ramsden (1992) has suggested six key principles for effective teaching in Higher Education one of which is for the student to have 'independence, control, and active engagement' (1992: 100). This assumes that deep learning is activated through the individual's unique imaginative spirit and practised through enquiry which involves choice over subject matter and control over which aspects can be focused on.

It is important to recognise that learning is a complex process and that understandings of that process have changed over time. In very general terms behaviourist theories of how we learn have given way to humanist theories. The former emphasise the active role of the teacher who dispenses knowledge compared to the more passive role of the student who receives it. In this scheme knowledge often equates with truth, and is independent of both teacher and learner and is, therefore, the same for all learners who are all aiming for the same point of understanding. Humanist theories, on the other hand, are largely post-modern in philosophical outlook and reject the positivism of empirical research and locate learning within the complexities and uncertainties of the individual learner's social context. Learning is embedded within the individual's experience and within the resources and conditions of the learner's situation including interpersonal relationships. Consequently, learning is not determined by external influences but created within each of us as we observe and reflect on experience to construct meaning and sense which is applied to the world around us. This is the learning cycle suggested by Kolb (1984), from experience through critical reflection on experience to action which creates new experience ready for the next cycle. Embedded within this are individual intentions, goals and decisions concerning the reasons for learning. It follows then that knowledge is not an external reality waiting to be handed on by a teacher but is the personal construction of new perceptions.

The result of this process is that we construct various acts of knowing that are contingent and provisional, so that rather than validating knowledge itself we are left with the task of establishing criteria by which we can judge the questions asked and the answers arrived at in each specific case. One way of doing this is by assessing which acts of knowing carry personal experiential validity, i.e. make sense within our individual experience.

But is all learning, especially incidental learning that we all encounter every day of our lives, the same as education? Most people would say not and would agree that education requires some form of structure and is a more integrated process that requires planning. Rogers (1996) suggests that three characteristics differentiate education from informal learning:

1. Education is both sequential and cumulative, it progresses through making connections between pieces of information and experiences.
2. The educational process operates within general principles so that methods and conclusions can be applied elsewhere within an established framework of knowledge.
3. The educational process is at the same time both capable of being completed and yet remains incomplete. Individual learning episodes can be completed with goals reached, satisfaction attained and a sense of fulfilment achieved and yet there is always a next stage, new doors open, there is always more to learn.

Learning is not just about cognitive gain, although this is what is likely to be tested or assessed in a formal way, but can involve many qualitative processes that may not be obvious during the actual learning experience. This could raise awareness about a variety of social issues including one's place in the world through ethnic, gender and other power relationships; it can re-affirm existing views and consolidate previous knowledge; it can initiate new interests and change perceptions and connect with the wider life-web of social and aesthetic learning – none of which are easy to assess.

Accepting that learning is about enquiry, it is important to realise that everyday modes of enquiry are rapidly changing and to assess how these changes have and will impact on university learning and teaching. The book is no longer the cultural paradigm that it has been for many centuries, and as shown by O'Donnell (1998) the implications for universities in the future are profound. Most Western students these days have to some degree moved 'beyond the book', and exist in a complex world of digital and analogue information sources. Not surprisingly in the capitalist West much of this is driven by consumerism and profits so that in the league of financial returns the book comes fourth behind television, cinema and video games (Landow 1996) and probably scores low according to other measures for many people as well. These moves away from the book can be seen as part of the wider post-modern experience in which traditional high and low culture are constantly mixed, re-constituted and contextualised in ways meaningful to individuals. It is interesting to note that while it is mainly middle-aged academics that write about post-modernism, young people live it and may not elevate the book above other information sources but integrate it within them. It is from this changing cultural background that students bring their attitudes to learning, and for them the shift from the printed page to the digital hypertext may not be as significant as it is to course designers.

This leads us into the world of digital learning and teaching and the way Information and Communication Technology (ICT) is contesting traditional relationships between teacher and student and offering ways of putting educational theory into practice. In the important book, *Rethinking University Teaching* (1993), Laurillard talks of the 'wretched experience' of the traditional didactic lecture, both for the lecturer and the student. The total lack of dialogue makes it a deeply unsatisfying isolated experience for the former while the student is faced with the one opportunity to capture that chunk of knowledge before it is gone forever. She suggests fundamental changes through computer-based methods that will force changes in the relationship between lecturers and students and in the way both participate within the process of learning and teaching. In essence, lecturers will have to take responsibility for how students learn and not just what they learn, and students will have to think more constructively, critically and reflectively. It is central to this approach that both actively engage in the creation of knowledge as a shared experience. The unhappy experience of both parties in Laurillard's scenario is improved by a redefinition of their roles and relationship from:

> Teacher as banker – depositing information with students hoping
> for a future return to Teacher as midwife – assisting in the birth of
> ideas which are nurtured and grow within a supportive environment.

This is a democratic approach to learning that resonates with George Landow's (1996) vision of hypertext as a diffusing and democratic technology consisting of multiple conversations in which no one ideology dominates. This is a fine ideal but one that is proving difficult to realise. Computer Assisted Learning is not just simply producing a multimedia interactive and letting students get on with it, but introduces the notion of teaching being 'mediated learning' in which the teacher becomes a moderator or facilitator. This challenge for many established university lecturers calls not only for competence with the technology, and the design of purposeful on-line learning tasks (difficult enough in themselves) but also a change from a transmission mode of delivering knowledge to a constructivist approach of collaborative learning. This acknowledges existing knowledge and experience that students bring with them to learning and the complexity of the process of knowledge construction for each individual. Marton (1981) coined the term 'phenomenography' to explore the concepts of reality that students have already acquired when they enter a learning situation and focused on the complex web of interaction between the students, the tutor and the learning resources. Setting up the interaction is crucial as is the role of dialogue so that the moderator's role is one of enabling constructivist learning through effective collaboration between students, tutors and learning resources.

None of this is particularly new within archaeology, for as a discipline we have been experimenting with multimedia and Computer Assisted Learning (CAL), or Computer-Based Learning (CBL), for some time now (Lock 2003: Chapter 7). Multimedia, including the production and 'reading' of hypermedia documents, is a medium which is still in its infancy, however, when compared with established forms of communication such as novels, feature films and TV documentaries which have all developed accepted conventions (Liestøl 1995). A key characteristic to the future development and acceptance of hypermedia documents is the integration of the two established and independent traditions of text with still images, based on the printed page, and the audio-visual tradition of moving images and sound. A typical hypermedia design distinguishes between the characteristics and structure of information, and the structure of the user's acquisition of information and how that generates understanding and meaning. Different types of information, and combinations of types, have developed specific strengths so that, for example, video and audio are good for capturing interest and for presenting quick introductions at a fairly superficial level, whereas text and still images are recognised as better for in-depth information.

In traditional linear media, such as books or videos, the structure and order of the information contained within the document is the same as the structure and order of the user's acquisition of information and, therefore, the accumulation of knowledge (and drawing conclusions from that knowledge) can be more tightly guided than in a non-linear web of information where the two structures are not related at all. A hypermedia document is a static structure consisting of nodes of information with links between them and it is the user's discourse within the structure that creates a story. That discourse will be influenced by the types of information available and the constraints and freedoms programmed into the links between them, and it is establishing a balance between these resulting in a rewarding experience that makes multimedia design a specialist activity. The major component within this is, of course, the user whose personal experiences and circumstances will influence the story created. The first information encountered is likely to be audio-visual which provides a lot of general information quickly with little user interaction required. The aim is to grab the user's attention and encourage exploration of the next layer which comprises text and images and eventually leads to the third layer which is fully exploratory, producing a sequence of increasing interactivity with related increasing depth and richness of information.

General concepts of hypertext and interactivity have been the mainstays of the attempts to introduce CBL into archaeology dating from the CTI initiative starting in the 1980s, through the TLTP (Teaching and Learning Technology Programme) products which are still available to the more recent LTSN (Learning and Teaching Support Network) subject centres. At one level TLTP was successful in producing an innovative range of interactive modules although uptake and usage of them has not reached anywhere near its potential, partially due to the unresolved question of the integration of the modules into existing teaching practices, whether these could really replace lecturers and lecturer contact or would be more effective as add-ons to existing lectures, practicals and tutorials. Surveys have shown considerable staff resistance to substitution but general support for supplementation. After a period of deliberation and practical experience based mainly on the TLTP products, it has been suggested that the use of CBL benefits four areas of archaeological teaching: the *simulation* of work that would not be possible otherwise; *practical work* that may be constrained by the availability of teaching collections or the fragility of materials; *repetitive teaching* of the same material to small groups; and *specialist areas* that may not be taught within a department (Campbell 1996).

One important aspect of CBL, as the name suggests, is that it is a learning, rather than a teaching, technology which enables interaction with the material. The student is required to assume responsibility for his or her own learning and make decisions; the constructionist approach to learning outlined above. The introduction of such radical change needs careful management and is not always seen as positive. Surveys have shown that human contact is an important element within teaching and learning – students like to talk to their lecturers and vice versa. The integration of CBL within a structured course that maintains human contact was demonstrated at least a decade ago by Anthropology 3 at UCL Santa Barbara (Fagan and Michaels 1992). This introductory course attracted many hundreds of students at any one time and was designed to give an appreciation of how archaeology works, the major developments in prehistory, an understanding of the origins and nature of human biological and cultural diversity in the past, to examine the role of archaeology in contemporary society and encourage students how to think about archaeology. From being entirely lecture based the course was re-designed to be computer-based but retained a single weekly lecture and seminar during which the week's work was outlined, thus providing the intellectual cement to entertain and motivate the student. All course material was available on computer (in labs and initially on disc to take away, although now this is online) and using a paper study guide and human teaching assistants, the students worked through the week's assignment and compiled a journal which is an accumulating record of their learning experience. The important lesson here is that using computers as a supplement to the existing lecture course probably wouldn't have resulted in the mind shift necessary to make CBL an effective learning option in this situation of large student numbers. The course had to be re-structured so that the computers were central and the lectures and seminars played a supporting role.

As with many other technologies, Interactive Multimedia was introduced within a haze of hype and excitement producing initial claims that have since been re-evaluated as experience of using the technology increases. For example, Banks (1994) has argued for a re-assessment of the benefits of non-linear enquiry, suggesting that an analysis needs to progress in a linear fashion where pieces of data are compared and arranged in an order, and that abandoning linearity is a return to the stamp collecting mentality. He is also sceptical about the wider claims of Interactive Multimedia as a teaching tool seeing it as a tool of control and boundedness rather than being educationally liberating. The benefits of education lie within the wider areas of enquiry, personal enlightenment and maturity accessible through libraries and the traditional academy rather than within the bounded constraints of a hypertext program reflecting only the horizons of its programmer.

The rapid development of computer networking, especially the Internet and the WWW, since the mid-1990s has had a profound impact on the potential and implications of Interactive Multimedia and CBL both within structured learning environments and as free standing learning resources and support materials. Rapidly improving functionality within a WWW environment now allows full hypertext capabilities including moving video, animations and sound so that as the new millennium progresses it is the Web that appears as the medium of the future with CD-ROMs becoming increasingly peripheral.

The Web has also enabled new methods of online course delivery, often referred to as Distance Learning. Internet-based distance learning, although still in its infancy, promises at the minimum some useful additions to the traditional distance materials and methods, with the possibility of providing a model for all future university teaching (O'Donnell 1998: Chapters 7 and 8). Not only will course materials be available online as is often the case now, but with the development of live voice and video links the possibility of online lectures, seminars and tutorials with synchronous interaction is becoming a reality to enable the virtual classroom. The challenge facing archaeology is whether we can alter our concepts of teaching and learning to operate in a virtual world.

Examples of good practice are beginning to emerge which postdate and draw from the initial years of hype and political rhetoric that surrounded the birth of CBL in general and in archaeology in particular (Kilbride and

Reynier 2002). These attempt to integrate the values of a 'traditional' structured approach to learning within the functionality of the WWW. A major strength here, and one that is just beginning to be exploited, is the ability to link between information resources so that data can be accessed, viewed and understood within an interpretative framework. An example of this is the PATOIS suite of online tutorials offered through the Archaeology Data Service (ADS) (Kilbride *et al.* 2002). These cover the four areas of: Monument Inventories: a resource for learning and research; Excavation archives: a resource for learning and research; Electronic Publications; and Inter-disciplinary resources at Christ Church Spitalfields. Each has been carefully chosen to exploit and demonstrate the diversity of data sources, interpretative approaches and variability within archaeology as a broad discipline. The areas of Cultural Resource Management, excavation, publication and integrating field archaeology with historical sources form the basis of the four modules. Each contains links to a range of appropriate resources and datasets offering the student endless possibilities to explore aspects of interest to a variety of depths. These are not just electronic links but also traditional bibliographies, accepting that students still need to develop library-based research skills. There are many innovative CBL aspects to these modules such as Monument Inventories being linked to the main ADS Archsearch so that resource discovery skills that are more widely applicable are developed and applied. The inclusion of original data as downloadable files means that students can organise and analyse the data within their own interpretative frameworks, as well as move on to understand the use of databases, GIS and other software applications. While each module has built in 'assessment' in the form of exercises and questions, they are flexible and data-rich enough to be used within a teacher-led environment so that the concepts of mutual learning described above can be explored. The potential within this last point is far-reaching because although the links to resources are within the structured framework of the tutorial, once entered they can lead in directions that neither student nor lecturer can fully predict. It is this balance between a structured learning environment which includes high quality content and the opportunity for the student to have 'independence, control and active engagement' (Ramsden 1992) that indicates the increasing maturity of CBL.

To conclude, I have no firm suggestions for what are the best ways of learning and teaching archaeology although it is clear that understandings of how we learn and teach are not objective givens but are part of wider shifting agendas. These changes in understanding are creating opportunities from which we are all learning about issues such as course content, modes of delivery and student/teacher relationships. These changes can, and have, proved fruitful and constructive without the use of computers, small group project work for example shifts the focus from lecturer delivered knowledge to exploratory investigation. The emerging maturity of CBL in archaeology, however, is making it a more realistic tool within a university context and although it is now widely accepted that it is not going to be the only solution, it is certainly one tool within an increasing range now available.

References

Banks, M. (1994) *Interactive Multimedia and Anthropology – A Sceptical View.* Online at http://www.rsl.ox.ac.uk/isca/marcus.banks.01.html [accessed 1st November 2003].

Campbell, E. (1996) 'Using hypermedia in archaeology undergraduate teaching: the TLTP Archaeology Consortium', in T. Higgins, P. Main and J. Lang (eds) *Imaging The Past. Electronic Imaging and Computer Graphics in Museums and Archaeology.* London: British Museum Occasional Paper No. 114, pp. 159–64.

Entwistle, N. (1992) *The Impact of Teaching on Learning Outcomes in Higher Education.* Sheffield: Committee of Vice Chancellors and Principals.

Fagan, B. M. and Michaels, G. H. (1992) 'Anthropology 3: an experiment in the multimedia teaching of introductory archaeology', *American Antiquity* 57(3): 458–66.

Kilbride, W. and Reynier, M. (2002) 'Editorial – keeping the learning in computer-based learning'. *Internet Archaeology* 12, Education and Archaeology Special Issue. Online at http://intarch.ac.uk/journal/issue12/index.html [accessed 1st November 2003].

Kilbride, W., Fernie, K., McKinney, P. and Richards, J. D. (2002) 'Contexts of learning: the PATOIS project and Internet-based teaching and learning in Higher Education'. *Internet Archaeology* 12, Education and Archaeology Special Issue. Online at http://intarch.ac.uk/journal/issue12/index.html [accessed 1st November 2003].

Kolb, D. A. (1984) *Experiential Learning: Experience as the Source of Learning and Development.* Englewood Cliffs, NJ: Prentice-Hall.

Landow, G. P. (1996) 'We are already beyond the book', in W. Chernaik *et al.* (eds) *Beyond the Book. Theory, Culture and the Politics of Cyberspace.* Oxford: Office for Humanities Communication Publications No. 7, pp. 23–32.

Laurillard, D. (1993) *Rethinking University Teaching: A Framework for the Effective Use of Educational Technology.* London: Routledge.

Liestøl, G. (1995) 'Multipublication and the design of hypermedia documents', in D. Bearman (ed.) *Multimedia Computing and Museums. Selected Papers from the Third International Conference on Hypermedia and Interactivity in Museums.* Pittsburgh: Archives and Museum Informatics, pp. 235–47.

Lock, G. (2003) *Using Computers in Archaeology: Towards Virtual Pasts.* London: Routledge.

Marton, F. (1981) 'Orientations to studies, approaches to texts – learning as seen from the learner's point of view', in M. Panhelainen (ed.) *Higher Education as a Field of Research.* University of Jyväskylä: Institute for Educational Research Bulletin, No. 179, pp. 3–12.

O'Donnell, J. J. (1998) *Avatars of the Word. From Papyrus to Cyberspace.* Cambridge, MA: Harvard University Press.

Ramsden, P. (1992) *Learning to Teach in Higher Education.* London: Routledge.

Rogers, A. (1996) *Teaching Adults* (2nd edition). Buckingham: Open University Press.

12

WHAT'S ANOTHER WORD FOR THESAURUS?

Data standards and classifying the past

Andrew Baines and Kenneth Brophy

Introduction

Most archaeological institutions now make use of electronic databases for storing information about sites and monuments. Digital media offer huge advantages in storage, ease of access, space saving and, importantly, searching over traditional paper-based media. However, in order to ensure consistency, both internally within a database and between databases maintained by different institutions and individuals, it is necessary to apply some form of data standard. Central to the application of data standards for digital media in archaeology has been the construction of thesauri controlling the nomenclature of site and monument types. The importance of such thesauri lies in the fact that searching by monument type is easily the most common way in which archaeological databases are interrogated. In the absence of controlled terminology, searches of this kind are unavoidably compromised.

This chapter takes as its starting point the shared experiences of the authors, who both worked on the compilation of the *Scottish Thesaurus of Monument Types* (STMT) at one time or another, albeit in different roles. The STMT has been developed by the Royal Commission on the Ancient and Historical Monuments of Scotland (RCAHMS 2001) as a source of controlled terminology for future use in heritage recording in Scotland, both within the National Monuments Record of Scotland (NMRS) and elsewhere in Scottish heritage recording. This nascent Scottish Thesaurus provides the source material around which our argument revolves. However, this paper will address some wider theoretical issues concerning the nature and role of thesauri in particular, and data and information standards in general.

Perhaps a useful place to start would be by outlining what we think data and information standards should be, and how they should operate in archaeology and heritage recording. The MIDAS data standard for heritage recording defines information standards as follows: 'a list of *what* information should be recorded and *how* it should be recorded' (English Heritage 2000: 9; original emphasis). We take the concept of data and information standards to refer to the form in which the various statements that are the product of archaeological investigation are recorded, stored and made available to both archaeologists and non-archaeologists. This definition seems relatively non-contentious, and we have no fundamental problem with it. However, we suspect that many theoretically informed archaeologists distrust the idea of data standards, as well as other attempts to standardise archaeological practice. This distrust springs from a more general resistance to the imposition of controls or restraints that restrict the freedom of archaeological research and interpretation (Hodder 1999). Indeed, among many so-called post-processualists there is a resistance to the idea that archaeological data, in the form of an 'archaeological record', exist at all (Patrik 1985; Barrett 1988).

We share the theoretical standpoint of many interpretative archaeologists, but we see no reason why such a theoretical position should prohibit the use of data standards as a *progressive* tool. However, we also believe that such progress is conditional on the adoption of a view of archaeological data, indeed of the objects that are the subject of archaeology more generally, which has been characterised, most notably by Richard Rorty (1999), as *anti-essentialism*. For anti-essentialists:

> ... there is no such thing as a nonrelational feature of X, any more than there is such a thing as the intrinsic nature, the essence, of X. So there can be no such thing as a description which matches the way X really is, apart from its relation to human needs or consciousness or language.
>
> (Rorty 1999: 50)

The implication for archaeology of this argument is that we need to acknowledge that our data are not merely more or less accurate descriptions of things. Archaeological data do not exist as independent, non-relational aspects of the real world, but are brought into being by the kinds of technical and conceptual schemes and practices we archaeologists use in our engagements with the world of material culture. Archaeological data are not essential truths about past objects, nor did they exist in the past. Rather, they are our attempts to use language as a tool to *redescribe*, and in so doing *contextualise*, the mute objects we encounter in such a way as to further our goals as archaeologists. Generally speaking, we try to describe material objects, and relate them to one another, in such a way as to evoke past worlds – often in the process invoking familiar aspects of our own world (Baines and Brophy forthcoming). The corollary of this claim is that our data are not immutable, but are the result of the way in which we choose to describe the world. In changing our descriptions, then, we can change our data in order to serve better our purposes as archaeologists.

We think that the concepts of data and information standards should be revised in the light of this anti-essentialist and pragmatic view of knowledge. They should be judged as to their relative utility in allowing us, archaeologists and non-archaeologists alike, to compose more interesting, imaginative and useful accounts of the past. If a data standard contributes, as we think it should, to the goal of creating a language for archaeology that allows us to best and most freely express our ideas and opinions, and to justify them both to one another and to non-archaeologists, then we would argue that it should be welcomed.

But we reject the idea of data standards if it represents an attempt to restrict archaeological discourse to a vocabulary that can only be used to describe the past and its material traces as a collection of non-relational, objective facts. Rather, our function as archaeologists should be to develop vocabularies with which we may bring into view the possibilities of past material worlds. These vocabularies should make a difference to archaeological practice by the changing descriptions that are at the heart of archaeological discourse. In doing so they should help us in our attempts to capture the ambiguities inherent in that past, and in our interpretations of the traces of the past in the present.

In this chapter we intend to move towards such a pragmatic approach through more detailed discussion of the points raised so far, and through two case studies drawn from our own studies of aspects of Scottish prehistory.

What do 'terms' actually mean in relation to the past?

The 'linguistic turn' in twentieth-century thought centres on appeals to language and discourse as the source of knowledge and truth (Austin 1961; Rorty 1967) – what we can know about the world is limited by what we can say about it. Language has even been viewed as one of the only defining characteristics of humanity. For instance, the centrality of language to what it is to be human is dramatically illustrated by the importance accorded to the possession by Neanderthals of a complex language in debates as to whether or not they have a place in the bloodline of modern humans (e.g. Trinkaus and Shipman 1993: 391). The 'linguistic turn' emphasises that there are no facts other than linguistic descriptions, no realities other than those that may be described, but one doesn't have to follow the argument so far in order to appreciate its implications for an academic discourse such as that of archaeology. For instance, it encourages the belief that the goal of academic language, and hence academic discourse, cannot be merely to replicate the content of the world. Rather, language is a tool that we use to work on, and ultimately try to change, our world.

The centrality of language to this debate suggests that the way we use and abuse language within academic discourse should be taken seriously (Tilley 1999: chapter 3). The idea of a thesaurus, an attempt to institute a controlled vocabulary for the description of archaeological objects, may be a weapon in the battle over our use of language in archaeology, and how it can be made to work for us.

The kind of thesaurus we are concerned with here is intended to operate as a discrete sub-set of a shared language (in our case English), pertaining specifically to a shared discourse (in our case archaeology). Unlike conventional literary thesauri like *Roget's*, the function of such a thesaurus is not to expand the range of words available for the expression of a single concept, but rather to restrict it to a single *term*. The STMT (RCAHMS 2001) contains a relational structure of terms, which are un-punctuated and singular nouns or noun phrases describing types of sites and monuments. Each term is accompanied by a scope note, which is a definition of the term as it is used in the context of the thesaurus.

As we have already argued, one cannot assume that these terms can stand alone, as representations with a 1:1 relationship with things in the world. As Davidson (1984) has shown, words cannot be understood as referring directly to objects, but take their meaning from the way they are combined in sentences. So our thesaurus terms cannot refer to things, or types of things, outside of the descriptive sentences that make up the discourse of archaeology. These descriptions are themselves relational – the essence of a thing can never be described without enmeshing its description in a web of relationships to other descriptions of other things. Thesaurus terms would not even be able to function as simple labels without the wider language and discourse within which labels become meaningful. The relational properties of terms and descriptions find an echo in the hierarchical structure of the thesaurus itself, from which terms draw part of their meaning.

In the report on the STMT Pilot Project (RCAHMS 2001), one of us suggested that the thesaurus should follow current terminological practice, remaining interpretively neutral. However, it is now clear to us that this suggestion was naive. Thesauri are not simply neutral lists of words, any more than material culture typologies are neutral categories (Lucas 2001: Chapter 3). We think that such neutrality is unachievable, and probably undesirable, because any ordering of words places them in a relation to one another, thus drawing out nuances of meaning. If the use of language in archaeological discourse is the only way in which we can come to know the world as archaeologists, then using controlled language such as a thesaurus must always be an attempt to control, and thus to actively intervene, in that world.

If naming things brings them into being and delineates their boundaries, then naming things within the discourse of archaeology creates archaeological objects. We try to use language to impose order on the chaos of the archaeological record. By using our own terms, it is inevitable that we will re-create the past in our image, on our own terms. This need not be a problem. After all, archaeology is about creating narratives about the past, which we find useful and enlightening. However, we should be aware that the products of archaeological discourse, like the hierarchical and equivalence relationships of thesauri, may be seen as self-evident truths, discovered rather than created. There is a danger that thesauri may be taken implicitly to be *representation*s of an idealised, structured past rather than tools with which we attempt to order and work on the traces of the past in the present.

With this in mind, we think that a useful thesaurus should make explicit the assumptions on which it is based. It should draw attention to the archaeological discourse of which it is a part, and enable access to that discourse for the greatest number of people, archaeologist and non-archaeologist alike. In compiling thesauri we should take an active part in developing a useful and open vocabulary. One implication of this is that the potential multiplicity of interpretations is accommodated.

The multiplicity of interpretations

We are concerned that thesaurus structures tend to discourage ambiguous or multiple interpretations. Many monument types have been – and are – the subjects of controversy, often with at least two competing interpretations, from causewayed enclosures (Oswald *et al.* 2001; Waddington 2001) to hillforts (Hill 1995). Similarly, there are also problems in defining the boundaries of any particular monument class – when does a pennanular ring-ditch become a henge? This clearly presents us with a challenge if we are to develop a pragmatic, not idealistic, thesaurus.

One partial solution is to associate a series of terms with any given site, monument or object, documenting its interpretive biography – especially appropriate for terms and associated debates that are the subject of more or less general agreement. However, there can be no certainty that sites that appear to have been adequately described will not require redescription in the future. Furthermore, one only need think of the terms broch, cursus, henge, stone alignment and hillfort to realise that there are certain classes of site whose nature and meaning are not likely to be the subject of general agreement in the foreseeable future.

This would appear to give us a problem when deciding the location of these terms within the context of a thesaurus, especially since some sites will migrate between one term and another depending on one's interpretative viewpoint. With this in mind, it seems to us very important to distinguish between a thesaurus and the superficially similar structuring concept of a typology. It might be objected that a thesaurus is simply a typology of words, and that there is no real difference between the two. We disagree.

The concept of typology rests on the assumption that each type is physically and conceptually distinct, and that each may be represented by a single site or object that displays all of its defining characteristics, yet none that would cause it to be included within another type (Adams 1988). As we learn more of these sites and objects, however, this typological project becomes increasingly untenable.

So we would argue that it would be a mistake to assume that there can ever be a 1:1 relationship between thesaurus terms and anything but the most idealised of objects. Archaeological thesauri, contrary to many current examples, should not be structured along typological lines, simply reproducing traditional typologies. Rather, we should attempt to construct terms (and definitions) that describe not objects *per se*, cutting them off from their relationships with other objects, but rather that serve as descriptive shortcuts to archaeological discourse. Tools such as Internet hyperlinks could allow multiple interpretations and associations to be followed if the user desires. This would seem to be a way in which the competing claims that make up such discourse could be accounted for within the thesaurus. It might also allow new and more productive vertical and horizontal links between terms to be forged, the need for which we will flesh out in the case studies.

Alternative perspectives and exclusion

Given that thesauri are, in the main, established and maintained by governmental or institutional bodies, how may perspectives other than the 'establishment' version be taken account of in their vocabularies? This would appear to be partly a matter of the fitness of the language used for the purpose of creating as open and useful a vocabulary as possible. We would argue against the use of terminology that might exclude users who are non-specialists, or to exclude the possibility of alternative interpretations without major reworking of the thesaurus structure.

During our period working on the STMT, we experienced resistance to the removal or amendment of terms on the basis that their use was traditional within RCAHMS field archaeology. An example of this might be the term 'small cairn', used for clearance cairns related to prehistoric or medieval rather than post-medieval agricultural settlement. However, thesaurus terms refer to the function rather than the date or morphology of the things described so there appeared to be no justification other than tradition for the retention of this term. Such in-house subtleties tend to exclude the non-specialist lacking the knowledge of either the RCAHMS system or the history of the debate that brought them into being. This exclusion would not be intentional, but we would argue that exclusive practices based on tradition or mere oversight can never be justified.

The STMT was carried out under the supervision of an advisory group comprising varied members of the heritage community, and terms were posted to a wider advisory group for comments on their suitability. We would suggest that this advisory process should be extended further into the long-term development of the thesaurus in order to assure further its clarity and openness. We would also argue for the introduction of input from potential users drawn from the wider community, in order to provide a balance to the 'insider' perspectives which we all, as archaeologists, will inevitably share.

Some of these issues are best addressed within the framework of specific examples. Here we draw from our fields of research.

Cursus monuments

The classification and interpretation of Neolithic enclosures has long been problematic, especially when dealing with a primarily cropmark record (cf. RCHME 1960; Harding and Lee 1987; RCAHMS 1994; Darvill and Thomas 2001; Oswald *et al.* 2001; Gibson 2002). One of the more enigmatic classes of earthwork, the cursus monuments, is no exception. In the British Isles, cursus monuments are predominantly known only as cropmarks.

The term 'cursus' itself has a rather quaint and obscure origin, being a corruption of the Latin for circus. The antiquarian William Stukeley coined this phrase in the eighteenth century after he noticed a set of sizeable earthworks forming a large rectangular enclosure near Stonehenge (Stone 1947). The earliest examples discovered in the southern English chalk uplands were reckoned to be Roman chariot racing tracks, and fanciful explanations of round barrows and earthworks as 'grandstands' retained some currency until the advent of aerial photography and associated trial excavations in the 1920s–1930s (Leeds 1934; Atkinson 1955). The term has persisted, however, and has filtered into the archaeological consciousness as the term for a large rectangular enclosure of middle Neolithic date.

Although there are now over 220 known examples of these sites throughout the British Isles (Barclay and Harding 1999; McOmish 2003), there is little consensus as to what they were actually used for in the Neolithic. Cursus monuments have been regarded generally as having some kind of ceremonial or ritualistic purpose, and this is usually characterised as processional. Furthermore, no clear morphological boundaries have been placed on this type of monument, and a vast range of sites, from 60 m to 10,000 m in length, and with earthwork, pit or timber post boundaries, have all now been called cursus monuments. This is the type of ambiguous and problematic class of site that challenges the linguistic objectivity and clarity of a thesaurus. This is how the STMT (RCAHMS 2001) deals with 'cursus':

CURSUS

SN A long narrow rectangular enclosure of Neolithic date, presumed to be of ceremonial function.

CL RELIGIOUS RITUAL AND FUNERARY

NT PIT DEFINED CURSUS; DITCH DEFINED CURSUS

RT AVENUE; HENGE; PIT ALIGNMENT; BANK BARROW

Clearly 'cursus monument' is a term that the vast majority of public users have no knowledge of – it is a quasi-classical term made up, and used exclusively, by archaeologists, like 'megalith' (Tilley 1999). (There is not even any agreement within archaeologists how to correctly pluralise the word (Brophy and RCAHMS forthcoming).) Partially reflecting this, the term 'cursus' (note the dropped 'monument') scope note (SN) is brief and extremely vague, giving little information on size, the form of boundary, associations with sites and material culture, or function. One of us was heavily involved in the development of this economical description that, in hindsight, is banal to the point of uselessness. Scope notes for both narrower terms (NT), ditch defined cursus and pit defined cursus, are repetitions, differentiated only by the form of boundary (ditch and bank or, despite the name, timber post).

The vague definitions of these unfamiliar terms are of little help to the public. They also give the illusion that cursus monuments come exclusively in these forms, and yet even the terms further down the hierarchy (ditch and pit defined) simply do no have the flexibility to capture the internal variations within the cursus class. These are not merely related to physical appearance, but also to landscape locations, constructional differences, and practices of deposition and monument re-use (Brophy and RCAHMS forthcoming). Some cursus monuments have earthwork *and* timber elements to their construction, like Holywood North in south-west Scotland (Thomas 1999); whilst others combine characteristics of other monuments listed as related terms (RT). The Cleaven Dyke, Perthshire, is neither truly a cursus nor really a bank barrow (Barclay and Maxwell 1998); how is this dealt with in a thesaurus structure, and by what means can this be communicated to the user? So, the creation of a set of terms within the thesaurus hierarchy here is implicitly reproducing typological schemes that have so dogged Neolithic monument studies (Russell 2002: 1–2). Another problematic implication of this is that the use of the label means that these sites – to the user – are implicitly all functionally the same.

The inclusion of sites under the various cursus terms is based purely on the final ground plan of the monument. Yet we know from excavations at cursus sites in Scotland and England that this is often only the culmination of centuries of modification, burning, abandonment and extension. The Cleaven Dyke, for instance, was constructed from a series of round and long mound segments over an unknown period of time. The term 'cursus' may apply to its final form but initially it may have been a round mound or round barrow; and then a long barrow or bank barrow (Barclay and Maxwell 1998). Many other cursus sites have indications of unclassifiable (or un-named) earlier phases (for instance, a possible E-shaped post setting at Douglasmuir, Angus (Kendrick 1995)). There is a growing realisation that such Neolithic sites were uncompleted projects, not monuments (Bradley 1993); and that they marked places of significance (Tilley 1994). This is where it is important that thesauri incorporate – where excavation, field-survey or cropmark evidence is available – some kind of *biography* of monuments as a matter of course. The public perception of Stonehenge as a stone circle with trilithons overshadows its origins as both a timber circle and henge monument.

Whilst we are not disputing that these shorthand labels are useful search tools for the user, we would also suggest that traits other than simply physical form and dimensions must be used to determine where a specific site sits within the database. The possibility that sites of similar appearance need not have similar functions should be addressed, possibly through pointing users towards specific case studies or sites within the database, or using multiple images to help explain terms and variations. Where appropriate, some sites must be allowed to be defined using several terms. The Cleaven Dyke, for instance, cannot just be classified as 'cursus monument'; it also has to be described as 'round barrow (possible)' and 'bank barrow'. Associated records with site biographies (where available) could help navigate the user and bring them to a closer understanding of a site (and the relationship between terms). Cursus monuments can be accommodated within a monument thesaurus, but the way that the user engages with them cannot simply assume that the simple equation 'cursus = X' can ever apply.

Brochs

We have chosen the broch as a second case study in order to highlight some possible practical implications of some of the points made. Most people working in British archaeology will have some knowledge of the brochs, although perhaps the rather terse debate that has revolved around them over the past few decades is less well known outside Scotland. 'Broch', or *Brough* as it is sometimes written, is a dialect term, derived from the Old Norse *Borg*, meaning a defence or stronghold. Broch has traditionally been used, in areas of Scotland with a strong Norse linguistic influence, to refer to the remains of later prehistoric buildings, as well as natural features with the appearance of defensive strength. In areas with a strong Gaelic tradition, the word 'Dun' is used to refer to morphologically similar remains. Beginning with the work of Joseph Anderson in the late-nineteenth century (Anderson 1883, 1890, 1901), and continuing with the influential work of MacKie in the 1960s and 1970s (1965, 1971), the somewhat cath-olic vernacular term has come to refer to a specific monument type, defined by a specific range of structural and morphological features. In the current STMT (RCAHMS 2001), the term 'BROCH' is used as follows:

BROCH

SN An Iron Age round defended homestead, found mainly in the north and west of Scotland. Brochs have a tapering profile and thick, usually hollow dry stone walls which contain galleries, cells and a stairway, with guard cells at the entrance.

CL MONUMENT <BY FORM>

RT AISLED ROUNDHOUSE; GALLERIED DUN; WHEELHOUSE

BROCH

SN An Iron Age round defended homestead, found mainly in the north and west of Scotland. Brochs have a tapering profile and thick, usually hollow dry stone walls which contain galleries, cells and a stairway, with guard cells at the entrance.

CL DOMESTIC

RT AISLED ROUNDHOUSE; CRANNOG; DUN; GALLERIED DUN; SOUTERRAIN; WHEELHOUSE

To begin with the scope note, the first thing to notice is that the morpho-logical details specified refer to what might be called an 'ideal' broch. At only a few of the best-preserved sites can all of these details be seen, and more than half a century of debate has raged over whether or not the broch should be defined in these terms, and whether typological studies of these monuments in any way advance our understanding of them (Baines 2003). Putting aside the details of these interpretative differences, it seems likely that a user coming to the thesaurus without a detailed knowledge of the academic debate on the subject might conclude that the site she was inter-ested in was not a broch at all – given the absence of one or more of the defining features. Yet there is a strong thread in current academic opinion that suggests that such typological distinctions should be subordinated to a more general concept of domestic monumentality (Barrett 1981; Armit 1997; Sharples and Parker Pearson 1997). These tensions are not evident in the thesaurus entry, which, on the contrary, suggests a 1:1 relationship between terms and objects of the kind that we have already argued is unten-able. One way to indicate to the user that thesaurus terms are always part of a discourse, and draw their changing meanings from the way they are used in archaeological discourse rather than objective changes in the objects to which they refer, would be to include links to bibliographic references that indicate the main currents in the relevant debates.

The scope note above is the second that was written to illustrate the term 'broch'. The original scope note was as follows: 'A round Iron Age house found mainly in the north and west of Scotland. Brochs have a tapering profile and thick, dry stone walls that often contain galleries and cells.' This was written according to currently dominant interpretations, and stresses the domestic aspects of the broch. However, there is a traditional approach to these monuments that insists that they are primarily defensive structures, which still enjoys wide currency in Scottish archaeology. The scope note was therefore amended to take account of this, the word 'defended' being used in preference to 'defensive' as a compromise to indicate that defence should not be considered the only function of the broch. Nevertheless, the existence of somewhat heated and far from settled debate on the function of the broch is hardly hinted at in the scope note.

This introduces the question of whether definitions such as scope notes are the only way of describing site types. Among the different components of the thesaurus, the scope notes have certainly attracted the greatest attention from archaeologists who have seen the draft STMT. Of less interest to many have been the hierarchies into which terms are ordered. This may be due to our tendency, as archaeologists, to look for a single meaning for a term, and to seek to capture that meaning in sentences that express it. Hierarchies, used progressively, are another way in which meanings can be attributed to terms without losing sight of their relational properties. Again, it will be noted that, in both of the two general classes (**CL**) in which the term 'broch' has been placed, it has been considered to be a type of house, thereby privileging a domestic over a defensive interpretation. This certainly reflects the balance of present opinion. However, one way of capturing the nature of the discourse that underpins the thesaurus may be to use the horizontal connections created by the related terms to suggest linkages to other debates that might be of importance to the user. For example, 'FORT' as a related term might be a way into an alternative debate centred on the putative defensive function of the broch. Similarly, a relational link to the term 'CASTLE' might alert the user to the traditional notion, still held in some quarters, of these sites as impregnable fortresses, the homes of a foreign ruling elite (Childe 1935).

In sum, we advocate the retention of natural language terms such as broch, over convoluted morphological or typological neologisms. Such terms are in use within a broad range of linguistic communities, from tourists on day trips to professional archaeologists, and as such are a bridge between worlds that might not otherwise be connected. The lack of specificity of such terms is one way in which the 'fuzziness' that characterises archaeological discourse could be retained.

Conclusion

These case studies have raised a number of problems with the use of classificatory terms in archaeology. We have made suggestions as to how these problems might be approached within the context of a thesaurus of archaeological terms. We hope that the case studies go some way towards fleshing out the more abstract points we made at the beginning of the chapter. In general, we have tried to argue that the use of thesauri cannot escape integration into a wider human discourse. Rather we should consider how the descriptive power of this particular bit of the English (and indeed any other) language can help us to redescribe things in ways which are useful to us, as archaeologists and non-archaeologists alike. In conclusion, we would like to offer some thoughts on how the issues raised in this chapter might help us to further improve the use of thesauri in archaeological data standards.

One of the most progressive aspects of the STMT, in terms of assuring its utility to as wide an audience as possible, was the proposal that it be linked to a series of images to illustrate the various monument types. While applauding this approach, we would like to see this concept extended further, as we have already argued that thesauri should not be regarded as typologies where words have a 1:1 relationship with 'real' objects. In order to highlight the role that terms have in the discourse of archaeology, we suggest that thesaurus terms might be electronically linked to a range of bibliographic and literary information. This would assure that both the current debate surrounding terms, and their historical origins within archaeological discourse were clear to the end-user. Thesauri structure could well lead into discourse through an Internet structure using hyperlinks. For instance, terms could be linked in the usual thesauri structure but also include links to images and textual sources; these links could also cross traditional typological and disciplinary boundaries. On-line thesauri might also host, or be linked to, Internet discussion groups on the use of language in archaeology. Such innovations might lead to genuinely interactive and pragmatic databases, which would provide both data control and flexible interpretation. There is no reason why thesauri should continue to portray the myth that data can be viewed only as either black or white (Merleau-Ponty 1990).

Of course, such levels of engagement with the data are not of interest to everyone, and simple hierarchies, scope notes and pictorial images may be all that some users need for their purposes. But for others, the knowledge that there are decades of discourse and discoveries lying behind every database entry and thesaurus term, may offer them an opportunity to explore familiar words and ideas in more depth. Our engagement with the world does not exist in the structure of a database, with chains of unbreakable relationships and nested hierarchies. Rather, we understand the world through relationships, connections, even juxtapositions. Perhaps by allowing users (both archaeological and non-archaeological) to have access to databases of heritage information in more flexible ways, we can encourage more exciting and imaginative ways of understanding the past and our heritage.

References

Adams, W. (1988) 'Archaeological classification: theory versus practice', *Antiquity* 61: 40–56.

Anderson, J. (1883) *Scotland in Pagan Times: The Iron Age. The Rhind Lectures in Archaeology for 1881.* Edinburgh: David Douglas.

Anderson, J. (1890) 'Notice of the excavation of the brochs of Yarhouse, Brounaban, Bowermadden, Old Stirkoke and Dunbeath, in Caithness, with remarks on the period of the brochs; and an appendix, containing a collected list of the brochs of Scotland, and early notices of many of them', *Archaeologica Scotica* 5: 131–98.

Anderson, J. (1901) 'Notices of nine brochs along the Caithness coast from Keiss Bay to Skirza Head, excavated by Sir Francis Tress Barry, Bart., M.P., of Keiss Castle, Caithness', *Proceedings of the Society of Antiquaries of Scotland* 35: 112–48.

Armit, I. (1997) 'Cultural landscapes and identities: a case study in the Scottish Iron Age', in Gwilt, A. and Haselgrove, C. (eds) *Reconstructing Iron Age Societies,* pp. 248–253. Oxford: Oxbow.

Atkinson, R. J. C. (1955) 'The Dorset cursus', *Antiquity* 29: 4–9.

Austin, J. L. (1961) 'A plea for excuses', in Austin, J. L., Urmson, J. O. and Warnock, G. J. (eds) *Philosophical Papers.* Oxford: Oxford University Press.

Baines, A. (2003) 'The inherited past of monuments: on antiquarian discourse and contemporary archaeology', *Scottish Archaeological Journal* 24(1).

Baines, A. and Brophy, K. (forthcoming) 'Archaeology after 'isms', *Archaeological Dialogues.*

Barclay, A. and Harding, J. (eds) (1999) *Pathways and Ceremonies: The Cursus Monuments of Britain and Ireland.* Oxford: Oxbow.

Barclay, G. J. and Maxwell, G. S. (1998) *The Cleaven Dyke and Littleour: Monuments in the Neolithic of Tayside,* Edinburgh: Society of Antiquaries of Scotland Monograph.

Barrett, J. C. (1981) 'Aspects of the Iron Age in Atlantic Scotland. A case study in the problems of interpretation', *Proceedings of the Society of Antiquaries of Scotland* 111: 205–19.

Barrett, J. C. (1988) 'Fields of discourse: reconstituting a social archaeology', *Critique of Anthropology* 7(3): 5–16.

Bradley, R. (1993) *Altering the Earth.* Edinburgh: Society of Antiquaries of Scotland Monograph.

Brophy, K. and RCAHMS (forthcoming) *The Neolithic Cursus Monuments of Scotland.* Edinburgh: Society of Antiquaries of Scotland.

Childe, V. G. (1935) *The Prehistory of Scotland.* London: Kegan Paul.

Darvill, T. and Thomas, J. (eds) (2001) *Neolithic Enclosures in Atlantic Northwest Europe.* Oxford: Oxbow.

Davidson, D. (1984) 'Reality without reference', in Davidson, D. *Inquiries Into Truth and Interpretation*, pp. 215–25. Oxford: Clarendon Press.

English Heritage (2000) *MIDAS: A Manual and Data Standard for Monument Inventories* (2nd reprint). Swindon: English Heritage.

Gibson, A. (ed.) (2002) *Behind Wooden Walls: Neolithic Palisaded Enclosures in Europe*. Oxford: BAR.

Gwilt, A. and Haselgrove, C. (eds) (1997) *Reconstructing Iron Age Societies*. Oxford: Oxbow.

Harding, A. F. and Lee, G. E. (1987) *Henges and Related Monuments of Great Britain*. Oxford: BAR.

Hill, J. D. (1995) 'How should we understand Iron Age societies and hillforts? A contextual study from southern Britain', in Hill, J. D. and Cumberpatch, C. (eds) *Different Iron Ages: Studies on the Iron Age in Temperate Europe*. Oxford: BAR.

Hodder, I. (1999) *The Archaeological Process: An Introduction*. Oxford: Blackwell.

Kendrick, J. (1995) 'Excavation of a Neolithic enclosure and Iron Age settlement, Angus: summary report', *Proceedings of the Society of Antiquaries of Scotland* 115: 15–57.

Leeds, E. T. (1934) 'Rectangular enclosures of the Bronze Age in the Upper Thames valley', *Antiquaries Journal* 14: 414–16.

Lucas, G. (2001) *Critical Approaches to Fieldwork: Contemporary and Historical Archaeological Practice*. London: Routledge.

MacKie, E. (1965) 'The origin and development of the broch and wheelhouse building cultures of the Scottish Iron Age', *Proceedings of the Prehistoric Society* 31: 93–146.

MacKie, E. (1971) 'English migrants and Scottish brochs', *Glasgow Archaeological Journal* 2: 39–71.

McOmish, D. (2003) 'Cursus. Solving a 6000 year old puzzle', *British Archaeology* 69 (March 2003): 9–13.

Merleau-Ponty, M. (1990) *Phenomenology of Perception*. London: Routledge.

Oswald, A., Dyer, C. and Barber, M. (2001) *The Creation of Monuments: Neolithic Causewayed Enclosures in the British Isles*. Swindon: English Heritage.

Patrik, L. (1985) 'Is there an archaeological record', in Schiffer, M. B. (ed.) *Advances in Archaeological Method and Theory* 3, pp. 27–62. London: Academic Press.

RCAHMS (1994) *Southeast Perth: An Archaeological Landscape*. Edinburgh: HMSO.

RCAHMS (2001) *NMRS/RCAHMS Scottish Thesaurus of Monument Types Pilot Project: Final Report*. Web published consultation document (www.rcahms.gov.uk/ hesaurus.pdf).

RCHME (1960) *A Matter of Time*. London: HMSO.

Rorty, R. (ed.) (1967) *The Linguistic Turn: Recent Essays in Philosophical Method*. Chicago, IL: Chicago University Press.

Rorty, R. (1999) 'A world without substances or essences', in Rorty, R. *Philosophy and Social Hope*, pp. 47–71. London: Penguin.

Russell, M. (2002) *Monuments of the British Neolithic*. Stroud: Tempus.

Sharples, N. and Parker Pearson, M. (1997) 'Why were brochs built? Recent studies in the Iron Age of Atlantic Scotland', in Gwilt, A. and Haselgrove, C. (eds) pp. 254–69, *Reconstructing Iron Age Societies*. Oxford: Oxbow.

Stone, J. F. S. (1947) 'The Stonehenge cursus and its affinities', *Archaeological Journal* 104: 7–19.

Thomas, J. (1999) 'The Holywood cursus complex, Dumfries: an interim report', in Barclay, A. and Harding, J. (eds) *Pathways and Ceremonies: The Cursus Monuments of Britain and Ireland*, pp. 107–15. Oxford: Oxbow.

Tilley, C. (1994) *A Phenomenology of Landscape*. Oxford: Berg.

Tilley, C. (1999) *Metaphor and Material Culture*. Oxford: Blackwell.

Trinkaus, E. and Shipman, R. (1993) *The Neanderthals: Changing the Image of Mankind*. London: Jonathan Cape.

Waddington, C. (2001) 'Breaking out of the morphological straitjacket: early Neolithic enclosures in northern Britain', *Durham Archaeological Journal* 16: 1–14.

Part VII

CONCLUSION

AFTERWORD

Patrick Daly and Thomas L. Evans

The use of computing is becoming an increasingly standard part of many endeavours within archaeology. This is largely due to the digitization of the world around us, rather than due to any strategic implementation of methods or approaches. The world is now at a stage where one needs to make a conscious and concerted effort to avoid dealing with some aspects of digital technology; and one doing so would most likely be seen as an anachronistic maverick – an interesting twist as less than two decades ago a person who struggled to incorporate computers into archaeological field work would have been on the fringe.

As a number of the chapters have demonstrated, data captured in the field using 'real-time' digital approaches can be moved quickly and directly to GIS and statistical analysis, modelled in a virtual reality environment, and published over the Web for both educational and academic purposes in formats that traditional publishing could never match. Yet this increasing ease in the capture, analysis and transfer of information is far from useful if it is not used with intelligence and forethought. Digital technology is valuable only if it is incorporated in an intelligent manner that is purposeful and aimed at creating specific results. Indeed the creation of data for the sake of doing so merely hides the valuable information in a sea of meaningless quanta. It is only through the thoughtful integration of technology into archaeology that our ability to study the past is enhanced.

Digital archaeology not only impacts our methodological capabilities but also our theoretical development. It is redefining the relationship between the two, allowing more holistic and iterative approaches to be used and encourages hitherto abstract ideas to be meaningfully applied. It can only do this, however, if one remembers the theoretical while performing the method, and methodological while contemplating theory. Yet while new technologies solve many problems, and allow many new questions to be asked, they introduce new problems and can lead to us forgetting simple solutions with long and reliable histories.

We steadfastly maintain that digital approaches should not be pushed as replacements for traditional approaches, but rather that digital techniques should complement them. Just as understanding technology can add to one's ability to record, analyse and theorize about archaeology, so too does the understanding of traditional techniques add to one's ability to use appropriate technologies. New technologies should be added to our arsenal of methods, understood and applied when and where appropriate, not just thrown in as a blanket new fangled solution.

Many of the accoutrements that accompany an archaeologist into the field, office, or museum have had long trial periods. They have survived because they have proved that they can get the job done, and in the case of archives, because they have a durability that is not restricted by changing technology (i.e. slides, drawings, and field notebooks). It would be foolish to look for immediate replacements before a convincing case can be made that doing so is both necessary and advantageous. Additionally the results of these new methods must be accessible to future generations of archaeologists, not lost to the ever changing 'improvements' of different programs.

Furthermore, there are dangers to dependency on digital approaches. We have both met and worked with an individual who is completely at ease working with hand-held GPS, CAD drafting, complex database work, and GIS analysis; but when given a compass and a map has difficulties locating his position in a field. When this was met with our horror, his response was that he had never had to do so before – he has always had a device to do this for him. Along a similar line, the training of individuals in the use of standard dumpy levels on field school excavations is essential, even when it might be more efficient or precise to use a Total Station Theodolite. After all, without knowing how such basic approaches are conducted, how can one truly understand the meaning of the results? How can one tell when things go wrong? The careful integration of technology may be construed by some as reactionary, but we see it as an important step in defining what archaeology is and how it should be performed, rather than letting the tide of computerization do so for us. One should let technology supplement one's thoughts while avoiding relying upon it.

Black box techniques are seductive, and the myth of digital and ICT infallibility can be a serious liability, as indeed anyone who works with such facilities knows. Archaeologists need to fully understand what it is they want to do, and how the tools they use do it. The integration of technology adds to our strength and capacity to perform our tasks, but blind use of digital technology is not only bad archaeology, it can backfire, disempowering the archaeologist. It can leave individuals essentially ignorant of what they are doing or how to fix things when they go wrong. If you rely upon the technology without thought, it will always let you down. Even if it works properly, such reliance limits an archaeologist's ability to be truly innovative, and condemns one to mindless forms of entry.

If, however, the methods are understood and used properly, digital archaeology is truly a form of empowerment. As demonstrated by projects such as Framework Archaeology and Ian Hodder's work at Çatel Hüyük, technology can highlight the work of excavators, bringing them firmly into the interpretative equation. As used in cases such as the Ferrybridge chariot, it informs the excavators, allows them to modify their approaches and lets them publish results on line while the excavation is still underway. Furthermore, the digital dissemination of data in new interactive formats has the potential to alter the traditional boundaries which demarcate the archaeologist from the 'other'.

Digital archaeology expands our perceptions by allowing us to see data in ways we otherwise could not. Yet it only does this if it is used with true understanding, not just with the technophile's love of the gadget, nor with the technophobe's use of the 'expert' whose results are never considered in the final interpretations of the project. Digital archaeology is most useful if fully integrated into an investigation. It should not be used as a bolt-on, nor as the central showcase, but as a normal tool such as the trowel one digs with or the paper one writes on.

In the end we applaud innovation, but at the same time advise caution. As computers and digital techniques become more and more standard parts of our lives, we need to be diligent in defining carefully how technology should be implemented. It is, however, becoming ever clearer that a holistic influx of accessible, powerful and sophisticated digital tools and methods brings with it the potential to do very different sorts of archaeology than what has been done before. Just as embracing standardized excavation practices and modern scientific methods fundamentally shifted the practical and theoretical foundations of archaeology – digital technology is resonating at all levels within archaeology and is poised to initiate the next leap forward – where that leap takes us depends upon how we as a discipline decide to apply it.

INDEX

ADS *see* Archaeological Data Service
Ahmanson Foundation 220
analytical scale 128–30; *see also* Bronze
 Age pastoral patterns; mobile
 pastoralism
Anthropology 3 (UCL Santa Barbara)
 231–2
anti-essentialism 237–8
Antiquity 219
Archaeological Data Service (ADS) 55,
 218, 219, 233
Archaeology Disc 216
architecture 203
archives and archiving 54–6, 219, 220,
 254
Arras Culture 39
artistic illustration 194, 197, 203
Assemblage 217

Bacon, F. 28 n1
Balliot, L 67
Banks, M. 232
Banning, E. B. 216
Barceló, J. *et al.* 194
Barker, G. 99
Barthes, R. 195, 196
Bateman, J. 200, 206 n8
Bedouin Camp survey (Wadi Faynan)
 97–125; ʿAmārin 103; ʿAzāzma 101,
 102, 103, 110, 111, 121; camp
 location 121–2; change 120, 123;
 land use 98, 123, 124–5 n1;
 (contemporary and recent 100–1;
 modern land use 102–3; results
 103–4, 103*f*); material culture 98,
 104–20; (artefacts and activities
 107–20, 108–9*f*, 110*t*, 122; black
 tents 105–6, 105*f*; durability 106,

122, 123; refuse 107–8, 110, 111,
 122–3; site WF869 107, 108, 109*f*,
 110*t*, 111–16, 114–15*f*, 117*f*,122,
 123; site WF909 107, 116, 120*f*, 121*f*;
 site WF942 107, 108, 108*f*, 110, 110*t*,
 111*f*, 112–13*f*; site WF982 107, 108,
 109*f*, 110*t*, 116, 118–19*f*, 122; survey
 and analysis 106–20); methodology
 99, 102, 107, 123; results 120,
 121–4; Saʾidiyin 103*f*, 116; scales 97;
 sites 103*f*; traditional vs non-
 traditional factors 98; tribal groups
 101, 103, 103*f*, 123; Wadi Faynan
 Landscape Survey 99–100, 100*f*, 101,
 124
Bedul encampment (Petra) 122–3
Bennett, K. D. 173
Berners-Lee, Tim 214, 220
books 213, 228–9, 233; *see also*
 publication in archaeology
Boyle, Angela 43
Bradford University 43
Breedon, Christopher 43
British Museum 43
brochs 244–6
Bronze Age pastoral patterns (Eastern
 Eurasian Steppe region) 131*f*,
 135–46; basic assumptions 145;
 ecology and prehistory 135–7; Koksu
 River Valley 135, 137–45; material
 culture 136–7; mobile pastoralism
 136; modeling pastures and land-
 cover 138, 139–40, 139*f*; pasture
 accessibility and potential pathways
 140–1, 141*f*, 142*f*; ritual landscapes
 141, 142–5, 143*f*, 144*f*; scale and
 landscape 145–6; study zone 131*f*,
 138, 138*f*